OUTLAW TALES

of MONTANA

GARY A. WILSON

Published By

HIGH-LINE BOOKS®
Havre, Montana ™

Copyright 1995 by Gary A. Wilson

All rights reserved, including the right to reproduce this book or any part
thereof, in any form, except for the inclusion of brief quotations in a review.

Library of Congress Catalog Card Number: 95-61348
ISBN: 0-9632240-0-X

Published by High-Line Books, Havre, Montana, in cooperation with
SkyHouse Publishers, an imprint of Falcon Press, Helena, Montana.

Distributed by Falcon Press, P.O. Box 1718, Helena, Montana, 59624,
Phone 1-800-582-2665.

First Edition

Manufactured in the United States of America

EPIGRAPH

"The heyday of the cowboy-outlaw was short, lasting only about thirty years; and their actual numbers were comparatively small. Yet they left an indelible impression on the pages of Western history."

Charles Kelly
The Outlaw Trail

"Of all the figures of the American frontier, the badman with a single-action Colt's revolver in his hand has surest claim upon the attention of American readers. Without him, the more or less orderly process of settlement could have been as dull as neighborhood gossip in a country store. With him, the West was in ferment from the moment of its social emergence."

Ramon Adams
Six-guns and Saddle Leather

"They cashed in their chips under the smoke of the same weapon that let them live, and took their medicine without whining."

Charles M. Russell

"There is drama and excitement in the stories of Old West outlaws and gunfighters. I know that it is often overplayed; that such scenes were few and far between, that we sometimes make heroes of unheroic men. But there is glamour in gunplay, there is excitement in desperate escapes and long rides and shortcuts with posses—it's there, it was part of the old West and as long as people want to read about it, there will be those who will write about it."

Jim Dullenty, founding board member of the Western Outlaw-Lawman History Association and editor of its publication, *The Journal*

DEDICATION

To Hartman Larson, my "mean" Everett, Washington, junior high and high school history teacher, who taught me the beginnings of academic discipline and gave me my first real interest in history and historical research.

To the late Seattle University Society of Jesus professors "Father John" Carrigan, Owen McCrusker, Michael Toulouse, and the now Doctor John Fitterer. These highly intelligent, dedicated, and caring gentlemen had a major influence on stretching my mental parameters, although much of it would lie dormant for several years; and to the school itself, where I had several happy and rewarding years.

To Harrison Lane, Ph.D., my late friend, mentor, and professor at Northern Montana College, who honed the abilities in me (such as they are) that the others first stimulated.

And not to forget my parents, who dragged me as a boy all over the West to see and learn about its "dumb" history.

CONTENTS

FOREWORD

One of the products of the American spirit of independence and self-reliance is the hero worship of "the bad guys." Earlier this century, the myths of the heroes who lived outside the law extended to gangsters, such as "Pretty Boy" Floyd, Bonnie and Clyde, and Al Capone. A century ago, the myth of the heroic bad guy developed around numerous Western holdup artists, bank robbers, road agents, killers, and railroad thieves.

The benevolent thief of the California gold fields was Joaquin Murieta; the Robin Hoods of Missouri were Jesse and Frank James and their various gang members. Other areas saw the Clantons, the Daltons, the Younger brothers, and Billy the Kid. In Montana we had forays by Butch Cassidy, the Sundance Kid, and Harvey "Kid Curry" Logan. Interestingly enough, Kid Curry, the leader of the notorious Wild Bunch and the verified killer of at least ten men, grew up reading the Bible. He was regarded as "well-mannered," and received his early training as an outlaw from reading Ned Buntline's outrageously exaggerated wild tales of the West.

It is no small irony, however, that Montana's best-known outlaw was a law enforcement man turned gold thief and murderer. Sheriff Henry Plummer's career as a vigilante and elected officer of the law strikes a note of genuine terror, involving as it does the corruption of law enforcement itself. In his earlier book, *Tall in the Saddle*, Gary Wilson has already told the story of another law enforcement officer accused of becoming a horse thief. As Wilson demonstrated, the life of "Long" George Francis is truly more touching than it is frightening. Whether he was falsely accused or not, Long George was a figure calling for genuine sympathy.

In this book of Montanans outside the law, Wilson has chosen to tell the stories of a much less inviting crew of real bad guys with few noticeable redeeming social qualities. Fortunately, as in his previous works, Wilson tells the story straight, with careful research of all available facts and little inclination to indulge in perpetuating the myths of Western Robin Hoods. His work takes a big step toward laying to rest the idealization of these genuinely vicious figures, who should be reviled rather than idealized.

William W. Thackeray, D. A.
Professor of Humanities
Montana State University-Northern

INTRODUCTION

Montana has had many notorious yet colorful outlaws who have all but disappeared down "trails gone dim," as *True West* magazine puts it. This was because their lives were not easily documented, nor were their exploits well known outside their respective areas of operation. Usually, history writers who specialize in Montana outlaws dwell on Henry Plummer and his band of cutthroats, who operated in and around Nevada City and Virginia City during the gold-rush days. Harvey "Kid Curry" Logan, whose badman career bloomed in the Little Rockies, went on to become a major player in the notorious Wild Bunch. It seems that a supposedly definitive book on either man's life appears with regularity. Lesser note is made of George "Big Nose" Parrott, Robert Leroy "Butch Cassidy" Parker, and Harry "the Sundance Kid" Longabaugh's infrequent forays into Montana—although this is changing.

The romance attached to these individuals was both a creation of the people of the East (gleaned from the pulp Western novels they consumed greedily) and of the cowboy, who saw the outlaw-gunman as experiencing the best of lives with plenty of money, women, adventure, and freedom. The cowhand's life was not free and easy. It consisted of long, weary, miserable, and boring hours in the saddle for little pay and great potential for injury, making it a short-term career for most. The "home on the range" actually provided a restrictive way of life, with only brief periods of freedom in town. In reality, the cowboy was just another industrial worker, only with a different kind of uniform and workplace.

But the cowboy's conception of the outlaw was a myth, too, especially in the latter stages of the frontier when more people, farms, telegraph and telephone lines, roads, bridges, and barbed wire relegated the outlaws to only the most desolate places. Yet cowboys told and sang of the badmen's supposedly glamorous lives anyway, as balladeers and poets of medieval England sang about Robin Hood, the outlaw of the forests. Robin Hood and his band of merry men were luckier though: they didn't have to deal with law-enforcement agencies, both government and private, organized under the banner of the Pinkerton National Detective Agency, the equivalent of today's Federal Bureau of Investigation. "Wanted" posters and newspaper pictures took away the Montana bandits' anonymity, and there was always a Pinkerton man ("We Never Sleep") on their trail. Historian James Horan concluded rightly that without the Pinkerton Agency, parts of the West would have been under the outlaw bands' control for longer than they were.

The true tamers of the West were the cattle and railroad barons and the freighters, stagecoach drivers, and steamboat operators who made and lost fortunes by either driving Longhorn cattle north from Texas or hauling large quantities of foodstuffs, equipment, supplies, and mail to the new farming settlements and already-established mining, cattle, and railroad towns. But the public's attention focused primarily on the cowboy. Some heroes on horseback, some outlaws on horseback, and some a combination thereof were portrayed dramatically in the Wild West shows that toured throughout the country and overseas.

The true range cowboy became only a memory as he was swallowed up in the massive westward agricultural migration. Interestingly, the North Dakota Historical Society has no listing of the outlaws who roamed back and forth across the borders of Montana, North Dakota, and Canada. This land was developed by farmers who had no interest in preserving outlaw tales—even though they readily bought stolen horses until they could raise their own.

Outlaws reigned for others, though. As one unknown writer put it: "For a time they brought a burst of excitement and high adventure to a region that was about to be changed from frontier to the monotony of homesteading and dry-land farming." It's all in a person's perspective.

To help fill the void of Montana outlaw stories, I'll introduce and in some cases reintroduce the following characters in this book:

— The gunman-killer "Long" Henry Thompson, "the terror of eastern Montana," whose politeness in closing a Saco, Montana, saloon door led to his death.

— Con Murphy, "the Jesse James of Montana," who was hanged twice by a Helena vigilante group for crimes he didn't commit—although he certainly had committed enough of his own.

—"Dutch" Henry Ieuch and the outlaws of the Big Muddy Creek valley, who terrorized settlers of northeastern Montana, present-day Saskatchewan and Alberta, and northwestern North Dakota. From 1900 to 1906, this region was considered one of the high crime areas of the West. Dutch Henry, according to newspaper sources, departed this world twice officially; in other tales, he died at least twice more.

— A trio of amateurs who attempted a mining payroll robbery at Wickes, high in a valley of the Rocky Mountains. They bungled so badly and comically that the townspeople forgave them and went so far as to lie in court to get them acquitted.

— George "Big Nose" Parrott, primarily a Wyoming outlaw whose final capture in Miles City, Montana, led to his lynching and bizarre skinning in Rawlins, Wyoming.

— Harvey "Kid Curry" Logan, one of Butch Cassidy's Wild Bunch and a notoriously cold-blooded killer from the Little Rockies Mountain region, featuring lesser known stories of his life.

— And finally, transplanted Eastern dude Abe Gill of Landusky, Montana, who wasn't an outlaw, but who was originally thought to have been Kid Curry's most prominent victim. The final resting places for both Curry and Gill are clouded in mystery.

Take note, Old West enthusiasts. Montana has another chapter to add to the history of the West's cowboy-gunman-lawman, and you'll find it here, in *Outlaw Tales of Montana*.

MONTANA, CIRCA 1910

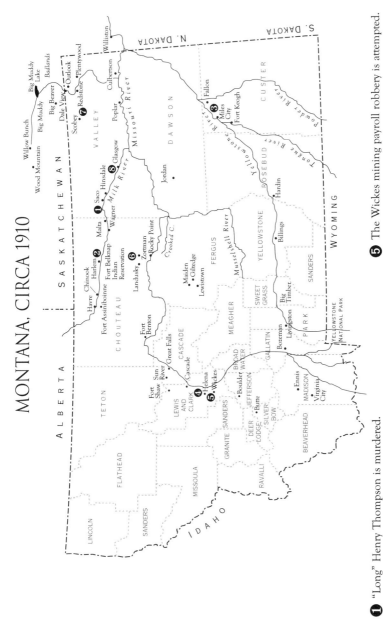

❶ "Long" Henry Thompson is murdered.

❷ "Dutch" Henry Ieuch departs for Minnesota, where he is killed.

❸ "Big Nose" George Parrott is captured and returned to Rawlings, Wyoming, where he is lynched.

❹ Con Murphy meets his demise.

❺ The Wickes mining payroll robbery is attempted.

❻ Abe Gill and Kid Curry collide.

❼ Outlaw leader Frank Jones is killed.

❽ Prisoner Brown is lynched at the Valley County jail, and outlaw George Whitney departs for South America, never to be seen again.

CON MURPHY

The Helena *Daily Herald*, newspaper of the territorial capital, proclaimed Con Murphy "one of the worst desperadoes that ever infested the [Rocky] Mountains, the 'Jesse James' of Montana." He bore another dubious honor: Murphy was Helena's last outlaw to be hanged by a mob, in 1885.[1]

By that date, the vigilantes of Montana's Virginia City-Bannack area had executed 22 thieves and murderers, and Helena's hangmen had added 13 more. Before Murphy, the last two, George Wilson and Arthur Compton, were hanged for the brutal beating and robbery of George Lenharth, an elderly prospector and rancher on the Missouri River. A crowd of more than 3,000 people witnessed the April 30, 1870, execution at the old Hangman's Pine tree in Dry Gulch. Six years later the tree was cut down by a Methodist minister named Shippen. However, the lack of a hanging tree didn't prevent a large number of men from hanging the 28-year-old Murphy—"a famous horse thief and badman," according to a local newspaper—from a railroad trestle across a small coulee between Helena and East Helena.

Versions vary somewhat, but what follows is the story of the relatively short and turbulent career of Con Murphy.

Known to his friends as "Red" or "Jack," Con Murphy was described as a slender but wiry and well-muscled man of about 150 pounds with an innocent-looking round face. His hair was a light reddish brown, and he had a matching mustache and closely clipped beard. The outlaw's complexion was described as both sallow and freckled, and his blue eyes (with red-hooded eyelids) were said to have produced a glossy stare. Murphy was supposedly good-natured and was not noted for either gunplay or killing, although he had briefly been associated with the vicious George "Big Nose" Parrott gang.

He said he took the name "Con" in Montana "because I fancied it." Murphy's real name was either Henry or John Redmond, and he reportedly came from a well-to-do family that lived between Hannibal and Palmyra, Missouri. He was said to have come west to live in southern Idaho at some time in his youth, possibly with relatives. In 1876, he became a teamster-packer with General Alfred Terry's Montana military command, campaigning against the Sioux (Dakota) Indians in the Yellowstone River country during the Great Sioux War of 1876-1877. He just escaped being dispatched with Lieutenant Colonel George Armstrong Custer and his Seventh Cavalry on their fateful ride from Fort Abraham Lincoln into the Little Bighorn River valley.

Murphy decided to abandon the military life while stationed at Terry's supply camp on the Yellowstone River, and he first began his outlaw career as a horse thief and later as a stagecoach robber. He also worked at legitimate jobs out of Miles City, Montana, such as driving a freight wagon, and apparently he owned some property there at one time.

As an outlaw, Murphy began operating in the Gallatin, Jefferson, and Madison river valleys of Montana. Then he went west to the Malad River and Big Camas areas of eastern Idaho. One writer, Andrew Garcia, said that Murphy knew every trail, hole, and corner of the freight-stage road between Corinne, Utah, and Virginia City, Montana, and that his earlier attempts at robbing heavily guarded stagecoaches had ended in failure.

Reportedly he also drove and sold horses to the Mounted Police of the Dominion of Canada's North West Territories. Murphy obtained some horses "legally" by trading with a few Indians and Metis (French-Indian) peoples for rotgut whiskey. He eventually drifted into the Helena Valley area—which proved to be a fatal mistake.

After three years on the outlaw trail, Murphy was captured in 1878, and in 1879 he was sentenced to the Montana Territorial Prison at Deer Lodge. He escaped—something at which he became an expert—after serving only seven months. He was recaptured about one year later by Lewis and Clark County Sheriff C. M. Jeffries in the Dearborn River country northwest of Helena. Murphy completed his sentence in 1882 and spent several months working as a cowboy in the Snake River country of Idaho and at other occupations at various mining camps before returning to the Helena area in 1884.

Upon his return he teamed up with the Edmondson brothers and a Texan named George Munn. The Edmondsons operated a ferry on the Missouri River near Spokane Creek. With Munn, Murphy robbed the Helena-Fort Benton stage on May 27, 1884. The holdup occurred at Mitchell's stage station, about 30 miles north of Helena in Prickly Pear Canyon on the Fort Benton-Helena stage line and the Mullan Road.

The bandits intercepted the coach about 600 yards beyond the stage station, just after the Helena-bound coach passed by. The holdup went smoothly, with no opposition. The booty consisted of registered letters containing money, and watches, revolvers, and $200 taken from the three passengers. Perhaps Murphy believed he had found an easier, more lucrative way of life.

But stage line superintendent Jacob Powers was determined to bring Murphy's new career to an abrupt halt. John Mead, the stage and ranch manager, gave Powers and two deputy sheriffs a detailed description of the two men and their horses and saddles. Mead said the bandits had arrived early in the morning on the previous day and had left about noon. Mead's suspicion was aroused in part because the thieves' horses were muddy, showing they had crossed the creek instead of using the road. In addition, he had observed that one suspect had a rip in one of his boot's insteps, and that it had been repaired.

The deputies stayed at the scene overnight, but Powers immediately began his pursuit. Two men had been seen riding in an easterly direction from the general area of the relay station after the robbery. Powers believed the pair might cross the Missouri River at the town of Canyon Ferry and set out for the Judith Basin country to the northeast.

The superintendent arrived at the ferry landing early the next morning, but no one had crossed recently. After resting briefly, he turned south and followed Spokane Creek, which paralleled the Missouri, to the old Helena-Bozeman stage station; it was run as a traveler's halfway house by Bruce Toole. Toole told Powers that Murphy often stayed with the John O'Neil family a mile and one-half northeast of Toole's place.

Powers had ridden over 100 miles in 24 hours with no sleep; he had talked with several ranchers in his line of travel, and he had located Murphy's and Munn's hideout. And what of the two deputies at Mitchell's? They leisurely returned to Helena, after spending the night in comfort and filling their stomachs. Powers also returned to Helena with the information he had rounded up and reported to the sheriff's office. Next, he traveled back to Toole's place with the two deputies to watch the O'Neil homestead.

Before arriving, the lawmen learned that two men matching Murphy's and Munn's descriptions had stolen two gray horses from the Clancy area south of Helena in Jefferson County. It was mistakenly believed they were returning to the O'Neil ranch.

Powers talked to O'Neil while the deputies stood by in the general area. After a lengthy, confidential discussion, O'Neil admitted that Murphy had stayed there and that the Edmondson brothers had collected all their stolen horses and had left for an unidentified park near the Snake River in the mountains of northern

Idaho. Murphy and Munn were to follow, he said, planning to add to the stolen horse herd on their way south. He told Powers that he doubted if the gang could be taken alive.

This ended Powers' participation in the search for Con Murphy, since the action shifted about 100 miles southward to Madison County, Montana. In spite of the fact that the outlaws were handicapped with both a large herd of horses and a covered wagon driven by John Edmondson, along with his wife and two children, the Edmondson-Murphy bunch was not detected until it neared Idaho.

Once they had located the outlaw bunch, the two Lewis and Clark County deputies took the train to Dillon, Montana, to cut them off, though they were too far to the west to make contact. A contingent of Jefferson and Madison county deputies finally caught up with them at Wall Creek in the Madison River valley and attempted capture on June 5, 1884. Many shots were fired (several hundred, some claimed), but no one was injured save a posseman who had his mustache singed by a stray bullet. The outlaw party lost some of the stolen horses in the fracas. But the outgunned posse couldn't dislodge the outlaws from their hiding place in a narrow canyon, and so, after expending all their ammunition, retreated. The $200 reward was hardly enough incentive to get shot.

The outlaw band continued 20 miles south, crossing the Continental Divide and going over Raynolds Pass into Idaho. They stopped at a naturally secluded park on Henrys Lake as originally planned.

The outlaws apparently thought the chase was over. But as they rested, a new 11-man posse was forming at the Madison County seat at Ennis, and was soon close behind them. The outlaws were spotted at their place of rest by local residents, the Switzer brothers, who passed the information on to the posse.

On July 9, John Edmondson's slow, lumbering wagon was at last overtaken one mile from Camas Station. It contained the camping outfit, rifles, and ammunition, and three stolen horses were tied on behind. The other outlaws had gone into town with just their handguns. They were captured the following day during a carefully staged ambush when they stopped for breakfast at the home of (LDS) Bishop Brigham Ricks in Ricksville (now Rexburg).

Murphy's partner Munn died in the exchange of gunfire and was buried in Idaho. His gear and personal effects were confiscated by Mormon authorities to defray the costs of an inquest and burial. Murphy (using the first name of Neal), Albert Edmondson, and John Edmondson were returned to Helena and incarcerated in the old wooden county jail on July 19.

Two nights later, Murphy cut his way to freedom through the jail roof. He wasn't missed until morning.

The Lewis and Clark County jail was described by a Helena newspaper as a "poor insecure building, no stronger than a pigeon box." It was learned that the night guard had left for a period of time to watch a boxing match. The U.S. Marshal's office had recommended that Murphy be kept in irons because of his frequent escapes. But this advice was ignored, and he was allowed to roam freely among the other prisoners and talk to outsiders as well. This must have allowed him to either plan a break with a confederate or to hire someone. The roof hole measured 14 by 16 inches, and a rope was dangling from the roof into his cell. The opening had been worked on from both sides.

A Helena paper called Murphy "the most hated villain in the county." The night of his escape, he reportedly rode 30 miles in the first two hours on his stolen horse, swam the Missouri River, and reached the Big Belt Mountains by daylight. The third day he arrived at Big Timber, Montana, having survived on berries and handouts from various farms. In Big Timber, he sold the horse and bridle for $75 to an Englishman and entered the Bliss Saloon to drink and gamble.

He did more of the former and so was no problem for the sheriff's department to arrest after local citizens telegraphed Helena. There was little worry of him leaving—they had tied him down.

Murphy stayed in the Silver Bow County jail at Butte until new steel-clad cells arrived in Helena from St. Louis and were installed. The jailers relaxed with Murphy in an escape-proof lockup—or so they thought. They should have been more cognizant of his determination to remain free.

When being transported back to Helena, Murphy had almost escaped from the undersheriff by jumping out the window of the train's water closet while fully cuffed and shackled. Three months later, when law officers entered his cell to take him before a U.S. grand jury, he had vanished. One report read that Murphy had skipped out the previous week; another said that he had secreted himself in the boxed compartment under the water sink and had only escaped after the cell was opened and they thought he had already disappeared. Apparently none of Murphy's jail mates had been invited along.

The reward for Murphy's capture was now boosted from $200 to $1,000.

Something else happened as a result of the jail break. Several arson fires occurred in Helena about the time of Murphy's escape, and a number of men—probably members of the fading vigilante movement—decided the outlaw must have set them. These men also surmised that the fires were to divert attention from a planned escape by the Edmondson brothers before they could be transferred to the state prison at Deer Lodge.

To further stir things up, Murphy's younger brother, whose name might really have been Con, appeared on the scene, trying to locate his brother. He had journeyed from Deer Lodge, and he told various Helena residents that their mother was very ill. She wanted her older son to return home to Missouri and mend his ways before she died.

Meanwhile, the Helena fires continued, and a witness claimed he saw Murphy at the scene of one. Hence the law and a resurrected vigilante "people's committee" made Murphy's capture (at the height of winter) a high priority.

Just before Murphy's second escape, the Jefferson and Boulder stagecoach had been held up by five or six masked men. The stage contained 15 passengers, nine on the inside and six on top, and two more wagonloads of passengers followed—along with two county sheriffs in a buggy. The group of prominent lawyers, judges, politicians, lawmen, and others were on their way to Boulder for the trial of the Edmondson brothers. This Helena group had transferred to the stage from a Northern Pacific train at Jefferson City.

The bandits were not after their money or valuables. They thought that John and Henry Edmondson and Con Murphy were aboard and had brought extra horses to rescue them. Warren Toole acted as spokesman for the passengers and asked the outlaws to be careful with their guns and not shoot anyone by accident. Toole told them that the prisoners they wanted were still in jail at Helena and warned them that more in their party were in wagons just behind the coach. The holdup men cut off their conversation with Toole and were about to beat a hasty retreat when lawmen arrived and opened fire.

One of the masked men, identified as Charley Warfield, was killed. Warfield had been one of the defense witnesses for the Edmondson brothers, and another Edmondson was thought to have been among the masked group, as was "Sleepy" Johnny Rothwell. The Edmondson brothers' trial was moved to Helena because of prisoner security problems and threats by the Edmondson brothers' father and friends against the judge, sheriff, and jury. But the trial proceeded, and the boys received prison terms of 14 and 12 years.

In the interim, jail escapee Con Murphy had been having a rough time surviving in the snow-covered and frigid Rocky Mountains. In January 1885 he stopped for two days at Paul's Saloon in Pipestone, a small community in Jefferson County near Whitehall. Murphy traded horses there and obtained a rifle and revolver. It wasn't until later that the saloon owner realized that Murphy had combined rewards on his head for $1,700.

Finally the cold and lack of food drove Murphy to return to the John O'Neil ranch on the Bozeman Road. There, somehow, his brother found him and convinced him to go back home. He bought railroad tickets to St. Louis for them, and they planned to depart from Missoula—where the outlaw Murphy was unknown.

O'Neil made contact with the Helena authorities, perhaps while buying supplies, and agreed to help in Murphy's capture if he would see the reward money. But Murphy's would-be captors were not Lewis and Clark County officers, but special officers George Bashaw and J. H. McFarland. Bashaw was a city policeman and McFarland was a liveryman. They were after Murphy for setting the Helena fires, not for the federal or state charges.

There had been about five arson fires in the vicinity of the county jail, and "people were in a state of alarm," according to a Helena paper. Henry Edmondson had escaped during the confusion generated by one of the fires, but he was quickly recaptured.

The three-man party of O'Neil, Bashaw, and McFarland set out in a sleigh for the 14-mile journey south and arrived at the O'Neil place early the next morning. The two officers waited in a nearby coulee while O'Neil entered the cabin and found the Murphy brothers still in bed. O'Neil asked the younger Murphy brother to feed the horses, and he was captured outside the cabin. Con Murphy was taken while still in bed. The party left the O'Neil place in the sleigh during a blinding snowstorm and was forced to lay over at Toole's halfway house, only a mile and one-half down the road. The two officers stayed awake all night with their prisoners.

The following morning after breakfast, Murphy had one of his handcuffs removed so that he could put on his coat. When Bashaw glanced out the window to see if the sled was ready, he allowed Murphy enough time to draw a secreted revolver from either a shoulder holster or boot. Murphy shot Bashaw in the wrist.

With his captor temporarily disabled, he ran up the stairs and hid in a closet. After several shots were fired up through the floorboards and walls, Murphy was told to surrender or the cabin would be torched. The outlaw said he would agree if promised safe passage to Helena and the return of his gun in the event a mob should attempt to seize him. Supposedly Murphy received such assurances, and he gave himself up.

Soon afterward, however, other law officers arrived from Helena and took custody of the Murphy brothers. The Helena newspaper's headline read "Con Murphy Will Be in the City This Evening, Dead or Alive." The twelve lawmen and their prisoners began the journey back to Helena on January 27, 1885, only to be intercepted by a "people's posse" of about 150 men. This occurred about four miles south of the capital city. The mob took the prisoners over the helpless peace officers' protests. Murphy's revolver was not returned, preventing him from going out in a blaze of glory.

A short trial of sorts was held. Murphy was questioned about the fires, denying any knowledge of them and not admitting to having confidantes who did. The mob leaders told Murphy that his career had ended and said if he had anything to say he should "make it damn quick." Murphy asked them to spare his younger brother because he was innocent of any crimes and asked for a fair trial. But the mob had already decided to hang him.

The crowd took Con Murphy to a nearby telegraph pole. A rope was thrown over the crossbars, and 50 men pulled him skyward. But the crossbar broke, and the half-strangled prisoner tumbled to the ground. After a short conference, the mob threw him back into the sleigh with the rope still around his neck and took a ten-minute ride to a nearby railroad trestle.

Before his second hanging, Murphy and his brother exchanged embraces and a few last words. Afterward, his swollen and purple-faced body was cut down from the 15-foot-high, makeshift gallows and removed to Helena to be put on exhibition, with the noose intact, at the old firehouse in Courthouse Square.

Con's brother, aged 23, was arraigned before County Judge Davis the following day for harboring and protecting a known criminal. He had not been harmed by the mob. The younger Murphy explained (in a different version of the earlier story) that he came from Morris, Illinois, at his coal miner father's request after he received a letter from Con after a ten years' absence. He said he had arranged a meeting near the railroad tracks 20 miles northeast of Helena, and that neither he nor his family knew anything of Con's outlaw career. Before he was scheduled to appear before a grand jury, he was released by Judge Davis, escorted under heavy guard to the station, and given a ticket to St. Paul, Minnesota.

Con Murphy was said to have been buried in the pauper's section of Helena's Benton Avenue cemetery, since apparently his family never claimed the body. In October 1894, old letters were found at the local post office addressed to J. T. Murphy; from whom was not revealed.

Whether Con Murphy, would have gone straight if he had returned to his home in Missouri (or Illinois) can only be speculated upon. We do know, though, that the outlaw once remarked to a fellow cellmate that he could have died an honorable death at the Battle of the Little Bighorn with Custer and saved the people of Montana much grief and expense. In the end, it was Murphy and his family who suffered the grief. His mother supposedly died soon after from a broken heart.

Special officers Bashaw and McFarland, who had risked their lives to capture Murphy, weren't happy, either; they were denied the reward money, which was to be given for a live capture only.

And lastly, the real culprits in the Helena fires were finally discovered. After the rest of the Edmondsons were banished from Montana by secret order of the Citizens Committee, the fires ceased.

The mystery of who helped Murphy escape from the Helena jail was never solved.

Although fate had dealt Murphy a dishonorable death, he gained a place in history as the last victim of the local vigilantes' rope—ironically, for crimes he didn't commit. After his death, it seemed the vigilante movement, which had begun in 1863, had run its course. Popular opinion weighed against it, and a strong court system replaced it. ★

"LONG" HENRY
THOMPSON

On a cold, crisp winter's morning in February 1902, a tall, slender cowboy in at least his mid-thirties exited from the Stevens Saloon and walked somewhat unsteadily but cautiously down the empty, snowpacked main street of Saco, Montana. His destination was the Valley Saloon. The man's partial Cherokee heritage gave his complexion a dark tint, as well as giving him dark hair and eyes, and he sported a wide handlebar mustache and chin whiskers that looked like the bristles of a paintbrush. He stood about six feet, four inches and was on the lean side, with a rugged look about him. On his gunbelt were two Colt .45 revolvers in low-hanging holsters tied to his trouser legs.

Once in front of the Valley Saloon, "Long" Henry Thompson hesitated, then opened the saloon door and entered. His right hand rested on his six-shooter. He stopped just inside and looked to his right, where several cowboys were either standing or sitting. Then he turned back to close the door. As Thompson's hand touched the knob, he stepped into eternity as the driving force of five pieces of lead ripped into his body. He staggered briefly, trying unsuccessfully to draw before collapsing. His still body lay in a pool of blood upon the roughhewn cottonwood floor. The terror of eastern Montana, one of the last gunfighters of the fading Western frontier, had died with his boots on.

This sounds much like a chapter from a Norman Fox or Dan Cushman paperback, but Thompson was a real person, and the event really happened, although some of the details have been disputed. Long Henry has not been kept alive in Western history books in the same way as Harvey "Kid Curry" Logan has, although Thompson's earlier reputation in Montana as a hard character was greater.

The *Havre Plaindealer* called Thompson "a bad man" and said that "a more desperate one never terrorized eastern Montana." The writer concluded: "The period that was placed on his life, in his last fight, ended an existence into which had been injected more thrills than to be found in a nineteenth-century novel."

The late Johnny Ritch—cowboy, historian, poet, miner, newspaperman, and Montana Historical Society board member—wrote another opinion in 1934: "There were gunmen. Most of them deadly sudden. Some of the lesser lights among them had only one notch on their gun; others had two, three, or four. Long Henry had six." Ritch further described Thompson as "a master craftsman with a six-shooter"—one of the quickest and best shots he had ever seen. "He was also fast with both hands and never missed his target, even though he never seemed to aim. He could fire twice before the average man could shoot once," he wrote.[1]

One cowboy companion, D. J. O'Malley, the "N Bar N Kid," described Thompson's Colt revolver as having both the trigger and trigger guard removed and the sight filed off. His swivel-type holster allowed the weapon to be fired by hitting the hammer from the hip without being removed from the holster. O'Malley agreed with Ritch on Long Henry's speed of draw. He said that Thompson always allowed his opponent to go for his gun first, so his plea would be self-defense. It was the philosophy of Ben Thompson, a notorious Texas outlaw.[2]

While Thompson's life in Montana is fairly well chronicled,

his earlier life is not. Thompson—whose real name might have been Westbrook, Brookside, or Pell—by his own account was born circa 1866 between Texas and the Indian Territory (present-day Oklahoma) on a strip of land claimed by no state and known as "No Man's Land." The lawless panhandle, a wide border between surrounding states and the territory, was barren, windswept, and lonely, and occupied by men who would "charge hell with a bucket of water." It was well known as a safe haven for outlaws, thieves, bootleggers, and other misfits.

Thompson was credited with saying that his mother cradled him in her arms while his father fought off desperate Apaches and even more desperate whites. Most who knew Thompson in Montana said one or both of his parents was of Cherokee heritage. Some said his father was white. Thompson spoke little of the past, and rarely of himself or his associates.

Others claimed that Thompson was born in the mountainous region of either Kentucky or Tennessee and drifted to the Texas-Oklahoma region,[3] or that he was born in the Weatherford, Texas, area, in Parker County near Fort Worth, where his parents still resided at the time of his death. According to the latter story, he had to leave there in 1877 after killing a rival for the affections of a prostitute.[4] He lived the next year in the Indian Territory and soon afterward drifted north to Wyoming and finally Montana. All versions of his story include killings and livestock thievery.

Regardless of how Thompson reached the Texas-Oklahoma area, he was credited with having belonged to the Henry Starr gang, which robbed trains, post offices, banks, general stores, express and post offices, and homesteads of whites and Indians alike, and stole livestock on the Texas-Mexican border and in Colorado and Arkansas.

The Indian Territory had been the rendezvous for the worst of the outlaw gangs in the Southwest for many years. Henry Starr was descended from the large Starr criminal dynasty that began with Tom "Giant" Starr and his son Sam. Henry had mixed Scotch, Irish, and Cherokee blood and operated in the Indian Territory until 1893.

It was reported in one version of his life that Thompson had fled from the Indian Territory after he had killed either federal or local law officers James McCarthy and Thomas White during a cattle-rustling attempt near the town of Okmulgee, the capital of the Creek Indian Nation. This is near the area where the Starr gang operated, on the Canadian River between Briartown and Eufaula.[5]

Thompson supposedly next went to Mexico for a period of time because of the $1,500 reward on his head—payable whether he was brought in dead or alive. Later he crossed into Texas and joined a Slaughter-Kyle Long S brand cattle herd heading north to the newly opened northeastern Montana grasslands in 1892. Their destination was a ranch south of the Great Northern Railway in the Larb Hills on Larb Creek.

Friend D. J. O'Malley, on the other hand, said Thompson came to Montana with a herd of Rocking H cattle owned by the N Bar N. (O'Malley appears to be the most reliable biographer.) These cattle had ranged on the Llano Estacado or "Staked Plains" of eastern New Mexico and West Texas, directly south of the Indian Territory's "No Man's Land."

An old-time cowboy of the Little Rocky Mountains country of northern Montana, Pink Simms, said he knew Thompson in Texas at the town of Higgins, in Lipscomb County, which also bordered the Indian Territory. Simms had been both a lawman and cowboy in Texas, once working for famed John Chisum's Jingle-bob brand. Simms also had a reputation as a reliable informant.

Yet another former lawman, Bob Ater of Hinsdale, said Thompson was in reality Texan "Big Foot" Wallace, who had been associated with "Billy the Kid" in the Lincoln County wars in New Mexico. However, he was wrong by all accounts. W. A. A. "Big Foot" Wallace came from West Virginia and had been a Texas Ranger, living in San Antonio. He was a light-complexioned and huskily built man, not tall and lean like Thompson. And Wallace died in 1899 at Austin, having lived 78 years. So much for that story.

Several other reports say Thompson stopped off in Johnson County, Wyoming, before coming to Montana. There, it was said, he was involved in an organized cattle- and horse-stealing ring. Possibly he rode with the "Red Sash" gang, headquartered at the K-C Ranch on the Powder River just 30 miles east of the fabled Hole-in-the-Wall country. Later it would be made famous by the Butch Cassidy, George "Flat Nose" Currie, and Kid Curry gangs.

Thompson's friend or acquaintance Ed Starr was certainly a member of the Red Sash gang.[6] Starr was described as a "vicious nonentity" and "a killer for killing's sake." Another supposed member of the Oklahoma Starr gang, Ed Starr was described as a small, dapper, dressy, and sociable individual who turned danger-ous when drinking—as most gunmen did. Starr was said to have been Thompson's equal with a handgun. Starr, calling himself Tom Dunn in Montana, gave his place of birth as Rockdale, Texas, in Milam County. Rockdale was about 60 miles south of Waco, and about 230 miles south of the Indian Territory.

One account said Ed Starr was the brother of the notorious Myra Maybelle "Belle" Starr, who was married to Henry Starr. This would have been quite impossible, though, since Belle's family name was Shirley and she was from Missouri; however, she did have a brother named Ed Shirley.

Starr was one of the three suspects accused of killing Special Deputy U.S. Marshal George Wellman on May 19, 1892, south of Buffalo, Wyoming, in Johnson County. Starr reportedly boasted of Wellman's killing and took the man's gun off his blood-soaked body. A reward of $1,000 was offered for Starr by the Wyoming Stock Growers Association.

When the large and powerful Wyoming cattle barons declared war on the small ranchers, cowboys, homesteaders, and rustlers of northern Wyoming counties without distinguishing among them, they began a conflict that culminated in the infamous Johnson County War of 1892. Because of the conflict, many Wyoming outlaws suddenly found eastern Montana to their liking. Some sources stated that Starr, Thompson, and mutual friend Armond Broome, along with Jack Teal and Clint Allison,[7] arrived in the Treasure State together.

The movement of about 50 major ranchers' cattle herds through Montana—an estimated 70,000 to 100,000 cattle— required the services of many cowboys, hired with no questions asked. It was easy to pick out the Texas cowboys because of their different dress and ways of talking, smaller cow ponies, and different methods of tending cattle.

Thompson, Starr, Teal, and Broome found employment with the Home Land and Cattle Company, owned by the Neidringhous brothers of St. Louis, who ran the N Bar N brand. They operated two Montana ranches during the 1880s: one on Rock Creek, north of the Milk River and the town of Hinsdale, and the other south of the Missouri River on Little Dry Creek. Also on the roster at times were "Dutch" Henry Ieuch and Harry "the Sundance Kid" Longabaugh, both future names in outlawry.

Eastern Montana was still a cowman's paradise where the large cattle companies had yet to suffer the devastating winter losses occurring on overgrazed ranges elsewhere in 1885-1886. And too, it was a place where an organization as powerful or vindictive as the Cheyenne-based Wyoming Stock Growers Association didn't control the range.

Many outlaws settled contentedly into complete obscurity, particularly in the newly settled area of northern Montana called the High Line (Hi-Line).[8] The shiny steel rails of the St. Paul, Minneapolis, and Manitoba Railway had recently stretched westward across this wide, roadless, and fenceless prairie, bringing the white man's "civilization" in the form of stations, roundhouses, water tanks, coal bins, and maintenance worker section houses. It was perfect for fugitives who wanted to go straight—or begin their careers anew—since there were few professional law enforcers and wanted men were even wearing some of the badges. Arrest warrants from Texas, Wyoming, and other places were unlikely to be served in this no-questions-asked country.

But a few outlaws, such as Thompson, shunned obscurity and even gained great notoriety in such an atmosphere. Thompson's career in Montana was marked with the same dramatic episodes that had characterized his earlier life.

The chronicles of Thompson before coming to Montana are vague at best.[9] He is reputed to have killed a trail hand named John Gallman in Wendover, Wyoming, as well as another victim at Chadron, Nebraska. These reported shootings took place in the area crossed by the Western, Texas, Jones-Plummer and Bozeman trails, and seemed to receive wide coverage on the informal but efficient cowboy telegraph from Montana to Texas.

The strenuous and boring life of a cowboy was relieved by news of such outlaw exploits. Impressionable young cowboys made up songs about the thieves and killers and gave them almost hero status similar to that of professional athletes today. Historian Richard White has called the bandits "symbols of masculinity" and "cultural heroes of the day."

Thompson's reputation was not that of a troublemaker, yet he never ran from trouble, either. He kept his cool when trouble courted him. One prime example of this was his run-in with fellow N Bar N cowhand Frank "Kid" Flannagan at their camp on Little Dry Creek in the fall of 1892. Flannagan, a Miles City boy, was a would-be badman who never quite made the grade, much like Johnny Curry, Kid Curry's brother. One night Flannagan got liquored up and decided to become a tough guy by picking on Henry Thompson, who had told him to go to bed or else he would take him over his knee. Flannagan pulled his gun, cocked it, and shoved it into Thompson's stomach. He declared that he would shoot Thompson for threatening to spank him. According to witness D. J. O'Malley, Long Henry looked Flannagan in the eye and said, "Kid, you ain't goin' to pull that trigger and you know it. If you did, you would be liable to hurt someone and that would be mighty bad." With that he grabbed the revolver barrel and twisted it away and out of Flannagan's hand as Frank pulled the trigger.

The bullet struck the side of the old ranch house nearby. With that, Long Henry ordered Flannagan to bed and the next morning gave him his gun back.

One of Thompson's adventures did not include gunplay. While guarding cattle somewhere on the Texas Trail in 1899, he was struck by lightning on the chest. The bolt went down his body, forked near his saddle, and arced down both his legs. It shredded his clothes in the process and burned the soles of his boots. He was unconscious for about six hours. Upon waking from near death and regaining his faculties, he reportedly exclaimed, "I guess none of those gunmen can kill me, and God Almighty will have to load His gun a little heavier if He does business with me."

There is another equally colorful version of this same story—unless the Lord went after Long Henry a second time. This version was related by a transplanted Texan, Plaz Price. Price, a reputed gunman, settled on Beaver Creek's Rocky Crossing (once known as the Fort Browning Trail crossing) west of Hinsdale in 1886. His ranch was located near a major crossing of the Milk River for those coming from the south along Larb and Timber creeks. Several outlaws from Wyoming and other places south stopped at Price's place on their way north into the North West Territories of the Dominion of Canada. Price said Thompson was one of the Wyoming cowboys blacklisted by the Wyoming Stock Growers Association, and that he came into Montana in 1891-1892, stopping first at Price's ranch. He said Thompson had killed three men before coming to Montana. Thompson settled in the Milk River country and often stayed with Price. Price described Thompson as quite dark, lean, and tall, but powerfully built.

During one such visit, a severe thunderstorm developed and a lightning bolt struck the cabin and entered just where Thompson's roundup bed was located. The lightning set off Thompson's loaded revolver under the bedroll and started a fire in the blankets. Price put out the fire and found that the partially paralyzed Thompson had lost his heavy body hair, the high heels of his boots, and the knobs of the ends of his heavy spur shanks (now melted). He was otherwise unharmed.

Thompson's first known Montana bloodletting occurred in September 1894. Tending cattle for the N Bar N brand between the Missouri and Yellowstone rivers on Little Dry Creek, Thompson got into a heated argument with the camp cook, George Dunman (or Denman), who was either part Black or Native American. The cook was described as a large, mean, powerful bully of a man. The altercation began at Charlie "Dynamite" Hanson's saloon in the town of Fallon, a cattle shipping point on the Northern Pacific Railroad line.

Thompson and his fellow cowhands, including O'Malley, watched the cook abuse a smaller, drunken Seven O L Ranch hand named Watson. Dunman whirled the smaller man around and laughed when he staggered, all the time buying him drinks. Finally, Watson fell hard enough to cut his forehead. Dunman threw whiskey in his face, saying, "There, cowboy, that will stop the bleeding. Get up and have another drink." Watson bellowed in pain from the alcohol in the cut and in his eyes.

Thompson went over and wiped the blood and whiskey from Watson's face. He then turned to Dunman and quietly said, "I guess this will be enough of this sort of fun with this man, George."

Dunman protested the interference, almost reaching for his pistol, but thinking better of it. Thompson returned to the bar, finished his drink, and left, passing within three feet of the cook. Dunman soon left, too, going from saloon to saloon, getting drunker and making threats against Thompson, but at last he returned to his rooming house for the night.

The next day Dunman continued the heavy drinking. He encountered Thompson walking down the street from his lodgings. The ranch cook, who had just mounted his horse, then grabbed for his rifle, which was already partially out of its scabbard, and warned Thompson of his impending death. However, Thompson shot him twice before he could fire. Thompson walked into Dynamite's Saloon and asked someone to notify the sheriff's office at Miles City of the shooting.

The Fallon-Custer County resident deputy sheriff, who was in Miles City at the time, returned and took Thompson by train to the county jail, about 50 miles to the southwest along the Yellowstone River. Three people immediately paid his bail, and a coroner's jury and a Justice Court judge, both ruling self-defense, cleared him.

Dunman was evidently buried next to the railroad right of way only a few feet from where he fell, and a fence was built around his grave.

Thompson was in worse trouble the following year. He was arrested for robbing the Lewis brothers' bank at Glasgow, Montana. Glasgow was a cattle and Great Northern Railway center of about two thousand people; it was the county seat of the original Valley County, and was located on the Milk River near the present-day Fort Peck Dam and Reservoir.[10]

One wintry day in November 1895, three masked and armed men entered the combination bank and general store at about 8 p.m. At first bank employees thought the cowboys were joking, but the nervous men who spoke in whispers and gestured with their weapons convinced them otherwise.

One man, thought to be Thompson, stood by the door after locking it and drawing the window shades. Another covered one clerk and two women customers, and the third bandit directed the other clerk to empty the cash drawers and vault. To the bandits' surprise, the vault was on a time-clock-controlled lock until the next morning—he even listened at the vault door to confirm it. So he took the bag containing the bank's change instead. It contained about $145.

Banker R. M. Lewis was in an adjoining office with a customer during the robbery. When Lewis entered the main banking room, the bandits greeted him with their guns and directed him back into the office. Not to be intimidated, Lewis jumped through the plate glass windows that faced the street and began yelling for help.

The startled robbers rushed out the door—one fell in the

stampede—and ran a block and a half to their horses. They headed for the hills north of town. A posse pursued them, but lost the robbers' trail in a blinding snowstorm.

Three suspects were arrested soon after the robbery. Thompson and Jack (Walter) Dawson were arrested at Charles E. Hall's sheep ranch on Porcupine Creek, near an N Bar N cattle camp northwest of Forsyth. The arresting officers were Valley County Undersheriff Milt Harrah and deputies Jack Caldwell and George Dunnell. Broome was arrested soon afterward in Glasgow. Dawson was a stranger to the townspeople, but the other two were well-known.

The town's residents were especially shocked at Broome's arrest. He had operated a saloon in town along with his brother Seymour, when not working for cattle outfits. Armond had cowboyed the previous summer for the N Bar N and had sometimes worked as a foreman. He had operated the Bank Saloon, previously owned by former sheriff Sid Willis. (Willis later owned the Mint Saloon in Great Falls.) A Glasgow newspaper reporter wrote of Broome: "He was always considered an honorable and upright young man and has many friends."

District Court Judge Dudley Dubose set bond for two of the captives at $5,000, but Broome's was reduced to $2,500, making possible his release from jail. Thompson and Dawson, who could not meet bail, stayed in confinement for about six months. Broome's defense attorney was granted a delay of trial until witness W. S. "Leather" Griffith (later a sheriff of Valley County) could be located.

The long-awaited trial in Fort Benton lasted one August day, and the charges were dismissed by Judge J. W. Tattan for lack of sufficient evidence. The trial location had been moved; County Attorney C. A. Evans didn't believe a conviction was possible in Glasgow because of Broome's popularity. The three suspects were represented by two Great Falls attorneys besides the one from Glasgow. Where the money came from for their defense is unknown.

Thompson, by all reports, kept out of trouble after the trial, except for an arrest for horse theft. In this case, he was found not guilty.

Thompson was said to have been a nice, cheerful fellow until he drank. Then he felt obliged to live up to his tough reputation, although his friend D. J. O'Malley said he drank very little and was not of a quarrelsome disposition. At local dances most of the women were supposedly afraid of Thompson, so he danced around and around by himself. Others said he was a good worker, even helping with household chores, but he always kept his Colt "peacemaker" close. Once he refused to dig a well because he would not have been able to see any potential adversary approaching.

O'Malley said he "found him as good a man to get along with as in any [cattle] outfit." Truman Cheney said Thompson was "among the highest paid, most dependable, and hardest working cowboys ... kept on the payroll during the winter when most of the cowboys holed up or rode the grubline."

The opinions on Long Henry were nearly endless: he would do anything for a friend; he was respected by law-abiding citizens since all his killings were in self-defense, and his victims were worse than he; he was a nervous person and rarely trusted anyone; he was the best of the bunch he rode with—although illiterate and not exceptionally bright, falling prey to Armond Broome's schemes.

Dunn, Broome, Thompson, and friends supposedly rustled livestock from all over eastern Montana, as far west as Havre in the north-central part of the state, north to Canada, and east into North Dakota. Broome seems to have been the dominant member of the gang, although he is a somewhat shadowy figure. Wally Blue, whose father operated a blacksmith shop near Saco, thought Broome was about five feet eleven inches, on the lanky side, with a long black beard. Broome listed his birthplace as Mississippi and gave his occupation as stock raiser on the 1900 census for the Saco township, located about 43 miles northwest of Glasgow on the High Line.

It was said he came to Wyoming from Texas, but whether as

a rustler or stock inspector is disputed. The Broome family homestead was about 50 miles southeast of Malta, Montana, on a small creek. The log buildings and land were sold to the John Etchart family in 1911, and became known as the Stone House Ranch.

Armond's father, C. L. Broome, had apparently died by 1900. Like Armond, he had earned the distrust and contempt of many people in Valley County. Armond's brother Seymour was said to have been mentally unbalanced and was killed by lightning while tending cattle. The only Broome to earn words of praise from area residents was younger brother Arthur, who was a good, honest cowpuncher.

One local writer, F. B. Gillette, ventured to say that Armond Broome was "one of the most calculating, cold-blooded and shrewdest personalities in the old Northwest." The early words of praise from his former Glasgow friends didn't apply here in Valley County, although Broome remained popular in Glasgow until its outlaw days were over.

Ed Starr, also known as Tom Dunn, was documented as having been in Johnson County, Wyoming, during the conflict with the owners of the large ranches there. There are two versions of one tale from that period. One has it that Starr and a cohort had a shootout in a Buffalo, Wyoming, saloon with U.S. Marshal Joseph Rankin and an unidentified deputy marshal. The deputy and Starr's companion were killed. In another more official version, Rankin and a posse had a gunfight with the two at a hideout on Crazy Woman Creek, but the outlaws got away. Starr's companion could have been either Charley Cruse or Black Henry Smith, his companions in the murder of special deputy U.S. Marshal George Wellman. Starr was never caught and moved on to Montana.

Before Starr moved to Saco from the Glasgow area to operate his Palace Saloon and livestock business, he had been appointed a stock inspector-range detective for the greater Glasgow district. He had been recommended by the N Bar N ranch manager, among others, and appointed by Chief Stock Inspector W. D. Smith of

Miles City sight unseen. Smith and Starr had known each other in Wyoming from opposite sides of the law, and Starr always had an excuse why he couldn't go to Miles City. After Starr's arrest and conviction for two major cattle thefts, Smith wrote Starr and asked him to meet him in Glasgow. Starr replied that he had to quit and return to Arizona because of his father's death. Then, in May 1897, he really moved to Saco, but not alone.

Starr married an Ohio-born 20-year-old of French heritage, Della Dehotell, then of Glasgow. Della had recently returned from Malta where she had worked at a hotel. Starr's Wyoming friends heard that she was a churchgoer and that she henpecked him something terrible.

Their marriage didn't keep Starr out of trouble. He received a $25 fine for disorderly conduct in March 1896 in Glasgow. He was accused of beating a man named Jack Allen on the head with his six-guns. Three months later he was arraigned before U. S. Commissioner Hall for attempting to smuggle drugs in from Canada. Broome's name was added to the indictment three weeks later. However, the case was dismissed for lack of evidence because it was determined that the white powdery substance was not a narcotic, but headache powders.

During the remainder of 1896 and early 1897, Della made frequent trips to Pearmond, an early settlement on the south side of the Missouri River about 45 miles east of Glasgow. The N Bar N Ranch had a cattle ferry there and had also consolidated its two eastern Montana ranches near that location at Oswego. Oswego consisted of a railroad depot, a trading post, and some shacks. Starr, Thompson, and Broome all worked there at times. The newlyweds plus Broome and friends attended dances at Pearmond.

Before moving to Saco, Starr and his wife stayed at the N Bar N Ranch on Rock Creek, north of Hinsdale. Starr and Thompson may have briefly operated a saloon at Hinsdale, but if so, they had a falling out and quit the business.

In May of 1897, Starr and Broome purchased 77 horses from

the N Bar N. Accompanied by a 19-year-old transplanted Iowan, Ed Shufelt, they took the animals to North Dakota to sell. Shufelt was believed to have been involved with a rustling ring, and he did business specifically with Broome. The young outlaw was listed as 22 years old in the 1900 census. He was described as about five feet, three inches tall, with dark complexion, eyes, and hair.

Shufelt was always on the edge of trouble. Two years earlier, he had been arrested for unlawfully branding cattle, but he was released because of irregularities in the prosecution of the case; a brother, Hank, was also involved. Another time, he was charged along with a "Kid" Oliver for stealing a mare. The Shufelt clan had a ranch at Nashua, Montana, about 13 miles east of Glasgow. Several different Shufelts are mentioned in early newspapers, and it appears that the parents of the boys were Theodore and Isabell Shufelt, formerly of Missouri, New York, and Iowa. The name was alternately spelled Shoefelt and Shufeldt.

Hank Shufelt was killed by a shotgun blast near Grinnell, North Dakota, in April 1898. The local newspaper editor pleaded self-defense. Shufelt had threatened him with bodily harm after the editor published an article calling the residents of Grinnell Bottoms horse thieves, and noting that Hank was their leader.

Ed and Hank Shufelt had a ranching operation of their own at one time, and they were well known in eastern Montana for their skill at breaking horses. They were also said to have been connected to J. P. "Doc" Smith's alleged major rustling operation near Culbertson on the Missouri River.

Hank Shufelt had been married to Minnie Christie, whose father Sam allegedly had an outlaw ranch in the northwest corner of Valley County. Hank and Minnie had one child. Minnie's parents moved to the Saco area after law officers told them to leave Valley County. One has to wonder what a Glasgow paper meant when calling the Shufelt family and its relations "highly esteemed members of the community."

Ed Shufelt married a 16-year-old girl by the name of Cary Pearl Chamberlin in February 1900 when he had just turned 21.

The wedding was held in Glasgow. The Chamberlins, originally from South Dakota, were residents of Dawson County.

Among Long Henry Thompson's cohorts, Broome and Starr appeared to get along well, as did Broome and Thompson; but the animosity between Starr and Thompson was getting worse, though they were still in the livestock business together. One story tells of a fistfight between Starr and Thompson in a Glasgow saloon. Starr lost and fired his revolver, but no harm was done.

The mounting animosity inevitably led to violence. Some said Broome fueled the flames because he coveted Starr's wife and properties. There are several versions of the confrontation. The place of the showdown was the Walter Ballard Ranch on the flatlands adjacent to the Milk River, west of Hinsdale. The date was August 6, 1898, a Saturday, and the time about 8 a.m. Thompson later said in a jailhouse interview with a Valley County Gazette reporter that the fight had occurred because Starr wouldn't pay him for helping to build a dance hall in Saco that summer.

Starr heard of the accusation and confronted Thompson at the Ballard ranch that morning. When Thompson acknowledged the complaint, Starr drew his revolver and fired three rounds at close range. Long Henry claimed that he was able to throw himself to one side so he only received minor scalp and side wounds and a hole in his hat; he then returned the fire, killing Starr. The reporter viewed the holes in his hat and clothing but saw no wounds.

The problem with this story is that Starr was an excellent shot. His shooting contests with Thompson, held outside the Coleman House in Glasgow, always ended in a draw, and each had to buy several rounds of drinks to pay off the bets.

In a second version of the fight, Starr and Thompson stepped down into a hollow near the corral and, each holding onto a handkerchief with his left hand, drew at Broome's command. A further variation adds an open grave for the loser to fall into!

In version number three, Starr was unarmed at his wife's insistence, his revolver and holster hanging from a nearby fence post. When Starr reached for his revolvers, Thompson shot him in the back and then put holes in his own clothes so he could claim self-defense. But Starr was probably without his gun because he was about to go in to eat, not because of any prompting by his wife. According to Della's family, she had only good words to say of her husband. She suspected foul play—at least on Thompson's part.

In version number four, which circulated widely (even back to Wyoming) and was the most popular version at cowboy campfires, Broome put blanks in Starr's revolver and changed them back afterward. A variation on this had Starr's gun empty or the powder removed from the bullets.

The fifth version has Thompson riding up with a small band of horses and leading them into the corral. Starr warned him to stay away, and he went for his gun. The reason for the fight was variously said to be either a dispute over the ownership of some horses, a quarrel over the distribution of the profits after the sale of some horses, or an accusation made by Starr that Thompson was robbing him.

In the sixth and final version, Thompson and Broome were haying at the Ballard ranch. Long Henry was on the stack when Starr rode up with a herd of horses and drove them into the corral. Starr had been told to stay away from the ranch for some reason. He removed his revolver and placed it on the corral fence after putting the animals away and then started for the Ballard house. As Starr walked up the path, Long Henry called to him from the haystack. Starr stopped, exchanged words with him, and continued on towards the house. At that, Thompson drew his Colt .45 and shot Starr in the back three times. Next he shot the holes in his clothing and hat.

In the last version, Mrs. Ballard reportedly observed all this from the doorway and called her husband, who rode to Saco and wired the Valley County sheriff's office at Glasgow. He made his wife promise not to tell anyone what she had seen. She only told the story after Thompson was dead and Broome had left the country.

When Sheriff D. Kyle arrived at Saco, Thompson surrendered and returned with him to Glasgow, where he was jailed without bail. Plaz Price, Jim Burnette, Walter Ballard, and Armond Broome were listed as witnesses, but only Broome was called to testify at the preliminary hearing before Justice Perret, since he was apparently the only eyewitness.[11] (Burnette and Price had been N Bar N cowhands, and Price claimed Thompson's friendship.)

Broome's testimony must have matched Thompson's story since the plea of self-defense was accepted. One can only speculate as to how they explained the results of the autopsy—that the bullets entered from the back.

Of course, it didn't hurt that it came out at the preliminary hearing that Starr had a $1,000 reward on his head for the murder of a law officer in Wyoming. Starr was also said to have been the head of a rustling gang operating north of Saco and Hinsdale.

Starr's burial service at the Highland Cemetery in Glasgow was well attended; perhaps his notoriety drew the curious.

Broome and Della were married the following spring in Glasgow in a joint Methodist-Episcopal ceremony. Broome now owned Starr's Saco residence, saloon, and Hinsdale property. Armond and Della each claimed one of Starr's two livestock brands.

With Starr buried and Broome settled comfortably in his house and bed, it is not clear where Thompson was hanging his hat. Saco seems to have been his home base when he wasn't working for wages south of the Missouri River. However, it appears that he moved on to Hinsdale after the killing. Perhaps he worked for the Pioneer Cattle Company, the successor to the N Bar N, owned by Kohrs and Billenburg.

Arthur Jordan, founder of the town of Jordan, which was located on Big Dry Creek south of the Missouri, said Long Henry often visited his ranch. Many of those on the wrong side of the law frequented the ranch and town, since it was the only main community between Glasgow and Miles City, and Jordan made them welcome. Jordan, in his autobiography, hinted at the fact that Thompson was in the horse-thieving business and may have had a remote "ranch" on Crooked Creek divide. Crooked Creek paralleled the Missouri River and flowed into the Musselshell about 45 miles west of Jordan and 70 miles south of Saco. A brief news item also mentioned Crooked Creek as the site of Thompson's ranch.

Those who believed that Broome had engineered Starr's death predicted that it was only a matter of time before he had Thompson killed, too.

In January 1901, Thompson was arraigned before local Justice of the Peace Wilson on a warrant issued December 25, 1900, for disturbing the peace. He had celebrated Christmas by firing his gun in the streets of Saco. The charges were dismissed due to insufficient evidence, according to the *Malta News*.

A month later, an article appeared in the Glasgow *Northern Montana Review* in which it was stated that Long Henry had been arrested Thursday morning, February 7, at the instigation of Broome, because "Henry had been making war talk." Thompson was to have a preliminary hearing before Justice of the Peace Freidl the following Monday morning. Bond was set at $250. On February 16, Thompson was placed on a $500 bond to keep the peace with Broome for one year. Six jurors were paid $1.50 each for the trial of the State versus Thompson.

There is no record of what transpired between Broome and Thompson, but one could speculate that Thompson was having guilt pangs about his cowardly killing of Starr. Perhaps seeing Broome marry Della and take over Starr's property made Thompson realize that Broome's motivation in urging the killing had been selfish. And so Broome became the whipping boy for Thompson's guilt. Of course, the complete story is buried forever beneath the western prairie sod.

The next chapter in Thompson's story comes from Clement "Tuff" Prentice, a trusted friend of Thompson. Prentice's parents were early Valley County residents, perhaps arriving with the railroad in 1879, and he inherited their ranch near the confluence of the Missouri and Milk rivers south of Nashua. Prentice had to abandon the property when Fort Peck Dam and Reservoir were built, and he retired to Glasgow where he owned the Mint Saloon. Bob Saindon interviewed him for the *Glasgow Courier* in October 1962.

Prentice agreed with O'Malley that Long Henry was born in the Indian Territory, that he was part Cherokee, and that he had come up the Texas Trail to Montana, stopping briefly in Johnson County, Wyoming. Prentice said it wasn't until 1902 that Thompson found out that Broome had arranged his killing of Starr. Apparently someone enlightened him while he was working for a cattle outfit south of the Missouri River. Tuff said Thompson learned "it was all a frame-up to get Tommy [Starr] killed, but Long Henry knew nothing about it."

Thompson hurried to Prentice's ranch, arriving late in the day. In the course of the evening, he told Prentice of his intentions to leave Montana after completing some business in Saco, presumably with Broome. A newspaper brief mentioned Texas as his destination.

Prentice tried to convince Thompson to "forget Saco and ride around it" or he would be killed. Thompson replied, "I've never ridden around a town yet, and I'm not goin' to now."

A suspicious rider showed up at the ranch about then, adding to the tension with a phony story about where he had traveled from that day. They assumed he was either a stock inspector or a spy in their employ. To avoid trouble, Thompson volunteered to sleep in the barn, but Prentice said no, believing he might need help. They told the stranger not to move during the night, or get up before they did. Prentice, if no one else, slept lightly.

Still, no trouble developed, and the stranger was fed breakfast and sent on his way. Soon after, Thompson saddled up, ready to leave for Saco some 70 miles distant. Prentice again tried to persuade him to do otherwise, but failed. When Prentice next heard of his friend, Long Henry was dead.

Thompson arrived in Saco on Friday, February 14. The story

of what led up to his death is murky, like the enigmatic killing of Ed Starr. It is certain that Thompson attended an all-night dance at the Valley Saloon, owned by Ed Shufelt and Andy Duffy. This is believed to have been Starr's former saloon, the Palace, sold by Broome. Broome himself was nowhere in sight.

Friends of Thompson claimed that Broome hired Shufelt to kill Thompson. Shufelt and his friends William Long and William Mason tried constantly to start fights with Thompson during the dance. Shufelt and his companions, on the other hand, claimed that the two quarreled over a woman named Georgia Grant.

The woman was supposedly keeping house for Shufelt in Saco, and Thompson would purportedly visit her on occasion. On this visit, Thompson was carrying several hundred dollars—no doubt the money he planned to use to winter in Texas—and the Grant woman showed her preference for Thompson at the dance. Shufelt reportedly slapped her in a jealous rage. Next Shufelt tried to make peace, offering Thompson a drink, but Long Henry slapped it away and pushed the much smaller man. Bystanders at that time separated the two antagonists. Georgia Grant stayed behind the bar during it all.

According to Shufelt, Thompson gave notice that he would be back in 15 minutes to "fumigate the dump," come in shooting, and/or clean the place out.

Thompson headed for the Frank Stevens Saloon and Restaurant-Hotel, down the street. Stevens, a former N Bar N foreman, was described as a heavyset six-footer. Stevens and his bartender, J. B. Northcutt, were friends of Thompson. There, after a few drinks, Thompson reportedly came near to a fight with William Mason, who had followed him; then returned to the Valley Saloon at about 8 a.m. Supposedly, friends stopped Thompson and warned him not to go in. Thompson replied, "Why, that blamed coyote couldn't shoot a crippled calf if he had it tied down!" Yet no such statements were presented later in the courtroom.

In the saloon behind the bar was Shufelt, his revolver lying on the bar top. Georgia Grant may also have been there washing glasses when Thompson entered the building, paused at the open door, and looked to the right where Shufelt's friends were congregated. He then half-turned back to close the door. At that instant, Shufelt opened fire. The first bullet entered Thompson's left shoulder and went through his body and down his arm. Thompson fell to the floor, his revolver not drawn, resting under his body. Shufelt fired more rounds into the downed man's back.

Most of the customers exited through the back door when the shooting started and claimed to have seen nothing. Shufelt left the scene, holding his gun and warning others away. His friends saddled his horse, and he went to Broome's house for a short time. He returned and surrendered to Valley County Sheriff W. S. "Leather" Griffith upon Griffith's arrival on the "Skiddo" local train from Glasgow.

It is interesting to note that the Malta *Enterprise* sided with Thompson and found much support for him in that locale, while Glasgow's *North Montana Review* editorialized, "He was a shiftless fellow, a dangerous man with a gun, and would resort to the taking of human life at the slightest provocation." The *Havre Plaindealer* concurred. Shufelt, though, was not popular in Saco, and was considered a rustler, smuggler, and general no-good. The locals there felt Thompson was foully dealt with, and that Shufelt wouldn't have had a chance in a fair fight, since he was no gunman.

The woman named Georgia Grant might have been the toughest one of the bunch if the following story about her is true. She supposedly said that she would shoot the first man who said she was the cause of the fight.

Frank Stevens was called after the smoke cleared. He moved his friend's body out of the open door and collected the outlaw's personal effects. His partner, Northcutt, who was justice of the peace, had Duffy secure the doors. The body was moved to the rear of the saloon and placed on a pallet. With Northcutt as acting coroner, a six-man coroner's jury was convened on the spot. None of the Shufelt faction was included. The dead cowboy's clothing was removed and the blood washed away so the wounds could be examined.

To no one's surprise, the jury found Thompson's death resulted from multiple gunshot wounds administered by Ed Shufelt, by his own admission. The only witness called was Austin Taylor, a local sheep rancher. Taylor had been following Thompson when he entered the Valley Saloon. The witness saw the revolver being fired from behind the bar, and he observed Shufelt leave the saloon through the rear door.

Pioneer ranchers Charley Hunter and John Taylor claimed to have served on that jury, but in fact they did not. Nor did Dr. Mark Hoyt of Glasgow, the county health officer, preside over it; he was a consulting physician during the official autopsy. The two ranchers said they had observed Dr. Hoyt probing Long Henry's heart for the slugs. They said the doctor sniffed, paused, and remarked dryly that "Long Henry always did have a bad heart."

The preliminary hearing was held on February 18, before ever-busy Justice Northcutt. Valley County attorney John Kerr represented the State, and George Hurd was Shufelt's attorney. Hurd was a prominent Glasgow criminal attorney and, along with his brothers, owned a ranch on Willow Creek.

It would be interesting to know whether Broome paid the defense's fees, which were undoubtedly costly.

An arrest warrant wasn't issued for Shufelt until February 17, and bail was provided on February 19 by J. H. Jordan, a Saco merchant, and E. M. Hammond, a Saco area stockman. Sixteen witnesses were called during the two-day hearing, starting with Sheriff Griffith and ending with Shufelt.

Shufelt's defense was that Thompson had caused the trouble in the saloon the morning after the dance, and that he had tried to pacify Long Henry by offering him a drink. But Thompson would have none of that and struck him. When one of Shufelt's friends tried to separate them, Thompson backed out the front door, threatening Shufelt and his friends. They claimed Thompson came back through the door about 15 minutes later, threatening Shufelt's life.

Shufelt claimed he had no choice but to shoot.

The state's witness said Thompson had no revolver out and said nothing upon entering and was neither angry nor drunk. Austin Taylor again told his story of following Thompson to the saloon and witnessing the shooting. He testified that Thompson was neither in an openly angry mood nor had he exchanged words with Shufelt at the saloon entryway. Nate Roach, owner of a small store just west of the Valley Saloon, concurred with Taylor that Thompson was his usual calm, quiet self.

Frank Stevens told his version of what transpired after he entered the saloon: He and three others moved the body, which was wedged between the doorway and bar, so the door could be closed. He also removed $200 from the victim's pocket for safe-keeping. Thompson's revolver fell out of his clothing on the right side when the body was moved. Stevens placed it on the bar top. It was fully loaded, and had not been fired. A layman's discussion of the examination of Thompson's wounds followed.

A witness named Ben Beam added a different view. Beam saw Shufelt with the others—including Duffy—standing in back of the saloon after the shooting with his revolver in hand. Shufelt's horse was being saddled at the time. A courtroom discussion followed as to Beam's visual acuity when drinking. He claimed it improved his vision, of course.

Shufelt's partner, Andy Duffy, claimed that he didn't see the shooting, only Thompson hitting the floor. He also didn't know who saddled the horse. He told of Northcutt taking charge of the crime scene. Duffy was the same age as Shufelt, twenty-two, and had come to Montana via Canada and England. The 1900 census listed him as a stock drover.

Doctors Mark Hoyt and George Clay presented their findings. They discovered five entry wounds: one in the right shoulder and the rest in the left side of the back. All five rounds were fired from behind. Two were horizontal and the rest downward wounds, so the first two were fired when Thompson was standing. This confirmed Taylor's testimony of initially hearing two gunshots, a pause, then three more.

Porter Roach, Nate's brother, testified that Thompson was angry and that Shufelt, as he backed out the front door, threatened to come back and shoot up the joint. Yet he couldn't remember who was at the bar at the time, nor did he have any information concerning Georgia Grant. He claimed to have left the building before the shooting, but he did observe Shufelt afterwards standing with his weapon while his horse was being saddled. He confirmed that Shufelt did go to Broome's and returned about 20 minutes later.

The five defense witnesses were Carl Sorrenson, William Mason, William Long, Walter Taylor, and Shufelt.

Sorrenson said Thompson came in threatening Shufelt, but he didn't see a gun in Thompson's hand. He admitted to saddling Shufelt's horse and related that Shufelt went to visit his sister at Broome's house. No one asked why Shufelt's sister was there or what connection Broome had to the affair.

Mason also told the story of Thompson's threats and his entrance into saloon, but in his version, Thompson had his revolver out. He admitted following Thompson to Stevens' place, where he observed him sitting by the stove. When Thompson refused to drink with him, he returned to the saloon just ahead of Thompson. Mason had tried to separate the two after Thompson pushed Shufelt, but Thompson told him to sit down since he wasn't the sheriff.

Long's testimony backed up Mason's, and he added to the list of threats that Thompson allegedly had made. When asked about Georgia Grant's whereabouts during the shooting, his memory was clouded, too.

Walter Taylor didn't make an especially good defense witness. He said Thompson had his gun out, but then contradicted Long and Mason by saying Thompson said nothing when he re-entered the saloon.

Finally, Shufelt took the stand. His version of Thompson's aggressive attitude was even stronger than Mason's or Long's, with

more violence, threats, and even graphic, foul language. He claimed
Thompson pushed him and gouged him in the face. His version of
the dialogue clashed with Mason's and Long's testimony; he said
Thompson didn't just exit the door, he tried to knock it down in
the process. He added a new wrinkle, saying Thompson had his
gun under his coat, and not out as his friends had said. In the long
examination by County Attorney Kerr, the only new fact presented
was that Shufelt had Mason's gun when he left the building, since
his was empty. Shufelt, too, had memory lapses over Georgia
Grant's activities. Perhaps he took her threats to shoot seriously.

The state felt there were sufficient grounds for charging
Shufelt with first-degree murder, and such an indictment was filed
in the Twelfth District Court in Glasgow. Hurd again represented
Shufelt. His bail was originally set at $10,000 but was dropped to
$5,000. Bail was provided by Glasgow merchants E. D. Coleman
and J. P. Truscott. Coleman, a hotel-restaurant-bar owner, and
Truscott, a department store owner, were both pillars of the
community and friends of Hurd. Shufelt's father, Theodore, also
helped pay the bail.

Since no transcript survives, the only available accounts of
the trial are brief newspaper stories. The witness list contained
the names of those who had testified at the preliminary hearing
with a few additions—among them, Georgia Grant. Surely her
testimony must have been illuminating. Broome's name wasn't
listed.

The unanswered question was, what was Thompson's plan
when he came to Saco? Had he been waiting for Broome to show
his face on the street for a showdown, but Broome had wisely
stayed home, protected by his wife and Shufelt's sister?

Fort Benton attorney F. E. Stranahan assisted Kerr in trying
to overcome the pretrial publicity of Thompson's previous killings
and how he was wanted for various crimes in Oklahoma and/or
Texas. Plus, Broome and the deceased had many friends in
Glasgow.

Thompson's killing was similar to Starr's in that the victim was an outlaw—the opinion was, "good riddance." But Kerr insisted it was a clear case of murder, since Thompson's gun was not out and he was shot in the back. Furthermore, Kerr said that it was a put-up job by a certain clique to murder Thompson, and that the main defense witnesses, William Long and William Mason, were liars. He pointed out that during the all-night dance they tried constantly to pick a fight with Thompson, and when that didn't work, Shufelt lay in wait with his revolver on the bar top to shoot him when he returned. Kerr said the Grant woman had nothing to do with the conflict; she was just a cover story for the cold-blooded murder.

The two-day trial ended with Shufelt being declared not guilty. Nine jury members voted for conviction and three for acquittal. This came as a real surprise to prosecuting attorneys Kerr and Stranahan. A discouraged Stranahan remarked to a Fort Benton River Press reporter that he had lost three cases during the district court sessions in which the defendants' guilt was clear-cut. A Glasgow paper called the verdict "another case of shielding from the intention of the law." Hurd was elected the first mayor of newly incorporated Glasgow the same year.

Those who thought that Broome was the mastermind behind Dunn's and Thompson's killings believed that he would next get Shufelt out of the way, too. But no physical harm came to Shufelt around Saco. He did manage to get into more trouble. Stock inspector Jack Teal made Shufelt his number-one target after Thompson's killing. He kept an eye on Shufelt's associates, too. Teal filed charges against Shufelt for taking horses to Canada without the proper registration papers. Shufelt was fined $50 in Northcutt's court.

Shufelt and Duffy finally left Saco and joined the "Dutch" Henry Ieuch gang, which was then operating out of the hills near the community of Redstone, in the Big Muddy Creek country of northeastern Montana.

Broome stayed in the Saco area until 1907, moving on to the new community of Scobey, located northeast of Glasgow. Redstone was another thirty-three miles to the east. Broome got into trouble in his new location for operating an unlicensed saloon with Gus and Charles Colon. He journeyed to Glasgow to pay a five-dollar fine for his tardy liquor license application. He sold his ranch south of Saco about 1911 and returned to his hometown of San Angelo, Texas.

There are two versions of Broome's death. According to one, he died from acid burns suffered during a dispute with a woman. In the other, he drank carbolic acid, mistaking it for whiskey.

Della Broome returned to Saco shortly after moving to Scobey and managed a "new hostelry recently built by Frank Stevens." She apparently received nothing from the sale of Broome's properties. She married a local rancher, William N. Taylor, in 1914. She and her new husband had ranch property south of Saco. In later years she operated a restaurant or two and did housekeeping for local families. She eventually returned to Kansas and worked as a cook for a railroad. She died in 1957 and is buried in a Kansas cemetery plot with her parents.

Except for their inclusion in local history books and in jubilee, diamond, and centennial newspaper editions, the characters in this story have been mainly forgotten. This is understandable, since homesteaders soon outnumbered cowboys and ranchers in the region, and the new settlers had little interest in the lawless element—except to say they were gone, and good riddance.

Long Henry's burial was a lonely affair. Only three men accompanied the body to the frozen, snowy prairie ridge two miles north of Saco. The lowering of the casket into the grave wasn't trouble-free, either. Luckily, a stranger came by and was hailed to help with the burial. He had come from the East to visit his sister, Mary Hunter, and her husband, Charley, who was one of the first cowboys and ranchers in the area. He scolded Hunter for bringing his sister to "a God-forsaken country where nobody cared when you died, where graves were dug only three feet deep, and where the whole burial ceremony took place without benefit of clergy."

Minnie Taylor, daughter of another Saco-area pioneer, remembered putting chokecherry blossoms on Long Henry's grave, yet not knowing the reason why. Local historian Dorothy Conlon felt it was because "being just a child at the time, she was probably intrigued by the emotional impact of the whole affair."

District Judge J. W. Tatten gave Long Henry's Colt .45 revolver to Glasgow banker R. M. Lewis (whose bank Thompson probably helped rob). Lewis in turn gave it to Sid Willis to put in his Great Falls Mint Saloon collection, next to some Charles M. Russell paintings.

Cowboy historian Johnny Ritch wrote what could be called a delayed epitaph. Ritch said that if Thompson had had as good a publicity man as "Wild" Bill Hickok had, Thompson would have been called the best in the West. In his opinion, never was there a gun artist so quick or so deadly. He concluded:

> None of the other alleged gunfighters from Bull Hook [Havre] to Mondak [a Montana-North Dakota border town] wanted to shoot it out with Henry. It was too much like suicide. They felt they didn't have an even break with lightning. With a publicity man, he would have reached to a height of fame more exalted than any other gunman who ever prowled the plains country.

One can't help but think that if Thompson had been that fearless, he would have faced Ed Starr in a fair fight. Yes, Thompson was wrongly murdered, but he hadn't given Starr any better. He was probably eastern Montana's number one badman. He also was a working cowboy par excellence.

Whether we look at Thompson as a symbol of a passing period, a romantic folk figure, or simply a product of frontier times, he certainly added color to the early development of eastern Montana's frontier. ★

☰

"Dutch" Henry Ieuch and the Bandits of the Big Muddy Country

Part I

January of 1879 was a quiet time in Dodge City, Kansas, cowboy-cow town capital of the West. It was halfway between the warm seasons when thousands of Texas Longhorns and hundreds of accompanying wild sons of the Lone Star State funneled through it. Down Front Street they came, between the typical western false-fronted wood and brick buildings and the tracks of the Santa Fe Railway. The saloons were all but empty, the girls all but gone, and no well-heeled cattlemen were yet in town doing their advance business.

But all those remaining, even from miles around, assembled at the train station to view the arrival of Ford County Sheriff W. W. "Bat" Masterson returning with the renowned outlaw "Dutch" Henry Born, who had been in jail at Trinidad, Colorado. Born had broken out of jail at Dodge City while awaiting trial on livestock theft.

Born cut a dashing figure as he stepped from the train in a black suit, white shirt, and tie. He was described as tall and hand-some, with black hair and mustache and a long face with a Roman nose. But the judge wasn't impressed with his fashion finery and bound him over for trial. However, Born's oratory was so impressive that the cowboys on the jury declared their hero not guilty. Before leaving town, he was given an ovation by those assembled on Front Street. All in all, it had been one of the best Januarys in Dodge City's cowboy days.

Dutch Henry Born was a good-humored German-American whose exploits more than rivaled those of Butch Cassidy and the Wild Bunch, if the stories are all true. He appeared on the Western scene about 1868 from Wisconsin and became a buffalo hunter, a civilian army scout, and a camp cook. He finally graduated to major horse thief-trader with a large gang operating between the Indian Territory and Colorado (particularly the town of Pueblo). His gang of an estimated 300 members was broken up into smaller bands and operated in their own districts.

Dutch Henry was wanted in several territories for horse-stealing, mail robbery, and even murder, along with jailbreaking, which he did on a routine basis. He seemed to lead a charmed life until the army captured him and Federal Judge Isaac Parker sentenced him to prison at Fort Smith, Arkansas. He married and settled down at Pagosa Springs, Colorado, upon his release. He first tried mining but eventually found his niche raising trout and two daughters. He died peacefully in 1921.

What does this have to do with the story of "Dutch" Henry Ieuch of Montana? Actually, very little, except legend-wise. Some Westerners confused the two outlaws, and Ieuch himself capitalized on their confusion by adopting Born's exciting early life on the frontier as his own. Actually, he was just a child in Switzerland at the time of Born's early exploits. And if this weren't confusing enough, there was a third outlaw named "Dutch" Henry—Dutch Henry Schmidt, who was considered one of the most successful early-day outlaws of southern Utah until he was murdered by one of his associates.

Montana's Dutch Henry Ieuch (pronounced "Yaw" or "Youch" and spelled a dozen different ways) wasn't tall and handsome but short and heavyset instead. But like Born, he did have a good sense of humor. No known pictures exist of Ieuch, although the North-West Mounted Police, or "Mounties," gave the following description of the 26-year-old in 1898: "Five foot six, 150 pounds, blue eyes, small mustache, gold-filled teeth, well dressed, and speaking with a German accent." He was also described as having light brown hair and a dark beard, and he may have been heavier than the Mounties described. In still another description, he was said to have been "a heavyset man, somewhat dark complexioned and coarse in manner." Also, he always had first-class horses and equipment.

It wasn't unusual for Ieuch to speak German, since it was the most commonly spoken language in the cantons of Switzerland, where he was born in 1873. He came to the United States in 1886.

Also like Born, Ieuch was a big-time horse thief, moving stolen stock back and forth amongst Montana, Canada, the Dakotas, Wyoming, and Minnesota. Still, Ieuch's and his associates' main area of operation was in eastern Montana, particularly the vast, thinly populated prairie of Valley County.

Valley County was created in 1893 from an even bigger county and was bordered on the south by the Missouri River, on the east by North Dakota, on the west by Chouteau County, and on the north by the future Canadian province of Saskatchewan, then called the governmental district of Assiniboia. The roughly rectangular county of about 14,000 square miles had its county seat at Glasgow. Glasgow was a small town on the Milk River with log shanties and ramshackle wooden huts. It was created in 1887 as a railroad siding for the St. Paul, Minneapolis & Manitoba Railroad, the "Manitoba Road," later called the Great Northern Railway. "Empire Builder" James J. Hill's railroad was moving westward from St. Paul to Everett, Washington. Later it would extend eastward to Chicago. It was not long before Glasgow had a railroad roundhouse complex and became a major cattle and sheep shipping center with substantial buildings of wood and brick. The sheriff's department had little control over the outlawry that went on within its borders—and it didn't seem to care. Glasgow was as much as 125 miles from the areas where outlaws such as Ieuch operated.

In the southeast portion of the county was the town of Culbertson, near the junction of Big Muddy Creek, which originated in Canada, and the eastward-flowing Missouri River.

Culbertson, like Glasgow, was helped into existence by the railroad and was a major livestock raising and shipping center. Most supplies and mail went north from there on a trail roughly following Big Muddy Creek, which paralleled the Fort Peck Indian Reservation. This area was called the Big Muddy country. It was basically a lawless land, from Culbertson in the south to Willow Bunch across the international border.

This all changed due to the efforts of a handful of brave, determined ranchers, stock inspectors, range detectives, Canadian Mounties, and an honest Valley County sheriff, who made the area safe for homesteaders and small ranchers.

George Hall, a one-time Havre lawman and well-known Glasgow-area stock inspector of that era, said Valley County was "the most lawless and crooked county in the Union, and the Big Muddy was the worst part of it." The Mounties established two strategic stations near the border just to combat the outlaw gangs. One was located in the Wood Mountain area near the present-day provincial park and town of the same name, and the other was at Big Muddy Lake to the east.[1] Both were in ranching areas that were just opening to homesteaders.

Regina became the capital of the North West Territories in 1882, thanks to the westward construction of the Canadian Pacific Railroad. The town consequently became the Mounties' headquarters and training center. Although small in numbers, the men in red patrolled the vast Canadian plains, regularly visiting almost all the farms and ranches. The Mounties' posts, located at 30-mile intervals, provided jobs and local markets for goods, and served as social centers much like U.S. frontier military posts.

Many of the ranchers dwelling in the highlands of Wood

Mountain were former Mounties. Unfortunately, a few turned to outlawry and joined their American counterparts. Unlike most of the law officers of Valley County, the Canadian officers were generally professional and well-educated, with high integrity and the respect and trust of the white and Native American inhabitants of the territory. They inspired fear in the outlaws across the line. For their harsh, demanding life, they made a salary equivalent to that of a Montana ranch hand.

The Mounties had all but eliminated the earlier whiskey traders from Fort Benton who were decimating the Indian population. Now the Mounties turned their attention to the American outlaws, who would learn what "Maintain the Right," the Mounties' slogan, meant. As a Fort Benton newspaper put it, the Mounties "fetched their men every time."

One fine example of a Mounted Police officer was Corporal Bird of the Big Muddy detachment. People found him at different times of the day and night in the most unlikely places—hence the outlaws respectfully called him "The Man Who Never Sleeps."

Combating livestock thievery was even more difficult for the Mounties because Montana ranchers could register as many brands as they liked for only two dollars and could place brands on any part of their animals. Many brands were unregistered, and often no brands were used at all. Few lawmen were brave or honest enough to cooperate with the Canadian authorities. Also, the Mounties were losing veteran officers to both the Boer War in South Africa and the Klondike gold strikes.

Among the hundred or so major outlaws of Valley County, Dutch Henry Ieuch is remembered (rightly or wrongly) as the principal among them. In fact, a saloon was named after him at Peerless, Montana; the establishment still exists and holds more than the town's small population. It is said to be the largest nightclub in present-day Daniels County, a part of old Valley County; also a roadway in the Daleview area of Sheridan County bears his name. That's more than any "Dutch Henry" in Colorado or Utah has!

As with many Montana badmen, not much is known about Dutch Henry Ieuch. There were no biographers or newspaper people following him around, nor did his exploits make newspaper headlines in Montana or the Dakotas. Most papers buried such activities in the back pages, since it was not good public relations for attracting settlers. Western pulp magazine writers would not have been welcomed and would have no doubt suffered grievously if they had attempted to either locate the outlaws' camps or talk to them. Due to this lack of specific knowledge, an aura of mystery surrounds Dutch Henry and his consorts.

Dutch Henry supposedly arrived in eastern Montana just after the owners of the "Manitoba Road" started building their rails westward from Minot, Dakota Territory, opening up the Fort Peck Indian Reservation to settlement. For his entry into Montana in 1888, or earlier, Dutch Henry may have picked the small High-Line community of Saco, called "the Hay Town," located about 45 miles northwest of Glasgow. The Saco area had mainly small ranches and farms on Milk River bottomland, producing nutritious blue joint hay guarded by hordes of mosquitoes. Here the teenage boy apparently worked for the Dave Kennedy Ranch on the Saco flats; it was one of the larger spreads.

After some "trouble," the Kennedys had come to eastern Montana from the Souris River country of North Dakota, changing ranch sites twice before settling on Beaver Creek southwest of Saco in 1886. The couple and their three children were generous people. They helped out cowboys who were on the out-of-work grubline during the winter. Mrs. Kennedy even washed and mended their clothes. It was said the Kennedys had to fire Ieuch because he was "too loose" with a branding iron.

One storyteller says that Dutch Henry left an uncle in North Dakota and came to Montana with a neighbor who settled in the Glasgow area. Another story says Dutch Henry helped drive a herd of unbranded cattle to the Glasgow area. They were turned loose on the range as ranch buildings were being constructed. However, come spring roundup, all the cattle under Henry's care were wearing the neighbors' brands. These ranchers claimed he had sold them the cattle and had bills of sale to prove it. Dutch Henry's response was that he was illiterate and didn't know what he was signing.

Another story tells how he spent two years in Idaho and left behind the girl he planned to marry. Since he was unable to read or write and didn't answer her letters, she thought he didn't care and married someone else. When he returned and discovered his sweetheart had married, he hit the outlaw trail seriously.

The illiteracy stories do not mesh with the 1900 census, in which Ieuch stated he could read and write, although not well. He probably didn't write from Idaho because he was in the Culbertson and Regina areas at about that time. Perhaps this story became confused with one involving Jack Teal, who lived for a while with friends in both Idaho and Utah in 1897. He may have suffered from a failed engagement at the time, too.

Also during this time, Ieuch broke horses for various Canadian ranches in the Big Muddy country. His principal employer was Pascal Bonneau (and sons), owner of the largest ranch in the area. Bonneau, a former Regina businessman, had been instrumental in the burial of Metis leader Louis Riel at St. Boniface, Manitoba, in defiance of the Canadian authorities after Riel's hanging at Regina. Bonneau began with four horses and four cattle in 1896 and had 400 of each by 1900.

Ieuch's next step was to work for one of the N Bar N Ranch camps located on Rock Creek, a few miles north of Saco. The Home Land and Cattle Company, owned by the Niedringhous brothers of St. Louis, reportedly was first headquartered on the Canadian side in the Wood Mountain area. The company was the largest single ranch operation in eastern Montana, with over 100,000 head of cattle in 1891. Its roundups required 11 chuck wagons, and it shipped as many as 20,000 steers to the Chicago market in the fall. Many a Texas cowboy came north with the N Bar N from Amarillo.

In 1962, Ieuch's friend Alf Watkins wrote to the Montana

Historical Society that Ieuch had returned to Chicago before relocating from the Saco area. This is the only clue we have as to the location of Ieuch's original U.S. home.

Watkins' father was an early rancher on the Milk River flats near Saco. The family moved farther west to the Harlem area where Dutch Henry was a frequent guest. Watkins and his brother Clarence later started a cattle ranch northwest of Saco. Their original family ranch site was later the scene of a gun battle between the notorious gunmen Ed Starr and "Long" Henry Thompson.

Unfortunately, Watkins didn't give any further chronology of Ieuch's activities until the outlaw's final departure from Montana.

About 1895 or earlier, Ieuch moved eastward to Culbertson, a more lively region with major cattle and horse outfits—and many outlaws. He quickly acclimated himself and established a ranch of sorts on Shotgun Creek, north of town in the Sand Hills. The area contains many canyons, gulches, and coulees that could offer concealment for lawbreakers. Dutch Henry may have had another hideout on Smoke Creek, a tributary of Big Muddy Creek to the northwest. His dugout was said to have been placed back into a hill so that only the smokestack could be seen.

This type of dugout consisted of a hole about four feet deep dug into a hill, with the walls built up about three feet with sod. A large ridgepole was placed across the center and small poles were laid across it. Brush, sod, and earth were placed on the poles to make a roof.

Here Ieuch began his illicit trade in earnest, stealing horses and changing their brands. No mere sneak thief, his admirers said, he stole large numbers of horses at a time. There was a big market for horses in the farmlands of Montana, the Canadian provinces and districts and surrounding states. A $9.00 horse could bring $200 in the right market. There was always a military demand for good horseflesh. Beef was in constant demand as well.

At some point in his horse-thieving days around Culbertson, Ieuch had a nosy neighbor who liked to tell everyone he met about the outlaw's activities. Ieuch obviously didn't appreciate this. He warned the man to mind his own business, but to no avail. Finally the outlaw kidnapped him and tied and tethered him outside his dugout with little or no food or water. When he released his captive, he showed him the east-west road, explaining that he could go either way as long as he didn't return—if he wanted to stay healthy.

West of Dutch Henry near Bainville was old J. W. "Dad" Williams' large and legitimate horse ranch on Shotgun Creek. His Diamond G brand was well-known in eastern Montana, and he conducted round-ups throughout the country. Saco was one of his stops. Williams was a big, gregarious man who always stopped by the newspaper office in towns he passed through to make their social page. He wrote letters to the editors of those he was unable to visit.

Shotgun Creek was said to have been named in "honor" of Williams. He often paid only a dollar for a hard day of haying, and when paytime came, he backed the salary up with his shotgun, asking if that wasn't enough pay. His workers never disagreed. Later, his famous shotgun was displayed in a Culbertson shop.

Early in his outlaw career, Dutch Henry rode for Williams and reportedly stole hundreds of horses from him. Legend has it that he broke Williams, yet the rancher was still going strong after Dutch Henry's demise.

At this time, in about 1895, Deputy Sheriff John Eder arrested Ieuch in Culbertson for stealing cattle from one or two local ranches. While Eder waited at a saloon for the county sheriff to pick up his prisoner, Dutch Henry escaped. He was recaptured three weeks later at a ranch on the Big Muddy, and this time he was put behind bars in the Valley County jail at Glasgow. Since Williams was one of those providing the bail, Ieuch must not have been stealing from the rancher yet or Williams wasn't aware of it. The charges were dismissed for lack of evidence—a common occurrence for outlaws, who rarely came to trial.

At about the same time, Ieuch told a local Glasgow reporter that the county was getting too tame, and he was going to join

Buffalo Bill's Wild West show. Perhaps he really meant the law was starting to cramp his style.

Also during this period, Ieuch began showing up around Regina, Saskatchewan, about 102 miles north of the Montana border. Ieuch brought a string of horses to Canada to sell and then decided he liked the country. According to several sources, he made friends with many there, having the knack of getting on the right side of people. Ieuch was described as being quite young and having a Dutch accent. He often remarked that he "found it easier to rob his friends than those with whom he was not visiting or on speaking terms."

Ieuch went from ranch to ranch in his buckboard, gentling stock with three other Montana men. The young cowboy was considered a top rider and ranch hand. He was always armed and was rumored to have been a wanted man in Montana.

From about 1897 to 1898, Ieuch rode for the Diamond Cattle Company on the Missouri River bottoms below Culbertson. The company was owned by Helena Valley rancher Henry Sieben and run by his nephew Frank Arnst. The Diamond company was the first large outfit to venture north into the Big Muddy country where the town of Plentywood is now located.

Ieuch is credited with naming the future seat of Sheridan County, although the details of how it came about varied from campsite to campsite. One version says some of the Diamond outfit cowhands were camped on an unnamed creek, waiting for the cook to serve a meal, but in the cold, damp weather, the buffalo chips just wouldn't burn. Things looked rather dismal since they were on a treeless prairie. But Dutch Henry, the wagon boss, jumped up and said, "Boys, if you'll go two miles up the creek you'll find plenty wood." So the camp chuck wagon and cook moved to where Henry directed. One story said they found no firewood there, either. "Plenty of wood, plenty of wood," laughed the cowboys. They were still hungry, but their morale was higher. The story circulated, and the stream officially became known as Plentywood Creek.

In another version, the cowboys found a stockpile of wood left by the site's previous inhabitants. Ieuch had discovered it while obtaining water. And in yet another version, a growth of small timber replaced the cache of firewood.

A post office was later established at a ranch on that creek, and even when the post office was moved six miles east to another ranch on Box Elder Creek, it and the town that grew up around it retained the name Plentywood.

This was perhaps the zenith of large-scale cattle raising. A June 1897 roundup in eastern Montana required 14 wagons, 80 riders, and around 1,500 horses. The largest outfits at the time were the Bear Paw and Milk River cattle pools, and the Pioneer, Coburn, Bloom (Circle Diamond), and Home (N Bar N) cattle companies and ranches.

In the Big Muddy country, besides the Diamond outfit, there were the Stevens, Slimmer and Thomas, and K P cattle companies. The cattle crossed the Big Muddy at Homestead after roundups, and were driven to Kenmore, North Dakota, for shipment on the "Soo Line" Railroad, which was officially called the Minneapolis, St. Paul and Sault Ste. Marie Railway. The crossing became known as the N Bar N crossing, since that brand was the largest shipper.

Early in his outlaw career, Ieuch was not considered a hard-core criminal. He was known for his sense of humor as much as for his other talents, such as riding and roping. Plentywood druggist and local historian Robert C. Mann wrote that Ieuch was "known as a first-class horse thief, but also as a humorist, storyteller, and all-around good guy."

One-time veteran Valley County Deputy Sheriff Hugh Calderwood agreed that Ieuch had a bent for humor. Calderwood said "it was so universal he could not control it."

Sometimes Ieuch didn't mean to be humorous. Once, early in his career, he worked as a camp cook. He was to set up a camp with a week's worth of supplies. He had forgotten the coffee grinder, however, and had to find an alternate way of grinding the

Arbuckle brand coffee beans. He tried grinding them with rocks, but that didn't work, so he finally decided to boil the beans. Since he didn't know the right mix, he added more beans, more water, and kept sampling his brew. That night he was so full of caffeine he couldn't sleep. When the men sampled his concoction the next morning, they found the thick, strong brew undrinkable—and cowboys were used to bad coffee.

One story of both Ieuch's sense of humor and his generosity concerned an early Culbertson-area rancher by the name of Jacob Bauer. Bauer purchased 100 head of yearling calves from Oregon in the spring. By fall, some had drifted, eating their contented way many miles west along the Missouri River bottoms. The rancher planned to take his sleigh on the snow-laden prairie, butcher the yearlings, and bring the meat home. But a day or so later, Ieuch brought in the rest of Bauer's cattle. The grateful rancher tried to pay Ieuch, but the indignant cowboy responded, "If I'da knowed you would want to pay me, I'd never have brought 'em down."

In another tale, Ieuch borrowed a rancher's fastest horse, then returned it two weeks later with $25 rolled up in its mane.

Though Ieuch had begun as a Midwestern tenderfoot, he learned quickly. W. S. Reed, late of Ottawa, was once a saddle mate of Ieuch's. Reed described Dutch Henry's talents this way: "He was a walking encyclopedia as regards the position of cattle on the range at certain times, approximate effect of winds in caus-ing them to drift." Reed went on to say that Henry "was a much sought-after man at round-up time or for ranch work of any kind." Ieuch was "a noble, tried, and trusted friend."

But the law-abiding citizens of the area had a more negative attitude toward Ieuch. "A funny horse thief," some called him. He would steal a team of horses and make someone a present of them, then he would steal them back again. Obviously neither the original owner nor the recipient saw the humor in it.

Ranchers who lived near Ieuch and were friendly with him also spoke of his generosity. He did favors in return for their help; however, if a resident did not want his ranch to be a robber's way station, or if he defied Ieuch in any way, it was a different story. That person would save himself and his family much trouble by moving elsewhere.

A Big Beaver, Saskatchewan, rancher wrote of his experiences with Ieuch. The town was situated north of Whitetail, Montana, in the Big Muddy badlands. He remembered the outlaw as having been "rather comical and partial to telling tall stories to kids." Mostly he told "lurid tales of Indian fighters." Perhaps they were stories of Dutch Henry Born. The rancher once stood vigilant all night on his porch, rifle in hand, because Ieuch threatened to burn his ranch to the ground. Ieuch had given no reason for the threat, and he never showed. Ieuch may have said it in jest, but you never knew about that Dutch Henry.

The same rancher said of Ieuch's outlaw talents, "Dutch never was on top as outlaws go, not compared to [Frank] Jones or [Charley] Nelson." The authorities apparently agreed, because the biggest rewards were always for Jones and Nelson.

Walt Coburn, Montana author-cowboy-historian, told of one Christmas when Henry played messenger, and delivered a greeting in the form of a bottle of Canadian whiskey to two old crusty cowboys. They were occupants of an isolated Circle C Ranch line camp at the confluence of Rock Creek and the Missouri River.

The whiskey was compliments of a Landusky saloon owner called "Dutch" John. Henry had taken his delivery fee out in sourdough biscuits, roast beef, and one-half of a raisin pie, since the boys were out on the range. Not that they would have argued anyway.

Henry also left behind his apparent trademark: one of his wanted posters, only the $500 reward offer had been changed to $5,000 with a challenge to anyone to dare try and collect it. The poster had one of the many misspellings of his name, "Euach."

When Ieuch wasn't doing favors for people, rustling livestock, or working as a legitimate cowboy, he usually went to Culbertson and boarded there. Henry and his outlaw friends were quite safe since the town was a long way from Glasgow and contained a large outlaw element. Anyone who stood up to them ran the risk of having his home or business burned—or worse.

A *Culbertson Searchlight* article of 1910 featured local citizens who remembered visits from Ieuch from 1902 to 1904, during which he spent the money obtained from his rustling activities. He was a fixture around the area in the late 1890s, too, stealing livestock more locally. He was listed as a resident of a town boarding house in the 1900 census. His brother Pete, age 24, lived in the Saco area at that time and was listed as a stock drover.

Sometimes Ieuch spent more than he made. Once he tried to obtain credit to buy groceries, but the feisty German store proprietor refused. In retaliation, Ieuch got a cart filled with garbage from a restaurant and dumped it on the floor of the general store. In a loud exchange of angry German words, Ieuch demanded groceries in exchange for the garbage, but the store owner held his ground. Bravely, he ordered Ieuch from his store, and the outlaw grudgingly complied. He had little choice since there was a crowd present, including women and children.

At one saloon Ieuch had been allowed to charge quite a liquor bill. Usually he only did that with his room and board, keeping current with his drinking expenses. He decided the debt had to be taken care of, but not in the usual manner. Instead, he went to the local mercantile store and selected a good, solid axe handle, lumberjack size. He then went to the saloon owner with axe handle in hand, asking about the bill. The owner quickly agreed that the bill must have been a mistake and said that all accounts were considered settled. That done, Ieuch returned the axe handle, remarking, "Don't need it anymore. Made $200 with it, anyway."

One time in Glasgow, Ieuch was celebrating heavily and decided to top off the night at a local restaurant. Intoxicated, he displayed poor manners and threw ketchup all over the establishment's white muslin curtains. The town marshal was summoned and he followed Ieuch, bringing the amiable drunk back to pay the charges. This was perhaps what the Glasgow *North Montana Review* writer was referring to when he said that "Dutch

Henry of Culbertson was in the city this week [January 1903] after a protracted absence of about four years. He took on the usual amount of distilled disturbance."

In another case where law and order caught up with Ieuch, he was caught rustling steers near the community of Lenark, east of Culbertson. He was sentenced—perhaps by the ranchers themselves—to digging miles of post holes with a guard beside him.

As previously mentioned, Ieuch was arrested by Deputy Sheriff John Eder in Culbertson in about 1895, but he escaped or was allowed to escape. Eder did not exactly have a respectable reputation. A treacherous, drunken, gun-happy coward was more on the mark as far as the cowboys were concerned.

The Mounties reported that Dutch Henry was released shortly after he was arrested. In the local "official" version, Ieuch's gang broke him out of jail the first night, galloping out of town on the deputy's favorite horse, which Ieuch sold to a Mountie once he was safe in Canada. However, in another version, Ieuch was with Eder in a saloon when he escaped.

When no alarm was sounded by Valley County Sheriff W. S. "Leather" Griffith, Glasgow-area stock inspector George Dunnell wrote to the North-West Mounted Police Commissioner Lawrence W. Herchener at Regina advising him of Ieuch's escape. Dunnell wanted the men of Herchener's command to be on the outlook, especially near the Wood Mountain area. Staff Sergeant Stewart was assigned to help Dunnell, and they met at Bonneau's ranch to start the search in the Big Muddy badlands.

A Saskatchewan provincial tourist brochure describes these badlands as "one of the eeriest and most storied areas of Saskatchewan." Its "rugged sandstone buttes, sheer cliffs, and rough-hewn hogbacks border the broad Big Muddy Valley. The badlands and its numerous caves made a perfect hideout for road agents [and] horse thieves."

The main valley starts southeast of Willow Bunch in Saskatchewan, stretching from Willow Bunch Lake southeastward to Big Muddy Lake and into Montana near Regway. Entering

Montana northwest of Outlook, it turns eastward near Redstone and goes southward near present-day Plentywood on its journey to the Milk River, west of Culbertson.

Plentywood-area historian Robert Mann described the Big Muddy Valley as quite wide in areas, averaging two to three miles across, but the Big Muddy Creek was narrow and averaged four to five feet deep. Its flow was restricted by its various curves, bends, and beaver dams. In the summer months, it went nearly dry in several places.

The Saskatchewan brochure called the valley "tabletop prairie," while Mann called it just "The Flats." The gentle, rolling prairie averaged about 2,000 feet in elevation. A prominent landmark on the Canadian side was Castle Butte, a 200-foot-high sandstone rock formation used as a landmark by lawmen, outlaws, and settlers alike.

In this rugged country Stewart and Dunnell captured Dutch Henry on January 30, 1898, six miles north of the border, where he was living in a dugout.

The *Regina Leader* called Ieuch "one of the most daring cow thieves Montana had ever known." In a dialogue with his captors, Ieuch said, "All right, boys. Two days ago my tent caught fire and I lost my outfit, gun, and all, or you would not have caught me so easily." And assuredly no one argued, since Ieuch knew the Big Muddy badlands so well.

Ieuch was taken to Glasgow for trial, and like his compatriot, Dutch Henry Born, he talked a good defense. He was acquitted. Why he wasn't charged with escaping custody isn't mentioned.

The *Regina Leader* also reported that Ieuch returned to the Regina area after the trial, where he lived for a few years and had many friends. Perhaps this was the "Idaho trip" mentioned before.

While living in Canada, Ieuch and associates were credited with running livestock from Buffalo Head, east of Willow Bunch Lake, to Indian Cliff and Snake Creek at the west end of Wood Mountain. Ieuch was also wanted for stealing horses still farther west near Swift Current, hiding out at Antelope Butte near the South Saskatchewan River. He may also have gotten into a shootout with the Mounties at one of the Canadian towns, escaping capture and driving stolen horses out of a livery barn corral. Ieuch also reportedly rustled livestock near Weyburn, north of the Ambrose-Crosby area of North Dakota.

The Canadian authorities called Valley County "one of the most lawless counties of that state." To them it was unbelievable and unacceptable that such "an organized band of horse thieves" was allowed to terrorize the city and county residents. And Culbertson was considered to be the toughest and most lawless of the cattle towns in the region.

Mountie Sergeant G. W. Byrne of the Estevan, Saskatchewan, detachment took a trip to Culbertson in 1899, looking for cattle stolen from a John Anderson of Wood End. Byrne posed as an Estevan merchant who was owed money by Anderson. Byrne's superiors warned him that he couldn't trust anyone in Culbertson since "they were all either owned by the gang or were afraid of them."

Byrne in particular was after outlaws Frank Wilbur and Frank Jones. Since Jones was considered the toughest of the Big Muddy outlaws, the lone Canadian lawman had quite a task before him.

The officer had to be on constant guard during his stay in town because he was under continuous surveillance. Not even the postmaster or train station agent could be trusted, he reported back to Regina. When Byrne was recognized by an outlaw-killer who had known him in Regina, several attempts were made on his life.

Byrne had no faith in Valley County Sheriff W. S. Griffith who he said could be easily bribed and spent most of his time in a Glasgow saloon (which he had owned since 1895), shooting craps or playing poker. Griffith's most famous establishment was the Sideboard Saloon, once owned by a previous sheriff, Sid Willis. Some Glasgow residents accused Griffith of smuggling coyote pelts into the U. S. from Canada, of using his badge to illegally obtain other people's money, and of acting as a point man for the outlaws.

In spite of having so much stacked against him, Byrne was able to capture Wilbur with the help of government stock inspector Harry Lund and the Chouteau County sheriff's office. The wanted man was found hiding in the Bear's Paw (Bear Paw) Mountains, between the Milk and Missouri rivers. Wilbur never made the Big Muddy "prominent" outlaw list; in fact, no information about him has survived.

Jones could not be found, according to the Valley County officers, although locals knew he was hiding at the Sam Christie ranch, located 50 miles north in the Big Muddy country and just short of the international border.

One of Byrne's worst nightmares was the local hotel where he was staying while conducting his investigation. The only stopping place in town, it was allegedly run by the head of Ieuch's gang, so Byrne got little sleep. Joint-occupancy rooms added to the danger, since any of his roommates could have been an assassin.[2]

Obviously, Byrne would have preferred to wrap up his activities as soon as possible. He had one prisoner, and after much legal fencing with Valley County authorities, he had some of Anderson's animals. The rest were trailed by the stock inspectors to their place of sale at a "notorious slaughterhouse near Williston [North Dakota]." Now, if only Byrne could safely leave Culbertson with his prisoner on the eastbound train to Minot, North Dakota.

Byrne took a different train than he originally intended because he had been warned of a last-ditch plan to ambush him. Stock inspector George Dunnell volunteered to accompany him, since the sheriff's department refused to provide an escort. Dunnell was returning the Mounties' favor of helping to capture Dutch Henry the previous year. Dunnell's reputation as a gunman—and his popularity around Glasgow—made him an excellent escort. It was probably he who had warned Byrne in the first place, thereby saving his life.

This incident shows how safe the outlaw gangs felt in that they would consider killing a Canadian police officer with no apparent concern about the international incident that would have resulted.

In his report, Byrne gave outlaw Frank Jones a compliment of sorts, writing: "He was the best shot, best horseman, and the owner of the best horse in Montana." According to Byrne, Jones had been an outlaw for several years but had never been captured. As long as Culbertson and Valley County stayed lawless, there was little chance of his apprehension.

Culbertson had 13 saloons, six other businesses, and a rail station-stockyard complex. The town was a supply center for the surrounding ranches, a recreational center for the ranch hands, a shipping center for livestock, and an outlaw center for the gangs operating in eastern Montana, western North Dakota, and up the Big Muddy into Canada. A ranch on the Missouri River south of town was said to have been an international headquarters for outlaws, operated by a former N Bar N foreman named J. P. "Doc" Smith. The ranch eventually burned down, and its owner moved north to the Big Muddy country.

Culbertson experienced around-the-clock shooting sprees, deadly gunfights, murders, and robberies on the streets and in the saloons. Local constables were the only lawmen, and they were basically powerless against the outlaw clique and Deputy Sheriff Eder, who allowed the outlaws to operate.

Glasgow was equally lawless. It took a courageous person to file a criminal complaint there. A rancher and Great Northern Railway fireman named James Sherry learned that lesson the hard way when he filed charges against brothers Ed and Hank Shufelt for illegally branding one of his calves. The pair were acquitted, and soon after Sherry was robbed of his watch and money by two assailants he refused to identify.

Even murderers were hard to convict unless they were outsiders, and those who were convicted might break out of the cracker-box jail before being shipped off to the state prison at

Deer Lodge. This was discouraging to the honest citizens of Glasgow and Valley County, and hardly attractive to potential settlers.

PART II

Walter "Leather" Griffith, Valley County sheriff in 1900, was considered as corrupt as they come by the North-West Mounted Police and others. The sheriff was a prominent member of Glasgow's high society, including the inner circles of various fraternal organizations and the Republican Party. Griffith had a ranch and livestock business with partners just outside of town. In town, he had operated such businesses as the Glasgow Meat Market and various saloons, eventually owning his own two-story building.

Griffith's nickname came from the fact that he spent hours sitting in a leather chair while playing poker.

But the winds of reform were beginning to blow. Pressure for law and order was already building from the state stock inspectors and the Mounties; and a few determined Culbertson citizens were galvanized into action by a series of events involving resident Deputy Sheriff John Eder. Eder gained office, it was said, by taking the gun and the badge of the deputy who tried to arrest him. The violence was tolerated until popular local cowboy Nolan Armstrong was killed. Armstrong, a former N Bar N cowboy, was working as a foreman for the Diamond Cattle Company. His killing was illustrated by Charlie Russell in the book *Good Medicine*.

One evening, Eder locked up Armstrong for drunk and disorderly conduct, but somehow Armstrong walked away from jail and returned to the party with his comrades. Eder shot him in the back with a shotgun, wounding cowboy Tom Reid in the process. Armstrong was unarmed at the time. Eder fired from behind a pile of bricks. The deputy ran away as the crowd returned the fire. He barricaded himself in his house, but no one pursued him.

The deputy claimed that a group of drunken cowboys was shooting into the air and refused to stop at his command, but no one agreed with his version. There was some talk of mob violence, but it never materialized. A petition to remove Eder, sent to Sheriff Griffith, was ignored. Next, the townspeople tried to have Eder arrested for murder. That didn't work either. Eder was absolved at a coroner's inquest and preliminary justice court hearing.

Perhaps Eder thought it was all behind him once Armstrong was buried in late January of 1900. He was wrong. He was shot to death by stock inspector Charles S. Stafford on June 25 of that year. Stafford was trying to serve a warrant on Eder at his ranch for driving Tom Cushing's cattle off the man's range. Cushing was a powerful Culbertson citizen, so the arrogant Eder had pushed his luck too far.

Eder showed his contempt for Stafford and the law by tearing up the legal paper and running back inside for a revolver "to blow [Stafford's] head off." When he reached for it on a table, Stafford fired, killing him instantly.

Stafford was a solid citizen and family man and was well liked by most except the saloon crowd. He had served as a county commissioner, and he was an area rancher. At the coroner's inquest, Stafford was exonerated, and the Justice Court judge ruled self-defense.

This wasn't good enough for Sheriff Griffith, though, and he filed murder charges. The saloon crowd wanted Stafford jailed, since they didn't want their authority challenged. Their plan backfired, however, and Stafford was acquitted. The outrage grew.

This seemed to give Stafford more determination. He went after the rustlers with a vengeance, particularly those operating across the state line at Buford, North Dakota.[3] Stafford went on to be the town's U.S. land commissioner and owner of the drugstore, post office, hotel, and real estate office when the outlaw clique was nearly only a memory.

Griffith's answer to the acquittal was to eliminate the deputy positions in both Culbertson and Malta. The people of Malta, 70 miles west of Glasgow, weren't any happier about this decision than the citizens of Culbertson. Malta formed the third spoke of the cattle empire wheel of Valley County. It was the weekend playground of many cowboys, from Havre west and from the Canadian line south to the Missouri River. Saloons outnumbered all other businesses, and the red-light district was behind them. Four large cattle ranches dominated the area: the Phillips, Coburn, Matador, and Phelps. Malta, like Culbertson, had to rely on town constables and the support of the stock inspectors.

One county commissioner, Harry Cosner, who lived in Malta, decided to do something about the Griffith situation. He ran for sheriff in 1902. Among other occupations, Cosner operated a saloon and restaurant in town. Previously he had worked for several western cattle ranches and had accompanied several cattle drives to northern Montana. He became a cowboy at age 15 and tended cattle along the Kansas-Nebraska border before arriving in Malta in 1889 with a herd from Cheyenne, Wyoming. At that time there was nothing to the town but a general store, a log saloon, a restaurant, and a boxcar along the tracks that served as a railroad depot.

Griffith's reputation perhaps suffered the most in July 1901 when Harvey "Kid Curry" Logan and three companions robbed the westbound Great Northern Railway Flyer between Malta and Wagner, Montana, at the Exeter siding on the Exeter Creek Bridge. While Logan and another robber directed the disconnection of the passenger cars from the express car and engine,[4] the other two covered the train, firing their rifles whenever a passenger poked his head out a window. A brakeman and two passengers and possibly a mail clerk were wounded. The express car entrance and safe were blown, and the take included some $65,000 in unsigned bank notes, money orders, gold watches, etc. Young fireman Mike O'Neil, who helped Curry at gunpoint, was suspected to have been a part of the robbery group, although no evidence was ever produced.

There are three versions of Griffith's actions during the robbery. In the first, he initially fired at the robbers with his handgun from the passenger car window but pulled back when fired upon with rifles; in the second, he considered firing on them, but thought better of it and pulled back; and in the third, he cowered inside the passenger car, begging other passengers not to fire.

Whatever transpired, a posse was immediately formed at Wagner. Griffith then raised two posses, one each from Malta and Glasgow, telling the townspeople that the railroad was authorizing them. The two posses joined forces before beginning to search in the Little Rockies country. But once there, the railroad's express company officials rejected the Malta posse. The unruly Glasgow posse, made up primarily of saloon-hangers-on, proceeded south. Curry said of them that "you could shoot a whole corral full of posse members and not kill a real man with guts."

The posse made poor time and didn't reach its destination at the Winters-Gill ranch until the third day. In the process the group suffered the effects of food poisoning and rotgut whiskey. One member reportedly shot himself in the foot; another shot a horse. That was the extent of their action.

A Chouteau County posse was organized at Chinook by Deputy Sheriff Erick Thorsen, but a jail break at Fort Benton prevented its participation. So the county in which the robbery occurred had no immediate representation. By the time Griffith returned to Glasgow, his pursuit efforts were being ridiculed as a complete farce.

The murder trial of Ed Shufelt for killing "Long" Henry Thompson didn't exactly bring glory to Glasgow's corroded wheels of justice, either. Shufelt was acquitted for shooting Thompson in the back in a Saco saloon. Shufelt owned the saloon, along with partner Andy Duffy. The verdict was a big surprise to those who viewed the trial, according to a Glasgow newspaper report. Rumors of jury tampering and bribery abounded.

Shufelt had an adversary who would not forget the murder, though. Jack Teal, one of the most controversial individuals in Valley County, was a prime example of a good badman. Teal personally exerted pressure on Shufelt and Duffy to leave the Saco area. He was a husky fellow with beady eyes who liked a good scuffle, especially with gunmen like Thompson who were no match in a rough-and-tumble battle. He dogged their tracks, even filing charges against them for illegal livestock activities across the international border. Teal called Shufelt's and Duffy's saloon "a murder house" and the headquarters for a gang running stolen horses across the Canadian line. Teal even brawled with one suspected member of the gang, Billy Mason, a suspected accessory in the Thompson killing. Teal's harassment and patrons who didn't pay their tabs convinced Shufelt and Duffy to leave town and (re)join the Ieuch gang.

Teal was a gentleman most of the time, but he had a mean streak and tended to go berserk at times. He was a vicious fighter with a revolver, knife, fists, or teeth. The tough cowboy was said to have fought in the Johnson County war in Wyoming. He came to Montana with Long Henry Thompson, Armond Broome, Ed Starr, and Al Tisdale (a.k.a. Clint Allison).

Teal's temper was at its worst when he lost at cards; that was always good for a brawl. But as a law enforcement officer he was tough on outlaws, at least after leaving Sheriff Griffith's employ. As a stock inspector, his involvement in the killing of a suspected rustler near Saco eventually led to the downfall of a large rustling kingpin at Williston.

When major rancher B. D. Phillips was suffering an epidemic of fence-cutting, he hired Teal to stop it. Teal's nickname was "Killer." Was there any doubt of his success? Teal at times owned pieces of Glasgow saloons, besides being a deputy sheriff, stock inspector, cowboy rancher, and ranch foreman. He apparently didn't engage in rustling himself, but had moral lapses in other areas.

Harry Cosner had a change of occupation, too. He became sheriff of Valley County, one of the few Democrats elected. Even Republicans voted for him because of his popularity. Griffith ran as undersheriff on a ticket headed by R. L. Cornwall, but the political maneuvering didn't work. Cosner announced that while he had no active arrest warrants, he would actually pursue the outlaws if complaints were filed—and many were.

The combination of the new sheriff, aggressive stock inspectors such as Teal, Hall, and Stafford, and the ever-present Mounties keeping an even tighter rein on the international line put real pressure on the outlaws for the first time.

How did this affect Dutch Henry? He moved north, leaving Culbertson behind, and merged with the Nelson-Jones gang.

Part III

About 30 men were associated with this outlaw band, supported by a few ranchers on both sides of the border who provided them with safe havens. Charley "Red" Nelson (really Sam Kelly) and Frank "Slim" or "Left-handed" Jones were the most notorious of the bunch; George Whitney (alias Tommy Ryan) was the most celebrated. Most of these men had either committed violent crimes or killed people. Ieuch, like Leroy "Butch Cassidy" Parker, was one of the few who wasn't gun-happy.

Jones used his gun often, but he was known as a Jesse James-type, friendly and generous with most people.[5] His gang operated on a large scale, never dealing in petty larceny. It was said that Dutch Henry didn't like Jones at all. At one point Jones was wrongly suspected of having been part of the Great Northern Railway robbery near Wagner, which had been committed by part of the Wild Bunch.

There are differences of opinion as to Jones' place of origin before coming to Montana, and dates vary widely. In one version, Jones got his start as an outlaw in Canada when a farmer refused to pay him the three months' wages he was due, and he stole 30 head of cattle as payment. This might have occurred in 1898 near Estevan, across the international border from the Crosby-Ambrose area of North Dakota.

On the U.S. side, Jones worked at the T. W. "Bill" Enright ranch on Porcupine Creek for perhaps four years. Enright owned and operated a saloon and an illegal gambling house in Glasgow. The ranch, under manager Jack Teal, was considered a haven for outlaws, including George Whitney and his sometime partner Johnny Woodruff.

There is little background information on Jones. The Mounties, who usually had good resources, had little information. They mistakenly called him Fred Jones. They said the "notorious" Jones was a gang leader and suspected killer. In Canada the bunch was called the Jones gang, in the U.S. the Jones-Nelson gang. The Mounties had neither a picture nor a good description of Jones. They knew only that he was "a medium-built man with dark hair and a mustache."

There isn't a western state that Jones didn't allegedly originate from, although North Dakota was mentioned frequently (specifically the Williston area) and perhaps Nevada before that. Jones was said to have brought a criminal record with him from both North Dakota and Canada, and had begun his outlaw career about 1893. Jones did have registered brands out of Buford City, North Dakota, near Williston. In Minot, Jones supposedly sold large numbers of other people's horses.

Jones was seen frequently on the range and in Culbertson. In towns he reportedly minded his own business and never drank to excess, but he always carried a pistol—and was good with it.

More is known about Nelson, since he associated more with local people. One Glasgow paper described him as "a tall, red-headed Irishman recently from Canada." His flaming red hair and beard did make him a standout. Others added that he was about six feet tall, weighed 180 pounds, hailed from Nova Scotia, and looked at people "with sharp eyes as cold as a fish." Nothing was known about his early life, either by the Mounties or the locals. Nelson was roughly in his late 30s when he arrived in eastern Montana. He also used the name of Nuskine, although his real name was thought to have been Sam Kelly. He owned property in Glasgow, presumably a saloon, but he sold the business and announced he was moving to South America. Actually, he started an area horse-thieving operation with George Trotter and Frank "Smithy" Smith. Trotter was described as a good-looking, well-educated, polite man who had been a grocery firm salesman in the Chicago area. Smith was apparently just a lowly saddle bum trying to make a name for himself.

Nelson's plans were disrupted when Trotter went to visit a friend, Charles Sapphic, who was being held in the county jail for a killing at Culbertson. Trotter was arrested on the spot for horse-thievery by Sheriff Sid Willis.

Nelson visited Trotter in jail and made an impression of the lock with candle tallow. He used the impression to fashion a key from a cut-up tomato can. Nelson and Smith camped within field-glass range of the jail and waited for Willis to leave. With only Mrs. Willis present, they released Trotter and Sapphic from jail.

An inquisitive cattle buyer tried to stop the jailbreakers and was shot in the rear end for his trouble. The outlaws first outran the sheriff and then eluded a subsequent posse. They disappeared into the Missouri River near the Musselshell River breaks after making a false trail towards the northern border. Smith's body was discovered south of Glasgow on Willow Creek. He had been murdered. Some said Nelson killed him, and that it was his third murder. Smith had apparently outlived his usefulness. A reward of $650 was posted for the trio.

After boating or rafting across part of Montana and half of North Dakota, the three split up near Mandan, North Dakota, on the Missouri River. Trotter headed back to Chicago, and Nelson and Sapphic went north. Trotter was recaptured and went to prison, but the latter duo remained at large.

A Valley County deputy sheriff, Clint Allison, heard that the pair were operating in western Dakota. He found their trail; it led to a coulee encampment about 50 miles northwest of Williston and 30 miles west of Stanley Station, near White Earth on the Great Northern Railway. Allison decided to go in himself, without calling for help, and ordered them to surrender. There was an exchange of gunfire; Allison's rifle and a hand were shattered. He retreated under a barrage of bullets.

The two outlaws boarded a train at Stanley and were on

their way to Minot before a posse arrived. They couldn't help but brag about their recent victory. They headed for Canada but soon returned to Montana and resumed their horse-stealing operations. The outlaw duo ranged from the creeks and hills north of the Saco-Hinsdale area, to Porcupine Creek north of Glasgow, to the Big Muddy country, to the White Earth River country of North Dakota, and into Canada.

Sapphic eventually vanished from the scene. He was either killed by Nelson or he returned to Iowa. It was at this point that Nelson teamed up with Frank Jones and associates, who were also busily stealing and trading horseflesh in Montana, North Dakota, and Canada. Nelson had finally met a man as good with a gun and as fearless and calculating as he was.

Before teaming up with Jones and Nelson, Ieuch pulled a big theft of his own. The victim was his old employer, Pascal Bonneau, the important Willow Bunch-Big Muddy rancher. Bonneau's ranch was located near the northernmost point of the Big Muddy Creek valley.

Bonneau had sent his brother Joe, a ranch hand, and Ieuch to purchase 250 horses for $5,500 in the fall of 1902, either from central Montana or western North Dakota. The animals were pastured on the Montana side north of Poplar on the Assiniboine (Nakoda)-Sioux (Dakota) Fort Peck Indian Reservation, because prairie fires had destroyed much of the grass on the Canadian side. The following spring, Ieuch stole the animals and took them to a Big Muddy hideout north of Redstone where they were reportedly kept until fall.

By stealing from Bonneau, Ieuch alienated himself from the friends he had made in the Big Muddy country. The North-West Mounted Police were powerless to help, and Bonneau probably didn't bother to report the theft to American authorities, either, probably fearing retaliation by the outlaw. But Ieuch's arrogance did him as much harm as the authorities could have.

Ieuch sold the bulk of the horses to Glasgow-area cowboy Ed Shufelt and his partner Andy Duffy. The men made a down payment, with the rest due perhaps when the animals were sold.

They had formerly operated the Valley Saloon at Saco, and more recently had worked for the C K brand in McCone County, south of the Missouri River on Redwater Creek. Now they too resided near Redstone, and were associated with Henry's gang. They had perhaps been members earlier.

That same year newly elected Valley County Sheriff Cosner decided to increase the pressure on the outlaws by forming a task force of special deputies. With a combined force of state stock inspectors, Indian reservation police, and the ever-present Mounties after them, the outlaws could no longer roam so freely. Now only a few safe havens remained. Even appearing on the streets of Glasgow, Culbertson, or other area towns was risky.

The only friendly place left was the isolated, northwestern sections of the Big Muddy Creek valley. The gang's main hideout was in what today is called the Daleview Hills, in a triangle formed by the communities of Redstone, Ranous-Daleview, and Outlook. From these hills the gang members could spot riders a long distance away. Dutch Henry had quite an extensive ranch operation near the future town of Daleview, as shown in a painting done by a rancher's wife, Ethel Hurst.

When Olaf and Mary Bergh opened their store and post office in newly founded Redstone, the outlaws and settlers gained a local source of supplies and mail, which were freighted up from Culbertson. The Berghs also opened a coal mine in the nearby red shale hills. They claimed that the outlaws "were treated the same as anyone else and never seemed to bother anyone."

Ieuch had another ranch in Outlaw Coulee off Whitetail Creek, which he sold to Andrew Goodale. It was located about five miles east of the community of Whitetail, northwest of Redstone. It consisted of a two-room shack, shed, and corrals.

Jones, not known to have owned property, seemed to favor staying at the Albert Tande ranch on Poplar Creek, about five miles northwest of the newly established town of Scobey. The ranch was located on the old Wood Mountain Trail from Canada to Poplar.

With their turf disappearing, the country becoming unfriendly, and big rewards on their heads, the outlaws held a summit at the Steve Scott ranch near Medicine Lake. Scott had a wife and seven children. Their ranch, sandwiched between the Indian reservation and the North Dakota line, was a stopping-off place for weary travelers on the north-south route. Present at the meeting were Frank Jones, Charley Nelson, Henry Ieuch, Frank Carlyle, and perhaps Ed Shufelt, Andy Duffy, and Thomas Reid.

The men debated whether to take their chances and surrender to Sheriff Cosner. Nelson was eager to do so, but Jones was not. Nelson threatened Jones, but to no avail. Ieuch and Carlyle sided with Jones, so Nelson left the group. He rode to Culbertson, took the train to Glasgow, walked into the sheriff's office, and surrendered to Mrs. Cosner. She had her young son find the sheriff for the formal arrest.

Nelson was represented at his justice court hearing by prominent local criminal lawyer George Hurd. Incredibly, Judge Freidl had to let Nelson go, since County Attorney Kerr couldn't produce evidence strong enough to convict him; so the alleged killer-rustler-jailbreaker-conspirator walked free, no longer a wanted man. In Kerr's defense, the attorney was in ill health at the time and unable to perform his duties as well as usual.

With Nelson out of the picture, Frank Carlyle assumed a greater leadership role in the gang. Carlyle was about 24 years old, roughly five feet, ten inches, and weighed 175 pounds. He had brown hair and eyes and a dark complexion. The outlaw came from Toronto, Ontario, Canada, where he had been a fireman for six years at a factory. He had come west to Regina, Saskatchewan, to join the Mounties, carrying a letter of recommendation from his former employer. But he was discharged from the North-West Mounted Police for fighting, among other infractions. He was said to have a hair-trigger temper, and he would threaten to kill anyone who offended him. He moved to the Willow Bunch area where he met Ieuch, who became sort of a mentor.

Meanwhile, the newly formed Ieuch-Jones gang committed

a brazen crime that further inflamed public opinion. Versions of the kidnapping of rancher and special deputy Frank King vary in detail, but the main facts coincide.

King was a member of the special task force formed by Sheriff Cosner; other members were John Davis, Billy Endendersby, Elmer "Hominy" Thompson, and George Laporte. They had all lost livestock to the outlaws, and Thompson had had run-ins with former sheriff Griffith. The plan was to patrol the perimeter of the region constantly while the Mounties kept the border closed to prevent escape into Canada.

The outlaws retaliated against King's involvement in the special force by looting his ranch. Elmer Thompson had suffered the same fate earlier. King reported his loss and was able to trace his stolen property to a ranch across the Canadian border. King traveled to the Mounties' sub-post at Wood Mountain and swore out a warrant.[6]

Jones was keeping a loose surveillance of these ranchers, and he followed them to a meeting at Elmer's shack near Whitetail Creek. Jones climbed onto the roof and heard their plan of action, including King's intention to file a complaint with the Mounted Police. Consequently the outlaws captured King between Big Beaver and the border. King was bound, blindfolded, and taken to a hideout for about two weeks. His clothes were exchanged for an old hat and some ragged overalls. A virtual slave, King was forced to dig post holes and build basket corrals (made by weaving willow branches to a fence and placing them at the ends of a draw). A nightly kangaroo court further terrorized King. All the outlaws would vote for his execution, save one, who would hold out. Finally King was released near Redstone—minus his two horses and fine clothes, of course.

Gang member Frank Carlyle had warned King that Jones intended to kill him, so King hid in some brush until nightfall. Once he thought he was safe, he walked for four hours until he reached the Jack Bennett ranch near Redstone, where he obtained transportation to Culbertson. A posse was formed to find his former captors.

King wanted no more adventure. With his father's help, he moved back to Tower City, North Dakota, believing the outlaw problem unsolvable.

The outlaws didn't stop with King, either. They burned the T. V. Girard ranch 10 miles north of Glasgow and made rancher Seth Folsom write a check for his entire bank balance. Then they told him to leave the country or he would be killed. On the Canadian side of the border, they showed their contempt for the Mounties, too, by robbing a cowboy of his horse and possibly wounding a constable. The Mounties increased their manpower and patrols to counter the escalated outlaw activities. However, none of the law enforcement agencies was able to catch up with the elusive outlaws.

The countryside now resembled a battlefield, with facts and rumors intermingled. There was a report of a Valley County man killed near the border by the outlaws. Somehow Ieuch and associates thought they could bully their way out of their troubles and return to their former "good times." Of course, getting a more friendly sheriff was still possible at the next election.

In one incident, the gang charged some Diamond ranch hands, who were escorting the chuckwagon, and chased them nearly back to Culbertson, minus their food supplies. One cowboy had his horse shot out from under him, and was nearly killed. They also drove some cowboys off of their range the same day outside of the town.

The arrogant group made another mistake. They not only put their stolen stock on the Fort Peck Indian Reservation, but in an almost direct challenge, they stole a prize horse from its stable at the reservation agency. The horse belonged to Superintendent-Major C. R. Scobey.

Until then, the outlaws' reservation camp had been unapproachable, since they fended off any range riders with warning shots. They also fired upon a party of men and women who were looking for homesteads and had wandered off course.

But since the most recently stolen herd consisted of both reservation and off-reservation horses, Scobey finally sent his Assiniboine (Nakoda)-Sioux (Dakota) reservation police force to shut the outlaw camp down. Reportedly, the superintendent didn't care whether the outlaws were brought back alive or not.

The outlaws didn't give ground easily, and quite a fire fight developed. The initial report from the area stated that two outlaws were killed and two more wounded. Andrew J. Duffy and Edward Shufelt of the Jones-Ieuch gang were identified as the wounded. Who died, if anyone, is not known. The Indian officers recovered about 200 horses. Apparently the thieves had grazed stolen stock there for years—but they had never stolen from the reservation agency before.

This was perhaps the only battle fought en masse between law enforcement officials and the Big Muddy outlaws. It was certainly the last.

No further contact with the outlaw gang was made until a Metis man reported seeing 14 government horses hobbled at the head of Beaver Creek, near the Big Muddy waterway just below the international line. Nine men headed north to retrieve the horses. They were heavily armed, rode top-quality horses, and had two weeks' worth of supplies. During their journey, they saw four different parties of outlaws, all of which fled at the officers' approach. Finally they found a deeply wooded coulee just below the future town of Ranous-Daleview. The party found a shack, stables, and corral made of thickly woven willows, making it visually impenetrable. Probably this was the recent home and handiwork of Frank King and his captors: Jones, Carlyle, Reid, et al.

The gang hadn't been gone for long—twenty-four hours or so—since the Indian officers found a recently killed steer with George LaPorte's brand on it. The outlaws had also left most of their camping gear behind, testifying to a hasty departure. In the camp, the policemen found bills for goods purchased at the Bruegger Mercantile Company of Culbertson and a letter to Frank

King from his father. Also among the equipment was a considerable supply of smokeless, high-powered "dum-dum" bullets.

The gang had the latest weapons, including Krag-Jorgenson rifles and semi-automatic pistols. Law enforcement agencies believed the gang had braved the Mountie border patrols and fled into the Willow Bunch country, where the Big Muddy valley begins.

Previously a sheriff's posse had discovered a winter hiding place at the junction of Lake and Alkalai creeks, located 35 miles northeast of Culbertson. When the posse arrived, the dugout had been burned, several quarters of stolen beef were left and a stove stolen from a county commissioner was recovered. There was no sign of the outlaws and their several hundred head of stolen horses, however. It was believed they retreated into Canada.

The Mounties eventually made an arrest in their own backyard. The Big Muddy detachment was boarding at the ranch of Joseph "Troublesome" Huntley. Huntley had worked for the gang right under the Mounties' noses, handling stolen horses and rebranding them. He made an effective spy in compromising the security of this "most important boundary detachment," as the Regina command termed it—until, that is, they captured him.

On the Montana side, Sheriff Cosner's efforts to suppress the outlaws' activities were definitely paying off. But in a separate series of events, tragedy struck, setting back his campaign but not stopping it.

In the spring of 1903, a William Hardee was arrested, tried, and convicted of a murder that occurred at Doc Smith's notorious ranch near Culbertson. Hardee was considered to be an insane and violent character, and he was headed for the county's gallows. He shared a jail cell after his arrest with two men, John Brown and a fellow named Davis. Brown, a commercial painter by trade, was a petty thief who was in jail for stealing a coat. The trio escaped by digging out the southeast corner of the building when the jailer left the facility for about ten minutes. While Hardee and Brown were promptly recaptured, Davis remained at large.

Brown received an additional three-month sentence for the

jailbreak, while Hardee continued to await his execution. Also in the cell block were George Pierce and Fred McKinney, both minimum-custody prisoners. Hardee was kept in a separate cell, and the others had the freedom of the cell block.

One night after supper, when guard Jack Williams went to the Truscott store to buy the prisoners some tobacco, the three short-timers attacked and subdued jailer N. L. Dillard and Undersheriff J. Harry Rutter. The trio released Hardee, who shot and wounded Williams when he returned. The group swam across the Milk River, then scattered: Brown west towards Hinsdale, Pierce east, and Hardee and McKinney south towards the Missouri River.

Pierce was never found, but Brown was recaptured in a haystack, and Hardee and McKinney were killed by a posse in a shootout on the prairie south of the river. A rancher named Hill also died in that exchange. Jailer Jack Williams died later from the wound he received.

The luckless Brown was returned to jail, though his stay was short. A mob of about 30 masked townsmen overpowered the two jailers and held them outside the jail for a half-hour. Meanwhile, members of the mob stuffed a rag in Brown's mouth, tied two ropes around his neck, took him to the second floor of the courthouse, and opened a window in the southwest corner room. They tied a hangman's noose with one rope, attached the other end to a nearby radiator, and pushed Brown out the window. His swinging body broke out the window of the county attorney's office below.

Sheriff Cosner was out at the ranch of Dr. Mark Hoyt and former sheriff William Griffith at the time of the lynching, obtaining more horses for posse work. No member of the mob was ever officially identified, but it was believed they were led by Griffith's old friend and former deputy, Jack Teal—according to the founder of Jordan, Arthur Jordan.

Pierce may have killed a billiard parlor owner at Buford City, North Dakota, during his eastward flight.

This mob violence didn't deter Sheriff Cosner from chasing after the Jones-Ieuch bunch, however; nor did he give up on finding Pierce. In fact, the outlaws didn't seem to get the message: Cosner meant to put them out of business. The best tactic for them was to lay low, or better yet, leave the country. At this point, after the Fort Peck Reservation officers' raid, there was no gang hideout.

The next major blow to the gang was inadvertent, thanks to Nick Moore, a Culbertson barber and town constable. Moore had it in mind to capture a member of the gang known as Kid Trailer. Trailer, actually Jack Winnefield (a.k.a. Charles Winfield), was wanted for a reward of $800. The Kid was the herdsman for the gang and performed other camp duties. The warrant was for cattle theft, to which he may have been only an accessory. Homesteader Marie Halverson described him as "a handsome young man of average build in his early twenties."

Trailer came into the area with a cattle herd. Born in England, he emigrated to Canada with a brother. He was a likable boy and attached himself to or trailed different groups of cowboys driving cattle, doing whatever he could to earn his keep. He was also appreciated for his fiddle-playing. Unfortunately, he wound up as the Jones-Ieuch gang's camp worker.

Moore heard that Kid Trailer was playing fiddle at a dance held at the barn on the Ed Sherman ranch on a snowy winter's night in January. Only Moore knew why he thought he could get away with waltzing into one of the gang's hideout ranches and walking away with the wanted man. But that's exactly what the constable did. He walked into the dance, disarmed Trailer at gunpoint, and drove away in his sleigh towards the Valley County jail at Glasgow.

The dance crowd was unhappy and wanted their musician back. Moore wouldn't have been as euphoric about the capture if he had known that Frank Jones had watched the whole affair. The group talked Jones into helping them get their fiddler back. Jones waylaid Moore down the road, returned the Kid to the dance, and took the sleigh and Moore's coat to boot.

One storyteller claimed that Moore walked the thirty-some miles south to Culbertson, but it is more likely he stopped at the nearest ranch for assistance. Meanwhile, the dance began in earnest again.

A posse of men from both Glasgow and Culbertson set out to find Trailer and Jones. It had no luck and returned home.

But Sheriff Cosner had an ace up his sleeve. Two special undercover deputies, George Bird and Frank Moran, were working the grubline from ranch to ranch, looking for Jones and the other gang members. The cowboys knew the country well, since they had worked for a rancher near Whitetail, north of Redstone. Most of the outlaws had apparently gone into hibernation in a dugout on the Big Muddy, somewhere near or across the border.

For weeks, the pair continued their sleuthing until they heard that at least some gang members might be in the vicinity of the train station at East Scobey on the east fork of the Poplar River.[7] The area was about 20 miles west of Redstone, where the outlaws had last congregated.

Bird and Moran moved northwest from ranch to ranch until they stopped at the Albert Tande ranch, four and a half miles from the depot. The date was February 10, 1904. The weather was still frigid and the snow deep. The north-south outlaw trail was close by. Tande and his son had about 250 cattle to tend until the spring thaw.

Nothing of consequence happened until the evening of the second day, when a stranger—at least to Bird and Moran—arrived from the north. There was speculation as to what words were exchanged between the elder Tande and the medium-sized, dark-haired and thickly mustached stranger. Supposedly the young Tande remarked to Moran, "There is the man who corraled a bunch of stolen horses here last summer."

Whether Tande welcomed Jones or tried to warn him off because of the two strangers' presence is not known, but Jones had ridden 35 miles that day, and neither he nor his horse could go any farther. Apparently Jones was still wearing Constable

Moore's easily recognizable coat.

That night the group played cards. When they retired, Bird, Moran, and Jones shared the same large camp bed on the floor. Jones had his semi-automatic pistol on his chest, so the deputies slept lightly with their hands on their revolvers.

Bird had volunteered to cook breakfast, claiming he was called the Pancake Kid and was the best cook around. At dawn, he began to make sourdough pancakes. Moran sat next to Jones while Bird cooked. They waited until Jones held a knife and fork before making their move. Bird laid his cooking utensils down ostensibly to roll a cigarette, but also reaching for his rifle situated close by.

Bird told Jones to throw up his hands, but he called him Carlyle, mistaking him for another outlaw. Jones ignored the order and went on eating. Moran drew his revolver and repeated the command. Jones tried to get up (or roll to the floor) as he went for his pistol, but both lawmen fired first. Jones fell back over the stove and onto the floor. His pistol was still in his belt.

The downed outlaw tried to speak, but the words wouldn't form. Some authors quote words he is supposed to have spoken, but they were fabricated, as brought out at the coroner's inquest. The unconscious Jones was wrapped in a blanket and canvas, and the two deputies, accompanied by the elder Tande, set out by sleigh to take him to Poplar. Jones never regained consciousness and died about 20 miles southeast of the ranch.

The party arrived in Poplar about 2 a.m. and telegraphed Glasgow to summon Sheriff Cosner. George Robinson, who worked at a local store, identified the body as that of Jones and not the larger Carlyle. Besides Moore's coat, the dead outlaw was reportedly wearing Frank King's vest. Before his burial, Ellen Scobey, daughter of Major Scobey, the reservation agent, reportedly insisted that a clean shirt be provided for Jones's funeral, which attracted a large crowd.

Once Bird and Moran were exonerated at the coroner's inquest and preliminary justice court hearing, they split the $1,500 reward for bringing down Jones. One report claims they returned to the scene of the crime in an attempt to backtrack Jones' trail north, but that seems unlikely because of the snowfall and their probable fear of retribution from Jones' comrades.

The saloon-cowboy crowd was not rejoicing at Jones' death and believed that in a fair fight Jones would have killed the pair. The story circulated that Bird and Moran went bad: one to the state insane asylum, the other drinking up his reward. But in the "official" version, they both went to Deer Lodge and became guards at the state prison.

After Jones' death, the remnants of his gang broke into the house of a J. P. Williams, a sheep rancher in the Medicine Lake-Reserve area. They demolished the doors and windows, wrecked his farm equipment, and mangled personal property—even pounding silverware into the house walls. Williams had twice sworn out arrest warrants for the Ieuch gang members, once for burning the prairie where his sheep grazed and once for horse-stealing.

So Sheriff Cosner continued his pursuit, arresting Ed Sherman for livestock thievery with the help of a state stock inspector named C. E. Tozier. After a stretch at the state prison, Sherman returned home only to be sent up again for wounding a man at a party.

Sherman was said to have been jailed previously for horse-stealing in Wyoming. He worked at Buford City, North Dakota, in 1899, before establishing his ranch near Reserve in 1900. He was described as a dark, heavyset man with few friends—and those few of questionable character. Sherman was always involved in shady deals and/or livestock thefts, according to his neighbors. He also provided a haven for his outlaw pals.

Ieuch and Carlyle were seen riding the range for several days in May 1904 about 25 miles northwest of Culbertson on the Fort Peck Indian Reservation. Ieuch was also seen alone buying supplies at Buford City.

Carlyle decided that he had had a bellyful of lawmen and returned to Canada. But the Mounties grabbed him for passing counterfeit coins, and he went to prison. Sometime after 1909, he reportedly returned to Valley County with some new recruits and planned the robbery of a GNR or Soo Line train in the northeast corner of Montana. The plan failed, however, because Carlyle got drunk and failed to blow up a bridge as planned. Supposedly, Carlyle's new associates tracked him across the border to a Big Muddy area ranch and killed him for his mistake. The coulee in which he died bears his name today.

Kid Trailer was captured near the Canadian line in May 1904 by John A. Davis, seemingly the only active special deputy left. Davis was instrumental in the arrest of several outlaws. They in turn must have respected his prowess, since no raids were reported on his ranch. Davis hailed from Minnesota and originally ranched north of Williston on the border with the province of Manitoba. His current ranch was 10 miles northwest of present-day Outlook, placing him close to the border and right in the heart of outlaw territory. Davis and his son John H. Davis helped establish the First National Bank of Plentywood. Like the few other dedicated and fearless lawmen who dared to challenge the outlaws, the elder Davis deserves to be more than just a footnote in the history of the Big Muddy country.

Davis next took Tom Reid into custody from the Mounties' detachment at Big Muddy, commanded by Corporal Arthur Bird, the policeman who never seemed to sleep and was everywhere at once. Bird was another officer who belonged in the same exclusive club with Davis, Cosner, Dunnell, Hall, Stafford, and others. Davis took Reid back to Poplar and by train to Glasgow.

In his appearance before Justice Freidl, Reid claimed that he had been working for a Canadian rancher for the past two years and didn't know Ieuch or the other gang members. The county attorney could not produce sufficient evidence to convict Reid of any crimes (again, perhaps because of his health problems). Reid returned to Canada a free man, only to lose his life when dragged by a horse he was training. Reid was rumored to have been wanted in Arkansas before he came to Montana.

Andy Duffy was still operating in the area, residing near Redstone. He brought horses into Culbertson to sell and still frequented the Saco area as well. His partner, Ed Shufelt, had relocated to the Wood Mountain area of Saskatchewan but was soon in the custody of the Mounted Police there, awaiting trial at Regina for the theft, importation, and possession of stolen horses. Shufelt was arrested with some stolen horses near a place called Buffalo Head.[8] Duffy and Shufelt had purchased some 450 horses from Ieuch, all of them stolen. Duffy wisely sold his share in Montana, but Shufelt was arrested for horse theft while trying to sell his animals in Saskatchewan.

Shufelt had a lengthy trial with a large number of both U.S. and Canadian witnesses testifying for both the defense and the prosecution. Shufelt stuck to his story that he and Duffy had bought the horses from Ieuch for $11,000, with $5,000 down from the sale of their Saco saloon. The Crown's prosecutor replied that there wasn't any evidence to substantiate Shufelt's claim and contended that whatever money Shufelt received from the saloon's sale was used to bribe jury members at his Glasgow murder trial. Also, the prosecutor said that Shufelt's character in the past had been "very bad" and that he had been a member of the Ieuch gang since at least 1902.

The first trial resulted in a hung jury, but in the second Shufelt was convicted and sentenced to five years at the bleak Stony Mountain prison, a half-day's ride north of Winnipeg, Manitoba, and located "on the slope of a small promontory. . . ." The Regina *Leader* said his conviction was a good example to others of doubtful reputation who were moving to Canada from Montana because things had gotten too hot for them in the U.S.

Shufelt threatened to kill members of the Bonneau family, to whom he had sold his horses, as soon as he was released. He also had it in for Ieuch and for Saco resident Armond Broome, who allegedly had framed Shufelt for the killing of Long Henry Thompson. However, Shufelt went insane after three years of confinement and was transferred to the the Kingston, Ontario, penitentiary. He died shortly before his scheduled date of release. Shufelt's cowboy friends didn't like that ending to the outlaw's story, though, so when they recounted tales of Shufelt's adventures, they changed it. They often said he died in a saloon fight somewhere in Colorado.

Duffy was said to have joined many outlaws of the region who went to more fertile pickings in the Argentine Republic of South America, since they were now welcome in neither eastern Montana nor Saskatchewan.

When Ed Sherman went to prison the first time in 1904 for horse theft, he was accompanied by Frank "Kid" Flannagan and Kid Trailer. Trailer continued his outlaw ways once he was out of prison, stealing horses mainly in the territory between the towns of Estevan, Saskatchewan, and Williston, North Dakota. He spent several years in the North Dakota state prison. He was wanted on a variety of Canadian crimes but never served any time there. He was said to have been active in the Plentywood area as a bootlegger during Prohibition, smuggling liquor in from Canada.

In 1934, Trailer showed up at his old haunts while on vacation. He was driving an old Model-T Ford, loaded with camping equipment. He stopped by Pete Marron's ranch to visit, but Pete had died. He told Marron's daughter Nancy that he had gone straight and was now a trapper in northern Canada. Plentywood historian Robert Mann places his death in Arizona in the early 1970s.

"Kid" Flannagan was at least as bad an outlaw as Trailer. His crimes included stealing horses, shooting up towns, wounding citizens, and attempting murder. Once a judge told him that he would be killed if he didn't reform, but of course he didn't take this advice seriously. Flannagan, like Trailer, was a good-looking, clean-cut individual, only slightly taller than the five-foot seven-inch Trailer. He was said to have been a native of the Montana smelter town of Anaconda.

Once out of prison, Flannagan decided to join the outlaw stampede to South America. In the meantime, he went to work at a ranch owned by a friend named Malcolm "Mac" Hunter. They both had once worked for the N Bar N Ranch. One day when both had been drinking heavily they got into an argument over who was best at breaking wild horses. Flannagan drew his pistol to shoot Hunter, but it misfired and Hunter shot him twice. A doctor was sent for, but Flannagan died several hours later.

Sheriff Harry Cosner's successful two-year term was nearly over, and he discovered that his election opponent was former sheriff William "Leather" Griffith. Cosner should have been easily re-elected, since the majority of the Big Muddy-Valley County outlaws were either dead, in jail, or in hiding. Even Ieuch's brother, "Coyote" Pete, had been arrested for possessing horses belonging to Special Deputy George LaPorte. Pete had been working as a camp tender for the J. B. Long Company before he brought the stolen horses to Culbertson to sell. The Long ranch was a frequent stopping place for Dutch Henry, George Whitney, and other men on the dodge. In return, the Long property and livestock were never bothered.

Yet the Republican newspapers in particular promptly forgot Cosner's accomplishments, perhaps because Griffith was chairman of the county's Republican Party and because the Glasgow area was the party's stronghold.

Two main complaints were leveled at Cosner. First, he was vilified because he had spent so much more money than the previous Griffith administration. This was true: Cosner spent $8,900; Griffith spent about $5,400. But Cosner's successful efforts to wipe out the outlaws had required many posses and much reward money. He argued that, in the long run, more people would settle in the country because it was now safer, and consequently the county coffers would grow fuller. Glasgow merchants would have more customers and thus would sell more goods.

Cosner was also mocked for "allowing" the jailbreak of Hardee and the others, as well as the lynching of prisoner Brown. Of course, jailbreaks had occurred during every administration, and the lynching had supposedly been led by Jack Teal, Griffith's former deputy and associate. Perhaps the real reason for the opposition to Cosner was that several of the larger area ranchers were involved with the rustlers and missed their cheap source of livestock for both resale and stocking their spreads.

Cosner lost the election by the slim margin of 594 to 532. But there were alleged voting irregularities, and Cosner's party contested the election. They contended that several votes were cast at Culbertson by non-registered voters—probably dead ones. Also, without notice, the regular Poplar polling place had been moved to the Fort Peck Indian Reservation. As a result, an estimated one hundred Cosner supporters were unable to vote. But Cosner lost his appeal, and Griffith was sheriff again.

Cosner became a game warden for eight years and operated a well-digging operation. He later became a major real estate developer at Malta and served as mayor of that town. Part of the town is laid out on his former homestead. Sheriff or not, he continued his search for escapee George Pierce. He found Pierce serving a burglary sentence in Harrisonville, Missouri, but Pierce broke out of jail and was never seen again.

Undersheriff Rutter became the postmaster of Hinsdale for several years. He originally came from Indiana and had been a cowboy-foreman for the N Bar N.

Griffith started his second term by losing a prisoner he was escorting back to Glasgow by train from Deer Lodge. The train was doing 35 miles an hour near Silver City, Montana. (He also lost Kid Trailer at Mondak, Montana, while engaged in a poker game.) The prisoner's name was Ed "Kid" Royals (or Royels). Royals was arrested by Jack Teal on a Great Falls warrant, but he escaped from the Valley County jail before he could be returned to the city. Teal found Royals at a ranch 40 miles north of Poplar and chased him for fifteen miles to the Poplar River. Here Royals made a stand, using his horse as a breastwork. Teal made the capture when Royals' rifle malfunctioned.

Royals was caught in Sweet Grass County and was returned to the state penitentiary for his other crimes. He escaped from custody several more times but was always recaptured. In 1908 he returned to Deer Lodge, served a five-year sentence, and then disappeared.

A distinguished-looking man with dark hair and mustache and sometimes a beard, Royals had originally ranched in the Judith River country of Fergus County. He was banned from the range for his thieving ways and had already served jail and prison time. He moved up to the Medicine Lake area of the Big Muddy Creek country. His new wife Emma drove the buggy, and he herded their 30 horses. But even with a good ranch site, a wife, two children, and uncles who had raised him living nearby, the temptation to steal was too great for him. He sold his livestock in 1902 and became a serious rustler.

Royals' wife got tired of being left alone when her husband was on the outlaw trail or in jail, so she divorced him. She married a neighbor, Arthur Charlesworth, who had looked after the Royals ranch while Royals served a prison sentence. He was also an alleged outlaw partner of Royals but had managed to avoid jail time.

There was much speculation about what happened to Royals, because his family never saw him again. Some said he left Montana and went to an adjacent state.

Jack Teal inadvertently helped bring down a North Dakota kingpins in an organization that bought most of the stolen livestock from the Valley County outlaws. It all started when Teal and fellow stock inspector George Hall questioned a suspected livestock thief near Malta. They decided to take him in for questioning and relieved him of his weapons, but he tried to escape and was killed. On the body they found papers identifying the man as John Cornwall, plus papers containing the names of all the outlaws involved in a large, interstate rustling ring, including the name of their main fence, William H. Denny. Denny was cashier and founder of the First National Bank of Williston and also mayor of the Missouri River town. The rustling ring dealt in hundreds of horses, selling them to farmers in North Dakota. A $10 horse in Montana was worth $200 on North Dakota farms.

Denny's name surfaced again when saloon owner George Miller went to the stock inspectors with information. Miller's saloon, between Hinsdale and Saco, served as a stopping-off place for the horse thieves. By 1905, George Whitney, alias Tom Ryan, was the major rustler in eastern Montana, now that Ieuch had disappeared. Whitney had Miller write a letter to Denny, because he had injured his hand. The letter told of some horses he had recently stolen that were now on their way to Denny, and it named the man making the delivery. To avenge the robbery of his saloon, Miller reported this, although Whitney had no apparent part in the saloon job. Miller even hired out to the Montana Stockgrowers Association and went to Denny's Williston-area ranch, representing himself as a friend of Whitney. Denny acknowledged receiving the horses and reselling them. Denny told Miller to tell Whitney not to come to the bank anymore for payment, because Montana authorities were breathing down his neck. He said he would notify Whitney of a new meeting place at a later time.

Convicting Denny would not be easy since he was a prominent citizen of Williston and had many powerful friends. Other ringleaders of the horse-stealing syndicate were said to include a doctor, a judge, a prominent butcher, a rancher, a lawyer, and the son of a respected pioneer. Another report mentioned that some of the county commissioners were supposedly involved. The stolen horses were shipped eastward from a Great Northern shipping point four miles out of Williston—probably at Wheelock—and also east along the Soo Line to Minot, towns in Minnesota, and beyond.

The area was booming agriculturally, with many homesteaders arriving daily on both train lines. Good plow and riding horses were in demand. Denny operated a land, loan, and insurance office in addition to the bank. He was also involved in an irrigation construction project at Buford City. Socially, he was the Exalted Ruler for the local Elks (B.P.O.E.) lodge. Once a cowboy in eastern Montana, he had ridden for J. W. "Dad" Williams (the Diamond G brand), Ieuch's old boss. He later contracted to sell Montana horses in North Dakota.

The Montana Stockgrowers Association filed charges against

Denny, and Governor Joseph K. Toole requested extradition to Montana for trial. North Dakota Governor Sarles granted the request, only to have Denny's lawyers block the action in court. Once free, Denny fled to his old residence, Benson County, where a friendly Church's Ferry judge issued a writ of habeas corpus. Denny was temporarily safe. He resigned from the bank, but continued as mayor in absentia.

A grand jury was convened at Williston, though no charges were filed and extradition to Glasgow for trial was denied. When additional evidence against Denny surfaced early the following year, he fled to Minnesota, but he soon returned to Church's Ferry. Meanwhile, the attorney general's office directed a Williston justice of the peace to issue a warrant for Denny's arrest. A local constable went to Church's Ferry and caught Denny just as he was about to board a train. Denny's friends had telegraphed him, warning him of the impending arrest.

The ex-banker was tried at Williston for having in his possession several stolen horses from Saskatchewan, yet renewed extradition requests for his Montana crimes were not granted. Denny never served his three-year term, thanks to his able attorneys and their delay tactics. He finally had the charges overturned in 1908. So Denny's prediction came true. He had said, "I'm too prominent. No one can convict me!" Still, physically and mentally he was a broken man, and he never recovered from the ordeal.

The legal action against Denny brought the outlaw George Whitney, alias Tom Ryan, into the spotlight. Whitney was a good-looking man, tall and light-complexioned with blue eyes. Other descriptive words included gentleman, man of refinement, good friend, and ladies' man. He looked more like an executive than a cowboy or outlaw. He dressed well, usually wearing a straight-brimmed Stetson, blue silk neckerchief, white shirt, and gray trousers tucked in at the boot. He carried two Luger semi-automatic pistols.

Whitney was a lovable rogue to many. He treated people well as long as they weren't lawmen trying to track him down. He was on the state stock inspectors' most-wanted list by 1902.

Whitney was said to have come to Montana from a ranch near "Lemon," North Dakota. Since no such town exists, it was more likely Lemmon, South Dakota, just south of the North Dakota state line on the western edge of the present-day Grand River National Grass Lands. Whitney had been a ranch foreman at Lemmon, the story went. He was framed for unknown reasons and became an outlaw. He had escaped from a Wyoming jail two years before coming to Montana; again the charge is unknown. Some said he rode for the XIT and C K brands south of the Missouri River; others said he rode for the N Bar N Ranch, circa 1899, and was their representative on the C K range. He and the Shufelt brothers were considered the best of the local bronco busters and were said to have worked together at one time.

Whitney ranged the Big Muddy country, the Saco-Hinsdale area, and south of the Missouri River. He especially like the town of Jordan and its founder, Arthur Jordan. The town was established on Big Dry Creek in isolated prairie country. There, Whitney was known by his real name and not the Ryan alias used farther north.

Whitney eventually found himself crowded into the northeast corner of Valley County, too, because of increased law enforcement pressure. He settled in with Andy Duffy near Beaver and Whitetail creeks and the Redstone community. Duffy seemingly led a charmed life, having outlasted all his former partners in crime. Additional campmates included Tom Reid and John Woodruff.

Whitney made no effort to hide his activities from the local Big Muddy residents. Ellis Hurst said he left empty stolen mailbags in plain sight in his cabin. But when strangers approached, he met them with his two Luger pistols out. "They're not going to find me hiding behind a bed or in the cellar," he said. Whitney would steal horses and retreat to a high hill near the Canadian border on his big chestnut horse and scan the horizon with his field glasses. Armed with a high-powered rifle and scope, he would wait for any lawmen to try to follow.

The Desonia family had a travelers' stopping place in the

present-day Daleview-Redstone area. Mrs. Desonia said Whitney was "the most gentlemanly man" she ever knew. Once she wanted some chickens killed, and he shot their heads off. He gave the family a motherless colt before he left the area. The Desonias' daughter Mildred kept the animal for twenty-nine years.

Both the state stock inspectors and the county deputy sheriffs had attempted to arrest Whitney, but they always came out second-best—minus horses, weapons, and even the warrant papers. Deputies Vasko, Dillard, and Calderwood learned the hard way just who they were up against; stock inspectors Smith, Oliver, and Berry also took their lumps. Though Whitney believed one of them may have been the culprit who shot him in an ambush, he never resorted to violence and peacefully recuperated at Jordan.

One of his would-be captors was Henry Peterson of Hinsdale. The enterprising Peterson operated the local barbershop, played at being a gambler, delivered rural mail to nearby Barr, operated a butcher shop, and was the town constable. He often informed the local citizens that he "intended to get Ryan [Whitney], dead or alive, if the opportunity should ever present itself."

And one day it did. Whitney walked in past "the usual group of stragglers and loafers engaged in gossip" and sat down in Peterson's barber chair. His pistol was prominently displayed and positioned within fingertip reach. Peterson's reaction was described as "goggle-eyed and breathless." During the outlaw's shave, not a word was spoken nor a movement made among the thoroughly intimidated witnesses.

Whitney broke the silence as he paid Peterson for the shave. He asked Peterson why he didn't try to take him prisoner, but Peterson said nothing as he literally shook in his boots. Whitney left, unmolested by the once-boasting barber or by anyone else. Of course, there was no way Peterson could have won even if he had captured the outlaw, since Whitney probably had more friends in town than he did.

In spite of Whitney's acts of bravado, he was tired of cat-and-mouse games with the law and decided to join the outlaw exodus to South America made popular by the outlaws Butch Cassidy and the Sundance Kid. Like others before him, he needed a stake for such a journey, since he wouldn't be receiving the rest of the money Denny owed him. So Whitney decided to rob a bank. He picked the First State Bank of Williams County, North Dakota, at the town of Crosby, the future seat of Divide County. Crosby was located in the northwest corner of North Dakota and was a growing regional trading and agricultural center, sitting at the railroad junctions of the Soo Line and the Great Northern Railway. The robbery took place on the morning of April 22, 1906, at 10 a.m. It was, and still is, the most excitement the community ever experienced.

Whitney and partner John Woodruff tethered their horses in a nearby draw and robbed the bank "James/Younger style," as the papers described it. They held up the two cashiers for the contents of their cash drawers, which contained anywhere from $300 to $7,000, according to estimates. The robbers didn't get the big money from the vault because either the lock timer was still activated or too many people became aware of the robbery in progress. They cleared people off the streets by firing their pistols as they exited and using the cashiers as shields. Nonetheless, Whitney was struck in the leg by a bullet before mounting his horse, and Woodruff helped him into the saddle. Woodruff dropped a revolver while escaping, as at least six individuals fired rifles at them. One or two rounds were returned.

A posse tried to follow but promptly lost the trail. Meanwhile, the outlaws were robbing a nearby rancher of coats and supplies. They broke open a trunk with an axe and found $100. "Sorry," they said, "but we need it more." Later they supposedly exchanged horses at an unoccupied ranch near Portal, leaving a note telling where to find the animals in Saskatchewan. This led lawmen to conclude that the pair had gone across the border. The problem with this story is that the boys were actually back in Montana at the J. W. "Bill" Ator ranch by that time. The property was north of Antelope and south of present-day Plentywood. The Ators carried the mail between Culbertson and the Plentywood ranch post office.

Whitney told the Ator family that he had received the gunshot wound when he stumbled and his pistol fell out and discharged. After Bill cleaned and dressed the wound, the family never saw Whitney again. Reportedly Whitney stayed at a Saco hotel until the wound healed. Another version of the story states that he hid in the Missouri River Breaks; yet another version says that the Windsor Hotel of Hinsdale was his place of concealment.

Whitney had second thoughts about continuing his outlaw life, and in a situation analogous to Butch Cassidy's failed 1900 attempt at amnesty, he arranged a meeting with the North Dakota attorney who had defended William Denny at Williston. The attorney now practiced law in Montana and had probably left the neighboring state to avoid any stigma caused by the Denny case. Their meeting occurred discreetly in the corral of the Windsor Hotel's livery barn.

The attorney advised Whitney that his Montana crimes could be cleared with minimal sentences, but the North Dakota bank robbery committed with a deadly weapon carried a 99-year sentence with no liberal deals possible. Whitney told the lawyer he would pay any price within reason to clear his name and go straight. The lawyer could give him no assurance of light sentences, but he did pledge to make every effort to get Whitney reduced sentences if he wanted to give himself up. Whitney said he would think the offer over and talk to him further that night. They met again, only Whitney had packed his gear and decided against serving any prison time, instead intending "to drop out of sight for all time."

"Thus did Ryan [Whitney] pass from the pages of Montana history," said one writer. But that's not quite true.

A year passed after the bank robbery, and a new Valley County sheriff had been elected. S. C. "Ski" Small, the former county treasurer, planned to be aggressive against the remaining outlaws, as Cosner had been before Griffith. The sheriff received word that Whitney was in Glasgow seeing old friends and buying clothes. The sheriff watched the stable for him, but Whitney took the train instead. He and Duffy and perhaps Woodruff embarked for the vast Patagonian plains of southern Argentina.

Whitney was never seen again by either his friends or adversaries. Word reached Glasgow that he was killed in South America with Harvey "Kid Curry" Logan and two others after a three-day gun battle with authorities. A battle of this sort did occur in the Rio Pico region of Argentina in December 1911; it may have involved two Montana outlaws. They had killed a third partner earlier. Since law enforcement officials determined that Curry wasn't involved, it is possible that it was our three Big Muddy outlaws who met their demise there.

Meanwhile, another Big Muddy denizen was actively working on having his epitaph written. In 1907, Regina Royal Canadian Mounted Police Superintendent Landers reported that the men most wanted for wholesale horse-stealing had been disposed of, except for Andy Duffy and a man called T. J. Birch.[9]

While the excitement of the Crosby bank robbery had faded, the neighboring community of Ambrose brought it all back again, thanks to the exploits of a man named George "Bloody Knife" Zegler (or Zeglin). Zegler was known as "Bloody Knife" because of the bloodthirsty tales he would tell when drunk. The name originally belonged to an Arikara-Sioux (Dakota) military scout who had served at Fort Buford, North Dakota, and died at the Little Bighorn battle with Custer's Seventh Cavalry. Ed Sherman was credited with giving Zegler that moniker.

Zegler was too crude and obnoxious for even the outlaws to accept, and he was hard on the eyes, too. He had quite a reputation as a petty thief, incurring the wrath of farmers and outlaws alike. His one chance at major outlaw status failed when he and two partners tried to duplicate the Wild Bunch's robbery of a Great Northern Railway train just outside Malta at Exeter Creek railroad siding. However, the authorities were warned in advance and Zegler spent a year in prison, thanks to lawman George Hall.

Zegler came to Montana with a local family who had hired him as a ranch hand from the stockyards at St. Paul, Minnesota, where he worked. Zegler went bad and spent most of his time drinking, gambling, and stealing horses, most of which he sold to farmers in the old Williams County towns of Crosby and Ambrose. He became upset with these farmers when he wasn't paid for recent deliveries of horses. They were having a rough time financially, due to drought and subsequent failed crops. Zegler would accept no such excuses and decided to show those hayseeds he was no one to fool with.

Zegler went on a drinking spree in Crosby on a Sunday in June 1908, and shot up a restaurant. Then he and an unidentified companion headed about ten miles northwest for Ambrose. They stopped at one farmer's place, trying to get him to join their drinking spree, but he refused. They stopped at another farm, demanding money or the return of the horses. Since the man had no money, they shot at his feet and unhitched his six plow horses. The operators of a nearby steam-tractor outfit breaking up new soil witnessed the goings-on, and one of them fired a shotgun at Zegler. He wasn't hit, but he headed for Ambrose without the horses; his companion wisely departed.

Zegler made his presence immediately known in Ambrose by riding into a saloon on his horse, demanding beer for both man and beast. Receiving no service, he pulled his pistol and began shooting into the ceiling, among other places. A number of towns-people heard the ruckus and armed themselves. Several of them entered the saloon and tried to persuade the medium-height, heavyset man to leave, but he shot at them, clipping off the fingertip of the local newspaper editor. The group pelted Zegler with billiard balls, frightening the horse and knocking Zegler off. In the process he lost one pistol as he scrambled out the door after his horse. He finally remounted and rode down the street with his other pistol in hand. Several shots rang out, and Zegler fell dead from his horse soon after. He was downed by an outraged citizen firing from his office window, the report read.

The coroner's jury ruled that Zegler was killed by a shot fired by a person or persons unknown. No one revealed that the shot had been fired by the town's jeweler, and that this was common knowledge. The townspeople remained divided on whether the shooting was justified. Newspapers of nearby towns proclaimed that the area was rid of one more lawbreaker. And the Mounties weren't in mourning, either.

Zegler's brother arrived and claimed the body for burial by the family in Minneapolis. He held no grudges against the townspeople and said his brother had been the black sheep of the family.

The last of the big-name Big Muddy-Valley County outlaws was the "Pigeon-toed Kid," who was actually J. C. Brown or just "Pigeon-toe." His outlaw career in Valley County was of short duration. Apparently he came from George Whitney's territory of Lemmon, South Dakota. No prior criminal deeds from there have been recorded, but he was wanted for horse-stealing in both Montana and Canada.

He was said to have arrived in Glasgow about 1906, after escaping from the Mounties during a train stop by jumping out a window. The wanted man worked his way down to Montana and, like Kid Flannagan, went to work on a ranch where the owners wanted him to steal horses for them. He decided to do it on his own and collect the full profit. That's when he fell in with the Big Muddy boys.

The sheriff and his deputies played hide-and-seek with Brown for several months before Deputy Sheriff Hugh Calderwood caught up with the bandit during the winter of 1908 at an unoccupied ranch located north of present-day Opheim, about 50 miles north of Glasgow. Calderwood was traveling by the ranch and noticed fresh buggy and horse tracks in the snow. Since Brown had recently stolen a buggy and a pair of horses, the deputy decided to investigate.

Calderwood spent the night in the barn, waiting for Pigeon-toe to exit the house. Calderwood had his chance the next morning when the outlaw came out for a load of wood to stoke the stove for breakfast. Calderwood confronted Brown when the outlaw had his hands full of wood.

Brown dropped his load to reach for his pistol, but Calderwood fired, hitting him in the hip. Seconds too late, Pigeon-toe's only shot went into the ground. He managed to escape without Calderwood pursuing and made it to a ranch two miles away, where he stole a horse and saddle. Calderwood rounded up the stolen stock and buggy and gave up the chase.

Four months later, the sheriff received word that Brown was hiding at the Camille Bonnabel ranch, north of Poplar on Poplar Creek. The sheriff and two deputies arrived at suppertime and entered the house. Neither Brown nor Sheriff Small recognized each other, but Calderwood and the fugitive did. Brown jumped to his feet, reaching for his revolver, but Calderwood had the advantage again and fired first.

The bullet passed through Brown and struck the hired man in the shoulder. Mortally wounded, Brown asked for a pencil and paper, but he lost consciousness and died within the hour. The Pigeon-toed Kid had kept his promise not to be taken alive.

Sheriff Small and his staff continued the crusade. They captured several outlaws and made Valley County and the Big Muddy country safer for settlers, completing Cosner's work. An extradition treaty with Canada helped in the quest.

And while this was happening, former sheriff Griffith lived in relative obscurity in Scobey, running a saloon. Like banker Denny, he had fallen from grace, and had been abandoned by his wealthy associates.

Part IV

Of the major outlaws who made northeastern Montana their stomping ground, Dutch Henry Ieuch is considered the main player and is still talked about today, as is Kid Curry in the Little Rockies and Long Henry Thompson around Saco and Hinsdale. Ieuch's disappearance was swift; a swaggering, gun-toting outlaw ranging the countryside one day and vanishing the next. The unwanted attention he received at Shufelt's trial at Regina must have convinced him to become scarce.

Apparently he went into hiding at the Watkins ranch, which was located a mile west of Harlem. Harlem was about 100 miles west of Glasgow, along the Milk River and Great Northern Railway tracks. Ieuch had gotten to know the Watkins family when they lived on the Milk River flats between Saco and Hinsdale. He had visited there periodically since 1899.

During this visit he was helping Alf Watkins round up horses for J. "Dad" Williams around Wild Horse Butte on the Fort Belknap Indian Reservation, near Peoples Creek between Harlem and the Little Rockies. They trailed the horses to another ranch on the Milk River where they saddled and pack-broke them. Ieuch gave the Watkins boy two colts for assisting him.

Ieuch left his distinctive buggy and fancy Bisley-model Colt revolver, too, both of which were too well-known for him to use any longer. He also left $100 for Alf's dad to send to a North Dakota town when Ieuch requested it. Saying good-bye, he left for Culbertson with two loaded packhorses.

He probably visited friends in Culbertson, then headed eastward, probably crossing the Missouri River into North Dakota by ferry at Buford City. It is likely he stopped there before heading northeast on the old Overland Trail towards Kenmore on the Lacs River. Ieuch knew Kenmore well since he had driven many cattle there for rail shipment east. There he left a horse, saddle, and weapons with instructions to the livery stable owner (or a farmer, depending on the story), saying that he would retrieve them later. Presumably he also divested himself of the other two horses and boarded a train for his journey to Ardoch, a small farming community in Walsh County near the Red River border with Minnesota. Whether he knew of the town from his North Dakota days or once lived in Minnesota as did his younger brother Chris is not known. Perhaps the town attracted Ieuch because of its predominantly Polish population. He may have felt safe there, so far from Montana and among people who spoke German.

Ieuch was calling himself John Stewart, a horse and cattle buyer from Sundance, Wyoming, where his mother owned a large ranch. He sent word to the Watkins family requesting the $100 in a postal money order.

At Ardoch he met up with Alec McKenzie and William Stephenson (or Stevenson). McKenzie and Ieuch had known each other in Montana. McKenzie had left his home on Prince Edward Island in Canada and ended up in the Glasgow-Culbertson areas earning a living as a blacksmith, farm hand, and general handyman. He was arrested in Culbertson for peddling whiskey. Later he lived in small communities in eastern North Dakota. It is not clear whether McKenzie was employed by Stephenson.

Ieuch and Stephenson appeared to be old friends. Stephenson may have acted as Ieuch's agent, selling horses for him. Stephenson was running a speakeasy at Ardoch in the officially dry state of North Dakota, and Ieuch took advantage of it, drinking heavily. They decided to spend some time at Stephenson's homestead near Palmville, Roseau County, Minnesota, to get away from the alcohol, and left on November 12. The county bordered the Canadian province of Manitoba. Ieuch settled his bills and paid their fares to Palmville with the money from the Watkins family.

From nearby Wannaska, Ieuch sent letters to friends requesting the money he had left with them, and a letter to the man keeping his horse and gear. He had McKenzie write the letters, since his writing ability was poor. McKenzie also sent a letter to the Valley County sheriff's office at Glasgow, asking if there was still a reward for Ieuch; he signed it "Bill Smith." He received an affirmative reply, but the reward offered was only $300.

The neighbors weren't overly impressed with young McKenzie, describing him as a "hanger-on" and "of little account."

Ieuch and Stephenson went back to the Wannaska post office on December 30 and picked up a registered letter with a $100 money order enclosed. Ieuch gave McKenzie $25 and told him he would have to shift for himself, but that he could stay with

Stephenson while looking for work. Up until that time, Ieuch had paid for McKenzie's room and board. Ieuch instructed Stephenson where to send the second money order when it arrived, but it never did.

The following morning at about 9 a.m., Ieuch started south for the town of Middle River on the Klondike Ridge Road to catch the train back to Kenmore, North Dakota. Stephenson accompanied him to the road junction, though McKenzie parted company at the barn, saying he was going to visit a neighbor. But, as was later determined, McKenzie instead returned to the house, got Stephenson's shotgun, and started after Ieuch.

Neighbors had observed a short, older man (Ieuch) walking down the road with a pack slung over his shoulder. He had a grayish beard and wore heavy winter clothing. Shortly after, they observed a younger man, later identified as McKenzie, carrying a gun and walking in the same direction. The younger man even asked one resident if he had seen another man pass by recently.

It is believed that once McKenzie caught up with Ieuch, he shot him in the side of the jaw. McKenzie placed the muzzle at the throat of his downed victim and fired again. He dragged the body in among some willows, put a knapsack over the head, and buried the body under the snow. He removed Ieuch's wallet from inside his coat pocket but missed $6.02 in change that was in his pants pocket.

A man living nearby heard the shots and decided to investigate. He found blood in the snow and tracks where something had been dragged away. He assumed someone had shot a deer and looked no further.

McKenzie left the next morning and took the stage to Roseau from Wannaska. He stayed there a few days, obtaining enough work for the fare back to North Dakota.

Once away from the murder scene, McKenzie wrote a letter to the man at Kenmore holding Ieuch's property, using the dead man's name and authorizing a John Commons to pick it up. This canceled the earlier letter McKenzie had written for Ieuch, telling the man to feed his horse oats because he was coming back to Kenmore. On March 1, 1906, McKenzie returned for the horse, paid the $17 feed bill, and then sold the animal for $100.

On April 24, a farmer found Ieuch's body while he was clearing and burning brush off his land. Once the Roseau County coroner and sheriff investigated, it didn't take long for them to identify McKenzie as the prime suspect.

Stephenson identified the body by its clothing and the gear in the knapsack. Residents of both Culbertson and the Big Muddy country also viewed the body. Special Deputy John Davis was the most prominent identifier mentioned. Ieuch's gold teeth played a major part in the identification.

McKenzie was finally found at Mekinock, North Dakota, after the Roseau County authorities had checked several towns around Ardoch. He was residing in a shed behind a livery barn, "drinking on a keg of beer" in the company of others. He must have sold Ieuch's belongings because none were in evidence. McKenzie offered the sheriff a beer before the law officer identified himself.

McKenzie, a "clean-cut, tall, lithe figure of a man," was returned to Roseau for trial. The court had to provide him with an attorney since he had spent all the money he had taken from Dutch Henry. McKenzie never admitted to the crime. He tried to blame the murder on Stephenson, but the evidence was overwhelming and the witnesses were sure of their identification, so the jury declared him guilty. The judge waived the death penalty, however, because of the influence of the bad company he had fallen into and since he had come from a loving, religious family.

McKenzie went off to the state penitentiary at Stillwater, Minnesota. There he was a model prisoner in transit who didn't require handcuffs as he walked through the streets, stopping at a restaurant and barbershop. After all, hadn't he killed a famous Montana outlaw?

Ieuch was buried at Wannaska, near where his body was

found. The Canadian Mounted Police reduced their detachment at Wood Mountain once they were sure it was really Ieuch who had been killed.

Ieuch stayed dead until January 1910, when articles appeared in the Culbertson S*earchlight* and the *Minot Journal*, datelined St. Paul, Minnesota and Moose Jaw, Saskatchewan, respectively. The stories announced that Dutch Henry had been shot and killed by the Mounties south of Moose Jaw. According to the more detailed version, a constable met up with Ieuch in the badlands near Willow Bunch on Big Muddy Creek. The outlaw opened fire with his rifle, downing the officer's horse, but the officer returned the fire and killed the shooter with the second round. Other reports had told of his continued outlaw activities in Saskatchewan in the previous few years.

The Royal Canadian Mounted Police commandant immediately wired the nearest local detachment for details. He received the following reply: "No foundation whatever for report about Dutch Henry." The Mounties were never able to determine the source of the story.

Some writers have said these tales about Ieuch's continued existence were the reason McKenzie was released from prison in 1913, but McKenzie was pardoned because he was seriously ill with tuberculosis. However, it is true that his parents kept petitioning to get their son released, putting political pressure on the Minnesota governor's office through Canadian officers and the British consul.

About the time of the report of Ieuch's death, George Whitney was said to have become a Hollywood western film star, using the name Red Murray. Also, a phony report circulated from Landusky, Montana, saying that the body of once-prominent resident Abe Gill had been found and his killer's apprehension was imminent. The cowboys were obviously bored and yearned for the good old bad-guy days. Making up such tales must have helped ease the monotony.

Brothers Alf and Clarence Watkins moved from their parents'

ranch and established their own place near Loring, Montana. In their possession were Dutch Henry's revolver and the buggy with a steer's skull on the front axle. Ieuch had used the wagon in about 1898, going from ranch to ranch in Canada gentling horses. The revolver was eventually presented to the Montana Historical Society, and the wagon was left to decay in a farmer's field.

Coyote Pete Ieuch was last mentioned in print in 1910. He was arrested for horse theft again but was not convicted by the Glasgow-Valley County court. His fate is not known.[10] He had come to the United States in 1888 at the age of 13. Dutch Henry was two years older and had migrated two years earlier.

The youngest Ieuch brother (or, perhaps, half-brother), Chris, came to America in 1901. He became a U.S. citizen at Crookston, Minnesota, in 1898. It was said he never approved of his brother's illegal occupation and was an honest, law-abiding citizen. He died at the Plentywood hospital in 1929 at the age of 58, and was buried in the Redstone cemetery. Chris Ieuch never married and left no children who could help historians with the Ieuch family history. His lifestyle had always been simple; he lived in a dugout on Buggy Creek, a mile from Daleview. He trapped in the winter and tended cattle in the summer, and always wore a leather cap regardless of the weather. He was about the same height as Dutch Henry, and he pronounced the family name "Yaw."

Chris lost his homestead plats a few years before his death and earned his keep by hiring out. He was a temperate man, except twice a year when he went on a "toot," as the locals called it. Attempts were made to locate his family at the time of his death, but to no avail. The Ieuch family, for all practical purposes, had disappeared from the Montana scene. ✸

IV

THE AMATEUR OUTLAWS OF WICKES AND THE WICKES PAYROLL ROBBERY

Not much has been written about the attempted robbery of the Wickes mining district payroll during the summer of 1890. The ill-fated holdup was staged by a few of the town's more covetous and larcenous, yet bungling and inept, citizens. The would-be criminals were easily captured, but not convicted. Their fellow citizens took pity on them and decided that their humiliating failure was punishment enough. Perhaps so.

The town of Wickes was about 25 miles southwest of Helena and six miles west of Jefferson City. The entrance to the former boomtown, which was established in 1876, is marked today by the remains of three tall smokestacks and the concrete foundations of a lead and silver reduction smelter. The smelter operation moved to Helena in 1889, and fires in 1900 and 1902 virtually destroyed the town of Wickes.

The mining camp was founded by George T. Wickes, a New York City mining engineer and partner of J. Corbin. Its leading merchant was T. A. Wickes; he settled in the valley in 1877. The town was said to have been named for another Wickes, "W. W.," who was an engineer and promoter of the Alta Mining Co.

Presumably they were all related.

Dominated by 5,644-foot Mount Alta to the north, and situated along Comet Creek in the Rocky Mountains, the mining community flourished for about 20 years, reaching a maximum population of about 1,500. Surrounding it were 25 operating mines that clung to the hillsides above the narrow valley floor. The premier mines were the Alta, Alta South, Comet, Custer, Gregory, and Rumley. Total silver, lead, and gold production from these exceeded $65,000,000 with the Alta contributing about half that amount.

Early Wickes had five dance halls and about 22 saloons operating 24 hours a day so that its miners could spend the $35,000 they collectively earned each month on rest and relaxation. Fights were said to have been so common that only the combatants took much interest in them. There were so many card games, according to legend, that a hired man with a wagon and team was needed to clean up the thick layer of cards that covered the street each morning. While the fabled cleaner tidied up the street, more than 350 miners—some no doubt bruised and hungover—trudged up North Hill with their lunch pails to the many mines that honeycombed the slopes with over 30 miles of tunnels.

Wickes was at its peak in June 1883 when a branch of the Northern Pacific Railroad arrived from East Helena via a newly completed mile-and-a-quarter-long tunnel through the mountains. From that day on, money for the local mining payrolls came unguarded from Helena on the train. The Great Northern-Montana Central Railroad followed the same route in 1888; its depot was isolated on a hill above town.

T. H. Kleinschmidt, assistant cashier for the First National Bank of Helena, along with a teller identified only as "J. W.," usually filled the Alta Mine strongbox with a small quantity of silver dollars and the rest in paper money. But on one unique day that July, the bank had an excess of silver on hand and decided to fill the steel strongbox with a small amount of bank notes and several thousand of the heavier silver dollars. This change of events was unknown to the three citizens of Wickes who had decided to steal the payroll.

The morning of the attempted crime was dusty and hot, without a hint of a breeze. The steam-engine-powered train labored up the track following the low lines of the foothills, snaked through the tunnel, and arrived at the sequestered hillside depot. Waiting by the depot in his one-horse wagon, just as he had for that last two mornings, was "Dad" Nixon. Nearby, also for the third morning in a row, was a young man loafing innocently on a log and whittling. Once the payroll box containing $13,000 was loaded onto Nixon's wagon, the youth asked Nixon for a ride back to town. Nixon consented, not knowing that this act signaled the young man's partners that the money had finally arrived. Meanwhile, the train had continued on its journey southward to Butte.

The wagon started down the depot road, passed the schoolhouse and doctor's office, and approached an empty shed near the Alta Mine's outbuildings. When the wagon drew abreast, two black-masked young men—one heavy, one slender, and both dressed in overalls—jumped out of the shed. One was holding a pistol. They silently motioned Nixon to get down from the wagon and took off with it and the money into a nearby gully that separated two ridges around the valley. The hitchhiking lad faded into the scenery.

In the gully, the robbers met J. W. Shreve, a Wickes merchant. He had left town early on his usual morning ride in a buggy drawn by two fast horses. The three conferred, reaching the apparent conclusion that Nixon's one-horse wagon couldn't handle the additional weight of the unexpected silver. So the chest was transferred to Shreve's buggy, and he took Nixon's rig back to town.

While he drove to town, rehearsing a plausible explanation for his vehicle change in case anyone inquired, his two confederates, Morgan Shreve and Barton Wilson, started up an infrequently used trail into the hills. The horses strained and the buggy creaked threateningly under the heavy load. Finally the men had to dismount and push the deteriorating buggy to relieve some of the horse's load.

Two boys hauling wood to town observed the spectacle; they didn't know the men, but they recognized the merchant's buggy. They noticed too, that the horses were exhausted and streaked with sweat.

The boys weren't the only observers the robbers had. A crew of men from the Alta Mine was repairing the road while some mine machinery was being fixed—another unexpected turn of events. From their vantage point, the workers observed the men and beasts struggle to the summit. Then the robbers turned the horses loose, abandoned the buggy, and disappeared from view.

Unseen, they buried the loot, dropped down the mountainside to where their horses were tethered, and rode back to town. The original plan had called for abandoning Nixon's wagon, so they did the same with their co-conspirator's rig (although they did release Shreve's horses). As they entered a barn on the west end of town, they were seen by a "Mrs. M.", who was out picking gooseberries—and whose son Harry and nephew Glenn were the boys they had passed earlier. The woman shouted a greeting, but the men didn't answer. She thought they looked shaken and were having trouble unsaddling their horses.

Meanwhile Dad Nixon had finally reached town and called Jefferson County Sheriff Dodley Halfard at Boulder while a Wickes posse was formed.

From Nixon's descriptions, the citizens immediately knew the masked men's identities. They were particularly surprised by Barton (or Buck) Wilson's participation because he had always been a friendly and upright citizen. But it appeared he had turned to crime, and they had to get the money back. The posse rode up the hill to the abandoned buggy and grazing horses. (Our would-be outlaws didn't take into account that the horses wouldn't leave the buggy, even if initially shooed away.) No thieves were to be seen, but one dismounted posse member fell into a freshly dug hole about the size of a strongbox. The robbers apparently had decided the hole wasn't a good hiding place after all. A further search produced the payroll box from a small mountain spring that paralleled the trail.

Later, when the sheriff arrived, no one seemed to have any idea who the holdup men were or where they had gone. A grand jury was convened at Boulder in the hope of getting at the truth, but no witness would identify the robbers—not even "Mrs. M."

The last witness called was young Harry, Mrs. M's son. Reportedly a hush came over the courtroom as he took the stand. County attorney M. H. Parker had heard that the boy wasn't going to tell what he knew. So Parker asked, "Harry, has anyone told you how to testify?"

"Yes, sir."

"Who was it?"

"My mother."

"What did she tell you to say?" Not a sound could be heard in the courtroom.

"She told me, sir, to tell the truth, the whole truth, and nothing but the truth." A muffled cheer went up around him.

"Did you know the men when you met them [on the road]?"

"No, sir," Harry said—which was the truth.

This ended any direct attempts at identification of the thieves. If the county attorney had questioned Harry further, he would have learned that Harry had been told their identities later.

The jury stayed out 20 hours and came back with a not-guilty verdict in spite of the strong circumstantial evidence. They were probably swayed by the lack of local enthusiasm to convict the men, by the fact that the money was back in the mine owners' possession, and perhaps by the knowledge that the alleged ringleader had recently lost his wife and child.

So life went back to normal at Wickes, with all perhaps forgiven—although the three fellows probably received some occasional sly digs. Besides, didn't the robbery provide the townspeople with a diversion from the usual fare of drinking, fighting, and card-playing? ✖

Helena, circa 1885, the Montana town Con Murphy was
framed for trying to burn down. Courtesy Western Federal
Savings & Loan Association of Montana, from the publication *Historic Helena,* 1978.

Fort Benton-Helena stage line, circa 1884. Perhaps the very
stage robbed by Con Murphy. Courtesy Western Federal
Savings & Loan Association of Montana, from the publication *Historic Helena,* 1978.

Lewis and Clark Jail, 1875. The "escape-proof" jail that could not hold Con Murphy. Courtesy Western Federal Savings & Loan Association of Montana, from the publication *Historic Helena,* 1978.

Valley County officials on the courthouse steps, Glasgow, circa 1898. Front row, second from the left, is Henry Cosner of Malta, then county commissioner, later sheriff, and finally game warden. Back row, right, is the later sheriff, S. C. "Ski" Small. From a *Glasgow Courier* photo.

The Valley County Courthouse from a distance, showing the courthouse, jail, and well for bath, circa 1905. From a *Glasgow Courier* photo.

Glasgow and its Great Northern tracks, circa 1889. From a *Glasgow Courier* photo.

Lewis-Wedum Building, where the Glasgow bank robbery occurred, circa 1899. From a *Glasgow Courier* photo.

County officers present during the 1903 break from the Valley County Jail. Seated, John Dilliard, deputy sheriff; left standing, Undersheriff Harry Rutter; and Sheriff Cosner to the right. From a *Glasgow Courier* photo.

The spot where Jack Brown was lynched at the Valley County Courthouse, June 18, 1903. Shown here is the southeastern corner of the building and the window (top center) from which he was thrown. From a *Glasgow Courier* photo.

Charles M. Russell's pen-and-ink depiction of the killing of cowboy-ranch foreman Nolan Armstrong by Deputy Sheriff John Elder at Culbertson, Montana. Drawing from *Good Medicine* (Doubleday & Co., Garden City, New York, 1929).

Supposedly a depiction of "Long" Henry Thompson, from *The Biographical Album of Western Gunfighters*, by Ed Bartholomew (Old Frontier Press of Texas, 1958). The drawing is attributed to a former lawman, Pink Simms, who knew Thompson, but it resembles a C. M. Russell sketch.

Big Muddy outlaw, George Whitney, alias Tom Ryan, 1906. Courtesy of Manson Bailey, Jr., Pioneer Museum, Glasgow, Montana.

Wyoming outlaw-Montana brand inspector Ed Starr, alias Tom Dunn, 1896. Courtesy of Manson Bailey, Jr., Pioneer Museum, Glasgow, Montana.

The town of Wickes, Montana, and its mill and smelting works. The Great Northern tracks are in the background, right. Courtesy Montana Historical Society. (H-1571)

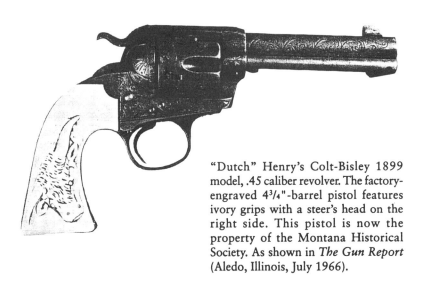

"Dutch" Henry's Colt-Bisley 1899 model, .45 caliber revolver. The factory-engraved 4³/₄"-barrel pistol features ivory grips with a steer's head on the right side. This pistol is now the property of the Montana Historical Society. As shown in *The Gun Report* (Aledo, Illinois, July 1966).

Charles M. Russell, *The Hold Up*, oil on canvas, 1899. This painting depicts the "Big Nose" George Parrott gang robbing a stagecoach on the Black Hills-Cheyenne Trail. Courtesy Amon Carter Museum, Fort Worth, Texas (1961. 212).

"Big Nose" George Parrott after his capture in Miles City, circa 1879. From the Union Pacific Railroad historical collection.

The Winters-Gill ranch in the Little Rockies, circa 1900. Courtesy Al Lucke Collection, Montana State University-Northern Archives (AL-896-653-1).

Barn on the Curry Brothers ranch opposite the Winters-Gill ranch. Courtesy Al Lucke Collection, Montana State University-Northern Archives (AL-896-23).

Winter scene, Landusky, circa 1896. Courtesy Al Lucke Collection, Montana State University-Northern Archives (AL-896-23-3).

Kid Curry photo, minus the half with his girl friend, Annie Rogers, Fort Worth, Texas, circa 1900. Used by the Pinkerton Detective Agency after the Great Northern Railway train robbery near Wagner. Jim Dullerty photo.

Kid Curry after his arrest for the 1897 Belle Fourche bank robbery. From the Union Pacfic Railroad historical collection.

"Curry Bros." saloon in Harlem, Montana (1899-1901). Alan L. Brekke photo.

(left)
Abe Gill just before his disappearance in the Little Rockies, circa 1905. Courtesy Al Lucke Collection, Montana State University-Northern Archives.

(below)
Olaf C. Seltzer, *Kid Curry Holdup,* oil, circa 1940. Depicts the robbery of a Great Northern Railway passenger train at Exeter Creek railroad siding in 1901. Until recently, this painting was still in the Great Falls collection of the Seltzer-Ervin families.

V

GEORGE "BIG NOSE" PARROTT

On a hot, dusty day in the summer of 1879, the U.S. Army paymaster's wagon proceeded slowly northeast on the rough, spine-jarring, Fisk, Montana–Minnesota wagon road. The journey had begun at Camp Ruger, located at Coal Banks-Missouri River steamboat landing near present-day Virgille; and would conclude at Fort Assinniboine, about 40 miles distant. The wagon, carrying the soldiers' first payroll, was escorted by a detail of Second Cavalry soldiers.[1]

The construction of the new ten-company military post on Beaver Creek, a tributary of the Milk River, had commenced recently on land formerly used legally as a camping and hunting site by the Blackfoot Confederacy[2] and by Gros Ventre (Atsina) and River Crow (Absaroke), and not so legally by the Assiniboine (Nakoda), Plains Cree (Kinnisto–no) and Sioux (Dakota) nations. The mostly brick fort would eventually have more than 100 buildings surrounding its rectangular half-mile-long by one-fifth-mile-wide parade grounds.

Waiting for the wagon in a coulee off Beaver Creek was a party of gunmen led by George "Big Nose" Parrott. They had been led to believe that the payroll would be easy pickings, with only a handful of guards. But the cloud of dust they saw coming from the south was too big for just a wagon and a few horses—in fact there were some 30 bluecoats guarding the payroll. Swearing profusely at their bad luck, the men spurred their horses and headed southwest, back towards the community of Sun River.

Meanwhile, the military party reached the fort site and reported seeing the men to their commander, Colonel Thomas Ruger. Since U.S. Deputy Marshal John X. Beidler of Helena was at the post on business concerning horse theft, robbery, and murder, Ruger told Beidler to go and investigate.

The short but stocky ex-vigilante was a brave man with a reputation for toughness, but he wasn't foolhardy. He asked Ruger for an escort but was refused; the commander said the men were needed at the military post since there were so many hostile Indians in the area. Beidler ended the conversation by telling Ruger that he wasn't yet prepared to meet his maker, and the gang was allowed to go on its way.

This was not Parrott's and his men's usual stomping ground. Parrott had been making his home at Miles City, Montana, since he was wanted for murder in Wyoming. The outlaw was about five feet, ten inches tall and weighed 160 pounds. He was in his mid-thirties and had a large mustache covering his mouth, dark curly hair, heavy eyelids, and a large potato nose. He was a little on the homely side.

Little is known of the early life of the man who also called himself George Reynolds in Montana, George Francis Warden in Wyoming, and George Manuse at other times. One historian states that Parrott was born in Indiana and reared in Iowa. Other reports had him living at St. George, Utah, once he came west. His earliest and perhaps only legitimate job would have been in 1876, as a bull team freight-wagon driver, or bullwhacker, carrying supplies to the gold-rush town and gulch of Deadwood, Dakota Territory, in the Black Hills mining district. Parrott probably hauled gold ore shipments south to the Union Pacific Railroad depots at Sidney,

Nebraska, and Cheyenne, Wyoming, also going eastward to a Northern Pacific Railroad depot at Bismarck (N.D.) and the steamboat landing at Fort Pierre (S.D.) on the Missouri River. Parrott quit this work after learning all the routes so he could easily ambush the gold-laden stagecoaches and freighters or travelers he came upon.[3] Ambushes were easy to execute from the trails through the dark and narrow gulches. However, the gold shipments were not easy to take since the gold came in 200-pound bricks; mine payrolls were easier marks.

Parrott's gang members at the time were believed to have been Jack Campbell, "Dutch" Charlie Burris (or Bates), Frank Towle (or Toule), and a man named McKinney. The gang reportedly had a robbers' roost near Cheyenne, Wyoming, close to the Black Hills stage route. They also had access to the old Oregon Trail along the North Platte and Sweetwater rivers, the north-south Black Hills-Cheyenne route, and the Bozeman and Bridger roads that broke off into Montana. They were said to have had another hideout in the Sheridan Valley on Goose Creek where the Bozeman Road skirted the Big Horn Mountains, and a third hideout shared with other outlaws in the lush mountain setting of Jackson Hole in the Grand Tetons of western Wyoming.

Parrott and his gang were well-known in the lower Yellowstone River valley once Milestown (later renamed Miles City) was established near Fort Keogh at the confluence of the Yellowstone and Tongue rivers. The same was true farther west at Bozeman, a farming community in the Gallatin River valley. Parrott and his band sold stolen horses from Wyoming in Montana and north to Canada, and they brought stolen animals back with them. In the winter months, they stayed at one of their hideouts, playing cards, drinking whiskey, racing horses, and fattening up horses to be sold in the spring.

Their exploits were recorded in the memoirs of Andrew Garcia in July 1878. Garcia had decided to leave the employ of the army as a wrangler-packer at Fort Ellis near Bozeman and had set out with a partner to hunt and trap in the Musselshell River country to the northwest. They fell in with five men who used them and their pack outfit as a cover while they peddled whiskey to certain Indian and Metis people, who in turn stole horses from the tribes for them. One of the peddlers was Parrott; another was Con Murphy, soon to be known as a notorious Montana outlaw. Yet another was Al Shinnick, who is believed to have had a brother, John, who had a saloon-brothel in Miles City. Parrott stayed there when in town. A man called Brock Adams, perhaps from Utah, was also traveling with them, as well as a Metis (French-Indian) called Hypolite La Brie, a most unstable and dangerous man.

These men kept Garcia's partner drunk during the trip—a feat which took little effort—and spoke freely to Garcia of their activities, perhaps trying to recruit him. They told him that they sold the ill-gotten horses to the Mounted Police in the North West Territories for about $100 each through a contact of La Brie. In addition, Garcia learned that Parrott and Shinnick had attempted several holdups of stagecoaches in Utah and Montana, but had failed at all of them. The gang claimed to be headquartered at Green River, Wyoming, near the Utah border.

Garcia and his partner were allowed to leave the outlaws after journeying south from Otter Creek to near Sweet Grass Creek, near the future town of Big Timber. La Brie was for killing the two, but Adams wouldn't allow it. Reportedly La Brie and Adams finally shot it out when they reached Canada, killing each other in the exchange.

The following month, Parrott returned to Wyoming and rejoined the old gang. After buying supplies at Medicine River, the group settled in a hideout in the thickly wooded Rattlesnake Creek canyon near the community of Elk Mountain in the Medicine Bow Range of the Rocky Mountains. It was believed that Parrott had previously been in the northern part of the Carbon County country, robbing stagecoaches after he left the St. George, Utah, area.

In the group besides Parrott were regulars "Dutch" Charlie, Frank Towle, a "Mack" (possibly McKinney), Jack Campbell, and two men identified as Thomas Reed and Sim Wan. Reed was supposedly a Younger Brothers gang member, and Wan was said to be an alias used by Frank James, the outlaw brother of Jesse James.

This bunch formulated plans to rob a special Union Pacific Railroad train carrying the railroad workers' payroll along a stretch of track west of the town of Carbon. Then a major coal-mining town, Carbon was six miles west of Hanna, where the rail section crew was headquartered, and about 40 miles west of Rawlins, the seat of Carbon County. The gang put its plan into action on August 19, 1878.

Using a James brothers technique, they pulled the rail spikes on a downhill curve and tried pulling the rails off, but their crowbars were not long enough to get sufficient leverage, hence they planned to build an obstruction of ties on the track to derail the train. But a section crew showed up before they could accomplish the work, and the outlaws had to lay low in a gully all day waiting for them to leave. The maintenance crew did not discover the loosened rails until they were ready to quit for the day. They hurriedly packed up and headed back to report their discovery. Meanwhile, the gang went back to work on the rails and once again had their plan thwarted when a passenger train came by and drove them into hiding again. Then, when the special didn't show up, and since the section crew had found the sabotaged track, they decided to head back to their hideout. What they didn't know was that the section foreman had flagged down the special and warned the crew of the danger ahead.

With the train stopped and the gang in retreat, the Carbon County sheriff instructed deputy sheriffs Tip Vincent of Rawlins and Ed Widowfield of Carbon, along with six special deputies, to proceed to the aborted robbery scene. The lawmen were fairly sure of their quarry since the Parrott gang had been seen earlier in the week at Laramie, about 80 miles to the southwest, and had left in a westerly direction.

Vincent and Widowfield became separated from the posse

when they struck the outlaws' trail, and they followed it to the gang's camp. Seeing no one, they advanced into the campsite and examined the ground, including the recently extinguished fire. In the ashes the lawmen found the remains of the railroad spikes the gang had cut off.

That was enough for gang member Frank Towle, who shouted, "Let's fire!" Both deputies were killed as the outlaws, who had been hiding nearby, emptied their guns into them. One officer was killed immediately, but the other made it about 50 yards on horseback before he fell to the ground, mortally wounded. The bodies were thrown into the thick brush and lightly covered, after being stripped of their valuables, weapons, boots, etc. The men hurriedly broke camp, took the extra horses, and started north, crossing the railroad tracks at Carbon and later fording the North Platte River above Muddy Creek.

By this time, the other posse members had returned to town, thinking the other two had done the same. Search parties were sent out to find the two deputies after three days, but their bodies weren't discovered for ten days. The dim trail of four of the outlaws was picked up but soon lost. A reward of $2,000 was offered for Parrott, and $1,000 was offered for each gang member, dead or alive.

Dutch Charlie was supposedly arrested soon after at Green River, Wyoming, and transported across the state to the county jail at Laramie. But another report is more likely: that Burriss was arrested in Laramie after hiding out for several months on Rock Creek. Carbon County Sheriff Rankin was in the process of bringing the outlaw back to Rawlins for trial when the train stopped at Carbon for fuel at 9:25 p.m., and a party of masked men broke into the baggage car. They took Dutch Charlie to the nearest telegraph pole and hung him high. He reportedly confessed his guilt before the execution, but would not identify the others. His body was cut down the next day and thrown into a Rawlins-bound coal car, the rope still around the neck.

It would have been useless for the sheriff to resist the mob, since, besides townspeople, there were several hundred miners to contend with.

The remaining gang members were credited by some authorities with robbing a stagecoach at Canyon Springs on the Deadwood-Cheyenne route near present-day Four Corners, Wyoming. Perhaps $27,000 to $40,000 was taken in the holdup. One outlaw died of his wounds. Frank Towle died near the Black Hills when the gang tried to rob a stagecoach bound for the Hat Creek sheep station in country south of Canyon Springs. The mysterious Mack died of fever in the Yellowstone country of Montana, according to Parrott.

The equally mysterious Reed and Wan apparently disappeared. However, they were hardly Younger or James Brothers gang members. The Youngers were in prison at the time after committing the Northfield, Minnesota, bank robbery; the Jameses were in hiding in Mexico until the summer of 1879, when they returned to their Nashville, Tennessee, homes, where their families were in hiding. From there they began a crime spree throughout the South before returning to Missouri, where Jesse James was killed. A Thomas Reid (or Reed) from Arkansas pops up in the Dutch Henry Ieuch gang at Culbertson, but whether there was any connection with the Thomas Reed involved with Parrott is unknown.

In the fall of 1878, Parrott and some gang members returned to the Miles City, Montana, area. When in town, Parrott frequented John Shinnick's saloon on North Fifth Street. John and Nell Shinnick's saloon and home ranch were widely known as desperado hangouts. Parrott stayed at Shinnick's cabin on the edge of town. The other gang members apparently had a hideout at Buffalo Rapids on the Yellowstone River.

Miles City, the seat of Custer County, was at the time a wild and rough young cowboy town near the end of Texas cattle trails. A combination of buffalo hunters, soldiers, and cowboys made it a lively place. Main Street had a solid block of saloons, brothels, and gambling dens. Its location at the mouth of the Tongue River made it an excellent fording place and steamboat landing on the Yellowstone River. Several large cattle companies established ranches near there because of the good grass and water. But at the time of Parrott's residence, it was still "a long way from nowhere," according to its residents.

If Parrott and his gang had indeed robbed the stagecoach at Canyon Springs, they were broke by the following winter. Perhaps their attempted robbery and a successful stage robbery by another gang became confused, because a bandit died in each.

Parrott probably believed his luck was changing when Morris Cahn, former Fort Keogh military post trader and then prosperous town merchant, decided to take a trip back East. Even better, the merchant wasn't well-liked and didn't have an honest reputation. Cahn planned to buy merchandise and feared carrying a large amount of cash on the first leg of the journey from Miles City, before he boarded a Northern Pacific train at Bismarck, North Dakota. His worries were legitimate worries, since the local people resented their money leaving town.

Cahn was able to hitch a ride with a military ambulance and an escort of 15 soldiers going that way to pick up the fort's payroll. Some claim that Parrott saw to it that each soldier was furnished with alcohol, but that cannot be substantiated. The party consisted of the lead scout, Sergeant Green, the ambulance carrying the officers, and Cahn, followed by the soldiers in the escort wagon.

About ten miles beyond the Powder River crossing, near present-day Terry, they came off a five-mile plateau into a steep-walled valley. Sergeant Green and the ambulance were stopped at the bottom at a sharp, dark corner by three men with rifles. When the soldiers in the escort wagon appeared, they also were captured. All the men were robbed, and Cahn was relieved of his $3,200 and some peach brandy. Adding insult to injury, the robbers took the sergeant's horse—but they gave the wagon driver a cigar.

Even though Parrott had the brim of his hat pulled down and stood in shadow, his big nose was still visible to the victims.

The gang crossed the Yellowstone River and doubled back

north, eventually reaching a ranch near present-day Kinsey, halfway between Terry and Miles City. The next day they reappeared in Miles City, spending freely.

For several years afterwards, when folks in Miles City wanted to treat a friend to a drink, they would say, "Come up, old boy, and have something on me, for I still have one of old Cahn's dollars left." And though Cahn lost his bankroll, he did have some solace: the coulee where he was robbed was later named in his honor.

Apparently Parrott was arrested and tried for the robbery (at least in a preliminary hearing) but was acquitted because of sworn testimony that he was at the Buffalo Springs camp at the time of the robbery. Cahn feared for his well-being after the trial, but to his relief, Parrott decided to move on four days later, broke once again.

Parrott's gang had good reason to move on. The army swore vengeance on the men; plus, with wanted posters still up in Wyoming, the Cahn robbery gave them unwelcome attention. And perhaps one or two gang members had bragged of their Wyoming killings one too many times.

The gang moved to an even more isolated area some 300 miles to the northwest. The community of Sun River was at the main crossing on the Mullan Road, which started at Fort Benton and ended at Fort Walla Walla in Washington Territory. More locally, it was the route of the Helena stage from Fort Benton to Sun River and south to the Helena-area gold fields. About five miles to the west of the Sun River crossing was another military post, Fort Shaw. The adobe post had been built in 1867 to oversee the Blackfoot Confederacy and protect the north-south trail.

The new Montana Central Railroad tracks were just being laid from Helena to Great Falls, Fort Assinniboine, and Pacific Junction where it joined the main east-west line. Since the tracks would bypass the old crossing, this was the gang's last chance at any treasure-laden coaches.

The Parrott gang established headquarters at the Hardy place, in the nearby hills at Rocky Gap. The gang members, except for

Parrott, took jobs at different ranches to allay any suspicion about their activities. They spent their free time at Johnny Divine's, the local saloon-hotel, planning to rob the army payroll from the paymaster's wagon bringing the money from Helena. The plan was to lay in wait in Prickly Pear Creek canyon north of Helena.

Their old comrade Con Murphy would rob a stagecoach in the same vicinity a few years later. Murphy's booty was sparse, and it was the beginning of the end of his outlaw career—and his life.

The story goes that Divine overheard Campbell telling of their plan, and being a former soldier, he hurried to Helena to warn the military authorities. Riding through the canyon, he was stopped by the gang, but he bribed his way through with whiskey and cigars. He arrived in Helena and warned the military of the outlaws' plan. A changed trip date and a more formidable escort prevented any robbery.

The original escort leader was to have been a Major Arthur, brother of then vice president and later President Chester Arthur. Major Arthur was deaf, and may have been killed in the holdup since he couldn't have heard the outlaws' orders to stop.

This story raises questions, however. Why would Johnny Divine journey the ninety-some miles to Helena when all he had to do was report to Fort Shaw only a few miles away? Fort Shaw personnel could have telegraphed to Helena to stop the shipment and sent out their own column to capture the outlaws. And was it usual for a horseman to carry whiskey and cigars? It would appear the storytellers embellished a bit.

The boys tried one more army payroll robbery in the isolated stretch between Fort Benton and Fort Assinniboine, but again the party had a large escort. The soldiers were lucky not to run into any of the hostile Plains Crees who were opposing the military move into north-central Montana. Since crime definitely wasn't paying well in northern Montana, the Parrott gang returned to Wyoming, despite the price on their heads.

At this point, the waters muddy considerably, since the lives of George "Flat Nose" Currie and George "Big Nose" Parrott merge at times. Currie was part of the Wild Bunch along with Kid Curry, Butch Cassidy, and the Sundance Kid. He had first operated out of the Hole-in-the-Wall valley in Wyoming's Powder River country. But the Bunch's notoriety came after the Parrott gang was all resting eternally in Boot Hill.

The Parrott gang went back to horse-stealing, though it is believed the stubborn outlaws planned yet another army payroll robbery not far from the site of the Union Pacific Railroad robbery attempt and subsequent murders. The payroll for Fort Fetterman, at the junction of the Bozeman and Oregon trails, came to the train stop at Medicine Bow and was taken from there to Fort Fetterman.

Because of the high number of robberies, the payroll was supposedly secreted on a freighter wagon, and the gang didn't find it in the teamster's grocery shipment.

Incidents of hot pursuit and shootings by ranchers and lawmen were also making horse theft tougher.

The year 1880 continued to bring the Parrott gang misfortune. In a saloon in South Pass City, Wyoming, northwest of Rawlins on the Continental Divide at the Wind River Range, Parrott and some new associates were fleecing a cowboy during a poker game. Finally cowboy Tom Albro accused gang member Tom Rutledge of dealing from the bottom of the deck. Rutledge went for his gun. Albro shot him, but Parrott then killed Albro and rode away in the dark before Albro's friends could find their target.

The following month Parrott and a sidekick named Bill Carey (perhaps he was actually old gang member Jack Campbell) were in the vicinity of Fort McKinney and the town of Buffalo. Here they reportedly stole a large amount of supplies from an old man camped near Deep Creek. With their new cache and a string of stolen horses, they headed north and dropped some of the animals off with a "squaw man friend" before following the Tongue River back into Montana.

However, the welcome mat was no longer out at Miles City. Reward posters for the Wyoming train holdup had reached Custer County Sheriff Tom Irvine at last. No one would harbor Parrott this time around.

Parrott arrived in town and stayed at the Shinnicks' cabin as usual. The stolen horses were housed in the adjacent stable, while Carey stationed himself at Shinnick's saloon-brothel. The law officers made a deal with a prostitute known as "Beavertooth," who was on calling terms with Shinnick's wife. The saloon woman was to frequent the cabin, report back on Parrott's movements, and keep Carey happy at the downtown saloon. Shinnick's cooperation probably wasn't hard to obtain since Parrott was sharing the cabin with Shinnick's wife.

Next, the sheriff hired two special deputies, Lem Wilson and Fred Schmalsle, both former Fort Keogh packers unknown to Parrott. The first trip to the cabin and grounds consisted of crossing the pasture to look at the horses. Parrott came out of the cabin with rifle in hand, but he believed them when they said they were prospective buyers. They had a friendly discussion. Wilson and Schmalsle returned the next day. This time, Parrott came out unarmed and the two arrested him either as they sat on the front porch or while talking horseflesh in the stable. The sheriff and his deputy came out of their hiding place in the nearby brush and handcuffed the outlaw. Carey was arrested at the saloon. As he lifted his beverage glass, a revolver was stuck under his chin.

Carbon County officials arrived to extradite Parrott after a local blacksmith riveted irons on his hands and feet. A large posse escorted him to the steamboat landing since there was still a significant outlaw element in the town. Parrot was taken up the Yellowstone River to the Missouri and down that river through the Dakota Territory to Omaha, Nebraska. What happened to Carey isn't clear. In one story, he escaped or was released; in another he was sent to prison for horse theft and later was transferred to the state mental hospital, from which he subsequently escaped. Whatever his fate, his part in the tale ended. Two other supposed gang members were arrested, one in Ogden, Utah, and one in Deadwood, Dakota Territory, but neither was convicted of involvement in the Wyoming murder and train robbery attempt.

At Omaha, Parrott was taken to the Union Pacific Railroad headquarters, where his only known photograph was taken. The authorities tried unsuccessfully to link him to other train robberies. He wouldn't even admit to the train robbery in Carbon County or to the murders. Departing Omaha, Parrott and his captors went by train to Cheyenne, Wyoming, where the lawmen tried to link Parrott with unsolved state robberies. Once again, they were unsuccessful.

The party left for Rawlins the next day, August 14, 1880, on the same fateful railroad journey that Dutch Charlie had taken and that ended in his death by hanging at Carbon. As the train pulled into Carbon for fuel and water, the passengers saw that the stores were lit up and a street dance was in progress. It is said the lawmen graphically recounted to Parrott how Dutch Charlie had been dragged off the train and lynched. As if on cue, a dozen armed and masked men entered the car. Another group had already neutralized the crew and conductor. It looked as if Parrott's fate would be sealed in Carbon, too.

But Sheriff Jim Rankin chose not to cooperate. He drew his revolver and called upon the compartment's passengers to help him resist the taking of Parrott. However, this proved fruitless, and his weapon was confiscated. Unable to find handcuff keys on the sheriff (another officer had them), the intruders broke Parrott's manacles with an axe, destroying his seat in the process. Parrott was marched out with a rope already around his neck.

Apparently, Parrott grabbed a revolver from one of his captors for a few seconds, in spite of overwhelming odds and being bound. Once outside, though, his toughness faded. He denied any involvement in the attempted train robbery or killings and asked to be shot rather than hung. He was taken to a corral and a rope was thrown over a beam. At that, Parrott changed his mind, telling the mob he was badly scared and wanted a few minutes to compose himself before confessing. The mob leaders told Parrott he could have all the time he wanted, within reason.

Parrott confessed to having been one of the party who had attempted the train robbery near Elk Mountain and killed the two law officers. He named the gang members, said that they had separated that fall, and claimed that most of them were dead. When asked why they had killed the lawmen, he replied, "On the principle that dead men tell no tales."

To Parrott's surprise, the group's leader ordered the outlaw returned to the sheriff's custody and sent on his way to Rawlins for a legal hanging. Back on board the train, Parrott slid down between the seats and burst into a hysterical fit of weeping.

A short intermission was called at the Carbon dance. The people expressed their satisfaction at how well the abduction had been executed and their relief that Dutch Charlie had actually participated in the murders. This was the first hard information that anyone had as to the gang's makeup.

One could speculate as to whether the Carbon County sheriff collaborated in obtaining Parrott's confession. The editor of the *Carbon County Journal* remarked that "the only wonder is that Big Nose George did not climb the golden stairs via that route."

While the town of Carbon outlasted Parrott, it began a gradual decline in 1902 when the coal mines closed. Soon, the town and railroad siding were bypassed by the new Union Pacific main line.

Perhaps it was a small consolation to Parrott that no mob waited at the Rawlins railroad station when the train pulled in. The outlaw was hustled off to the county jail. He pleaded guilty at his preliminary hearing in September 1880, fearing a lynch mob if he pleaded otherwise. Then upon legal advice, he recanted his confession and requested a trial. Judge William Peck stopped the trial to say it was useless to go on since he was satisfied with Parrott's guilt. The outlaw broke down again when he received his death sentence and had to be physically supported by two bailiffs.

For a short time Parrott tried a hunger strike, but gave up when it was obvious it wouldn't help his cause. Next he supposedly converted to Christianity. Perhaps because of this "conversion," his jailers relaxed and, as the months rolled by, even allowed him to roam the cell-block corridor.

Somehow between September and March, Parrott obtained a small case knife with one blade and a piece of sandstone with which to sharpen it. He used the knife to file the rivets on his leg shackles.

The night of Parrott's escape attempt, Sheriff Jim Rankin was out of town. The sheriff's brother, Robert Rankin, was the jailer on duty. When he entered the cell-block corridor to lock the prisoners in their cells for the night, Parrott came from the water closet compartment and struck Rankin three times on the head with the seven- to eight-pound shackles. However, the game Rankin turned, struck Parrott with his fist, and slammed him against the wall. Rankin's wife, Rose, heard the commotion and locked the outer corridor door to prevent an escape, then ran to grab her husband's revolvers. She covered Big Nose George while her bloodied husband exited the cell. Meanwhile, her sister ran for help.

Parrott returned to his hiding place in the water closet, but another prisoner was called out of his cell to light a corridor lamp and Parrott was found and ordered back to his cell.

Presently reinforcements arrived and new rivets were fashioned for Parrott's leg irons. He was returned to his cell for the night, and as an extra precaution, another guard was added. Parrott expressed remorse for attacking Rankin, although no one believed him. In fact, the townspeople were already on the streets in small groups discussing Parrott's irritating behavior—and how to end it.

Around 10 p.m., these smaller parties merged into a large assembly in front of the jail. About an hour later, there was a rap on the jail door, and several voices demanded entrance. A guard inquired who was there. The answer was, "Friends." The guard said it was too late to admit anyone. "The door was immediately burst open," the *Rawlins Daily Tribune* reported. The well-armed visitors covered the jail personnel and removed Rankin's keys from his room. They used an axe to enter Parrott's cell because they couldn't make the key work. The group—said to have been some of Cheyenne's best citizens—marched Parrott to a place near the railroad station where more than 100 people awaited him. A half-inch rope had been hung from a telegraph pole with an empty kerosene barrel as a platform for Parrott to climb.

On the first try the rope broke and Parrott went sprawling to the ground. Undaunted, the group obtained a 12-foot ladder and made Parrott climb it, with two men "assisting." The ladder was pulled away when the doomed outlaw was at the eight-foot level. In desperation, Parrott was able to untie his hands and cling to the telegraph pole, pleading to be shot. Finally, he lost his grip and agonizingly strangled to death.

The assembly dispersed, Parrott was cut down by the coroner, and his body was removed from the scene. Several other outlaws were said to have left the city in a hurry after word of the hanging spread.

According to local folklore, Elizabeth Widowfield, sister-in-law of one of the murdered deputies, kicked the barrel out from under Parrott, saying, "This will teach you to murder my brother-in-law!"

Rose Rankin, wife of the jailer and sister-in-law of the county sheriff, received a gold watch and key in a velvet-lined box for preventing Parrott's escape.

Ordinarily, this would have marked the end of Parrott's story, but there is a bizarre epilogue involving Dr. John Osborne, a recent arrival from Vermont. Osborne had witnessed the lynching, and he and his partner desired the outlaw's corpse for "anatomical study and dissection." When no kin claimed the body, Osborne took it and preserved it with a strong saline solution in a whiskey barrel. He made a plaster cast of Parrott's head and neck and then sawed off the top of Parrott's skull so he could supposedly examine

Big Nose George's brain to find out why he had such a mean disposition. He noted that Parrott didn't look very intelligent—but how many dead people do? He gave the skull cap to his young assistant, Lillian Heath, who used it at times for a doorstop or a container for rock specimens. (Heath later went on to become a doctor herself, specializing in obstetrics.) Finally, the physician removed skin from the dead man's thighs and chest and had it tanned for use in a pair of two-toned shoes and a medicine bag. Reportedly, he wanted to keep the nipples on the shoe skin, but the shoemaker ignored his bizarre instructions.

His body of no further use to the physician, George Parrott was buried, with the barrel for a casket, in a secret location. His remains had finally come to rest—at least until May 1950. That month, workers from the Metcalf Construction Company were digging a foundation for the stone Hested store on West Cedar Street in Cheyenne when they found the whiskey barrel with Parrott's corpse, minus the top of his head, plus other items of clothing and shoes. Dr. Heath's memento was taken to the scene and it matched perfectly. Parrott's bones were offered to the Carbon County Museum, which declined, and Parrott was reinterred in a more suitable but still undisclosed location. Like folks said, "Big Nose George Parrott sure has got around!"

And parts of him still are around: a piece of his tanned skin, his skull cap, and his leg irons are still on display at the Union Pacific Railroad Company museum at Omaha, Nebraska. The bottom part of his skull and the shoes he was wearing when he met his death are in the Carbon County Museum. And lastly, his death mask and the doctor's shoes made from his flesh are on display at the Rawlins National Bank.[4]

But what of Dr. Osborne? Did he go to Hollywood and produce horror movies? Or start a wax horror museum? No, none of the above. He became the governor of Wyoming and later assistant secretary of state under President Woodrow Wilson. He died in Rawlins in 1943 at the age of 89. And yes, he received a conventional burial.

If the local citizens thought the end of the Parrott gang spelled the end of outlawry in the area, they were sadly mistaken. Soon Butch Cassidy and associates were on the scene, rivaling the exploits of the James and Younger brothers. The latter gangs frequented the same country and became quite successful at robbing Union Pacific trains, as opposed to the Parrott gang's failures.

Nonetheless, Parrott's notoriety in Western outlaw lore was secure, not only because of his scattered remains, but also because of his frequent confusion with George "Flat Nose" Currie of the more famous Cassidy Wild Bunch. ★

VI

THE OUTLAW KID CURRY AND THE GENTLEMAN, ABE GILL

PART I

The Little Rocky Mountains of northern Montana attracted a diverse assortment of individuals in the mid-1880s, including gold miners, cowboys, ranchers large and small, merchants, homesteaders, and outlaws. Two of these early inhabitants brought together by fate were Harvey Alexander Logan, alias Kid Curry, and Abraham ("Abe") Ditmars Gill.

A poor, illiterate farm boy from Iowa and later Missouri, Logan headed west to be a cowboy and drove cattle north from Texas. He would become known as one of the most notorious outlaws and killers of the western United States.

Gill, a gentlemanly college-educated rancher from a prominent New York State family, would never be accepted by his fellow Westerners because of his different ways. These were manifested in his speech, clothing, naturalist philosophy, and strict sense of right and wrong. His tastes tended towards the classic poets and writers of Europe and New England Renaissance writers such as Ralph Waldo Emerson and Henry David Thoreau. He named his ranch "Paradise Lost" in honor of the great seventeenth-century English poet John Milton—a reference, perhaps, to the personal hell he found in the wilderness of the Little Rockies, with the role of the Devil and his demons played by Curry and his associates. Gill and Kid Curry would both die in unrecorded places of unspecified causes, though at different times.

The lava-formed mountains dated back about 90 million years. They were roughly 20 miles in length and 10 miles in width, averaging over 2,000 feet in height. The remote, timbered slopes came to be known as the Little Rocky Mountains because of explorers Lewis and Clark's mistaken belief that they had found the Rocky Mountains of the Continental Divide, actually some 200 miles farther west.

Some areas of the island-like mountains of the high prairie plains are considered sacred by the Indian peoples of the region, going back to their earliest ancestors; they contain pictographs/symbols on cave and canyon walls, dating back an estimated 3,500 years.

The wild Missouri River Breaks to the south, with their rugged, multicolored peaks, perfectly suited those traveling the outlaw trail. Once the cattle-raising and gold-mining frontiers opened, the various gulches, caves, and narrow canyons of the Little Rockies offered additional refuge to outlaws.

Father Frederick Eberschweiler, S.J., who established St. Paul's Mission just northwest of the Little Rockies, compared this "most beautiful country" with the biblical promised land of milk and honey. The country was blessed with heavy stands of timber, and "seven beautiful creeks" and fertile bottomlands. The priest directed the building of the mission at People's Creek, located near the mouth of future-named Mission Canyon, with its wider valley and arable land. But even his paradise was touched by corruption, as the Curry gang hid stolen horses in the coulees near the mission and had a canyon cave hideout nearby.

The peace of this promised land was shattered in 1884 when gold was discovered in the area, attracting hundreds of miners to the Missouri River port of Fort Benton and points west. Fort

Benton is the seat of Chouteau County, which includes the Little Rockies. Troops from the military posts of Maginnis and Assinniboine were unable to stem the invasion of Indian lands. The government "solved" the problem by creating a separate mining district outside the reservation. At least Father Eberschweiler talked the miners into helping with the construction of the mission buildings.

The first major gold strike was made by "Dutch Louie" Myers, Frank Aldridge, and Powell "Pike" Landusky on an old mining site at Little Alder Gulch on the eastern slopes of the main divide. Myers and Aldridge were suspected horse thieves, and they were trying to avoid the vigilantes combing the river bottoms. Landusky also operated a legitimate store and saloon in the newly established mining camp of Maiden in the Judith Mountains.

Landusky came to Montana in 1864 to join the gold rush at Last Chance Gulch in Helena. He later trapped and hunted in the Missouri Breaks and established a liquor-dispensing trading post in the area. Landusky, from Pike County, Missouri, was a powerfully built man of at least six feet and 215 pounds, with unusually long arms. He had a reputation as a ferocious fighter and saloon-brawl champion. The loss of part of his lower jaw had added to his tough image—and his bad temper.

The injury occurred during a battle with some braves of the Blackfoot Confederacy after Landusky killed a Blood war chief's wife while on a drinking spree. He was not known to have killed anyone before that; he had just beaten white men senseless. But Landusky deeply hated Indians. Sober, he was known as a kind-hearted person, but drunk, he was as mean as they came. He was also reputed to be proficient with firearms.

The gentler side of Pike Landusky's French and Polish heritage was reflected in his marriage to the French widow (or deserted wife) Mrs. Julia Dessery of New Orleans, Louisiana. They married at Maiden, and he inherited her brood of daughters. The family moved to a cabin on Little Alder Gulch, where Landusky and his partners had struck gold.

The placer strikes soon ran out and the prospectors left, leaving behind defaced stream and creek beds. But Landusky and his son-in-law Bob Ormond kept prospecting, in addition to working as ranch hands for the D Bar S brand of the Pioneer Cattle Company near Fort Maginnis and the Judith Mountains. They discovered a hard-rock deposit and named it the August Mine for the month it was found in 1893. The vein was located in the general vicinity of Gold Bug Butte, elevation 5,450 feet. They also had other mining properties named Little Ben, Gold Bug, and Julia.

Once again, a stampede of about 2,000 prospectors came to the Little Rockies. This time, the immigration was of a more permanent nature. The mining camp of Landusky was founded about 1,000 feet down the mountainside on the former site of a trading post made up of four cabins surrounded by a stockade. Other major strikes were made and developed on the eastern slopes by such men as O. "Pete" Zortman and George Putnam. The mining camp of Zortman came into existence at the foot of Ruby, Little Alder, and Pony gulches.

Soon, some 12,000 pounds of gold bullion were being mined each month and a $10,000 payroll of silver coinage was arriving for the miners. The ore was said to be similar to that found in the Black Hills of Dakota and the mines of Cripple Creek, Colorado.

Another major event occurred between gold strikes: the St. Paul, Minneapolis, and Manitoba Railway was built west along the Milk River. Railroad sidings were created every ten miles and some became major cattle shipping towns as cattlemen moved north across the Missouri River from depleted ranges into newly opened Indian lands. They brought thousands of animals to the last of the untouched ranges of the West. The cow (and railroad) towns of Malta, Chinook, and Harlem, located about 30 miles to the north and linked by dry-weather trails, also benefited from the sale of supplies to the mining camps.

Cowboys were attracted to the area as they moved north up the cattle, outlaw, and emigrant trails from Mexico, Texas,

Colorado, and Wyoming. Among them were the Logan boys: Hank and Harvey. The latter would become known as Kid Curry. Two more brothers came later: John and Lorenzo, or "Lonie."

The Logan brothers came west from Iowa. Their parents came from Rowan County, Kentucky. Their mother, Eliza, moved her family to Dodson, Missouri, after her husband's death or his abandonment of the family. She remarried but died soon after.

Hank and Harvey Logan first came to F. M. "Dad" Marsh's hotel, store, and saloon at Rocky Point in the summer of 1884. The town was a handful of adobe buildings located 20 miles south of the Little Rockies on the south cliffs overlooking the Missouri River. Some steamboats still stopped at the once-busy river landing for fuel and dropped off supplies, some for local distribution, some destined for Lewistown. Rocky Point was the supply point for nearby ranches and provided liquid refreshment for the cowhands. Whether Marsh was running his operation in its former livestock-rustler and outlaw-rendezvous tradition is not certain.

In Rocky Point, the brothers learned of job opportunities and found employment with the British-backed Circle Bar Ranch on Crooked Creek, which paralleled the Missouri River. They were laid off after the fall roundup and spent their idle hours at Marsh's place. Over the winter, they cut and hauled wood by sled from the Missouri River bottoms to sell to the steamboats that would ply the river come spring. Marsh also helped them to learn to read and write. Then the Circle Bar outfit hired them again, and they worked for several other ranchers over the next few years, including the Pioneer Cattle Company, McNamara and Marlow's ranch near Big Sandy and the Bear's Paw Mountains, and Coburn's Circle C Ranch east of the Little Rockies at Brookside. The Circle C was the successor to the D Bar S brand of the Pioneer Cattle Company.

About 1888 or 1889, brothers Johnny and Lonie Logan arrived from Missouri via Wyoming. Johnny worked for a ranch south of the river owned by James Fergus, and Lonie worked for the Circle Bar. Missouri friend Jim Thornhill came to the area at about the same time from somewhere south on the Texas Trail.

The Logan boys had been raised by an uncle and aunt, Hiram and Elizabeth Lee of Dodson, now part of Kansas City. Hiram was an invalid who spent the summer months in his rocking chair on the porch of their two-story hillside frame house. His condition may have been caused by wounds he incurred when he fought for the Confederacy in the War Between the States. The brothers helped their cousin Bob Lee work the farm.

Many reports refer to the Cherokee Indian blood that showed in the Logans' dark features, but some more recent researchers claim that this was actually due to their Welsh heritage, and that the Indian blood story originated with Pike Landusky.

The boys were quite different in temperament. Harvey Logan was quiet and reserved, Lonie was outgoing and mischievous, and Johnny was impulsive and quick-tempered. Older brother Hank was the level-headed one and attempted to keep the boys in line. All that is known about a fifth brother named James is that he worked in a store and never went west. Also in the family was a sister, Arda, called "Allie," and perhaps another older one named Mary. The three younger boys' personalities hardened after their mother's death, as evidenced by their tougher natures.

As a young man, Harvey reportedly almost killed another boy after a baseball game collision and some racial remarks that ensued; he also stole an old American Civil War vintage U. S. Navy Colt revolver from the town drunk. Soon the brothers and cousin Bob Lee were shooting up the nearby woods. Another story describes Harvey backing the town constable against a shed and threatening to kill him if he came to the Lee house with another complaint from the neighbors about the boys' behavior.

But happily for the mistreated lawman, the brothers caught the "Go west, young man" fever, and Hank and Harvey headed west, following friend Jim Thornhill's tracks to Texas. There they joined a cattle herd headed for Wyoming, but they stopped over at Pueblo, Colorado. There, while frequenting a tough saloon and dance hall, Harvey engaged in a gunfight. It was written that they left with "a lot of lead and dust flying." They completed herding the cattle to Casper, then traveled north to the legendary Hole-in-the-Wall country, perhaps already having met George Currie, the future horse-stealing king of Wyoming.[1]

Located in central Wyoming in the southern part of Johnson County, the Hole-in-the-Wall consisted of a roughly north-south valley about 30 miles long with a colorful, rugged, red sandstone canyon wall on its east side. The middle fork of the Powder River penetrated in several places. The outlaws' main entrance—a narrow, V-shaped notch in the wall just wide enough for two horse-men or one wagon to pass through—was several miles south of Barnum, Wyoming. This easily defensible opening led to the outlaw ranch: six cabins in the large prairie valley of Buffalo Creek.

Another trail led into the valley farther to the north and to a remote cave near another tributary of the Powder River. On the west side of the valley, several trails led through the rolling hills and into the the Big Horn Mountains beyond.

The outlaws' best defenses were their isolated location and the fear they had instilled in local lawmen. To the east were large ranches with foreign owners and many thousands of cattle on the ranges. Some of these cattle and horses ended up in the outlaws' valley, wearing the outlaws' brands.

Transplanted Nebraska resident George "Flat Nose" Currie was just beginning his outlaw career. Currie may have been moonlighting as a livestock thief while breaking horses on a legitimate ranch or ranches. However, he was finally banned from ranch work as the rustlers became better organized and began stealing in earnest from Johnson, Natrona, and Converse county cattlemen. The situation was made worse by the drought, economic downturn, and disastrously hard winter of 1886-1887, which decimated herds on the already overgrazed ranges and put many cowboys out of work. These cowboys turned to rustling. The Wyoming Stock Growers Association claimed all the unbranded mavericks and slicks on the range.

This situation, plus homesteaders' occupation of the open range, began the cattle barons' war of 1891-1892. It wasn't until about 1897 that the law gained control of the situation. Still, some large ranchers continued to employ killers as late as the turn of the century.

After coming west, the Logans took Currie's last name because of their friendship with him, modifying the spelling to Curry. The name change was believed necessary because of a warrant for Harvey Logan in Colorado for assault with a deadly weapon, or even murder. The brothers reportedly came to Montana with Currie, trailing a herd of cattle to the Miles City area, after a short stay in the Hole-in-the-Wall valley. Then they parted company with their namesake and headed for Marsh's place at Rocky Point.

The Curry brothers continued ranch work and worked for Robert Coburn's Circle C Ranch. Coburn had bought the holdings of the D Bar S brand in 1886. The Circle C was located on Beaver Creek, east of Zortman near the northeast stagecoach and wagon trail to Malta. Coburn had come west from Ontario, Canada, in 1859 to prospect for gold near Denver. He moved on to Virginia City, Montana, and to Last Chance Gulch (Helena). He continued his mining interests on the side, but turned his main attentions to cattle ranching, first on Prickly Pear Creek and then, in two successful ventures, near Great Falls and White Sulphur Springs. He eventually moved to the Little Rockies area with his wife Mary and seven children. Mrs. Coburn died in 1885, and he married Mary Blessing in 1887. He had two more children, Walter and Harold.

Thornhill and the Currys became good friends with Robert Coburn and his sons Wallace, Bob, and Will. Kid Curry made the connection even closer when he saved Bob Coburn's life during a snowstorm in which he was trapped under his crippled horse. Curry also rescued Thornhill, who was moving some cattle, from a watery grave in the Missouri River.

Hank Curry wasn't as lucky. He was suffering from tuberculosis, and had recently contracted pneumonia that got worse when he rescued a couple of bogged-down steers during a cold fall rainstorm. Hank was en route to Steamboat Springs,

Colorado, for hot springs therapy when he died in either late 1893 or early 1894. Reportedly, Kid Curry had sold his favorite horse to the Coburns to finance his brother's trip.

Thornhill was now the primary influence on the Curry boys. Harvey was 26, Johnny was 24, and Lonie was 22. Thornhill was only about 25 himself, and not the good moral example that Hank had been. If the earlier death of the boys' mother had in fact turned them (especially Harvey) surly, the death of their older brother may have been the finishing touch.

Kid Curry had the reputation of being a tough customer who had a volatile temper made worse by heavy drinking. As one cowboy put it, he was easy to get along with as long as he had his own way. Johnny Curry tried to be a tough guy and exhibited a tendency to be gun-happy. It was his ambition to become a famous gunman. Lonie had a mean streak to match his brothers', but didn't always show it.

Looking back on the boys, District Judge Dudley Dubose of Fort Benton expressed a different view. He considered Harvey "the best of the lot" and thought he "might have turned out all right had he been separated from the bad men that infected that section of the country." Dubose didn't elaborate as to who those bad men were. On the other hand, the judge had no use for Johnny and Lonie, calling them "bad eggs who are good now because they are dead."

Lee Self, another member of the Curry gang, was also from Missouri. He was married to the Currys' sister Allie. She eventually left him, returned to Dodson, and remarried. Self may have operated a business in Landusky. How major a role he played in the Currys' life isn't known. Apparently, he died in 1909 of a self-inflicted gunshot wound.

The gang basically stayed to itself, except for Thornhill and the Coburn boys. Actually, it was quite a formidable group. The Coburn brothers alone inspired fear in the normally tough local saloon owners. Chouteau County records show several assault charges leveled against the group members, including some for pistol whippings. In September 1893, "Dad" Marsh of Rocky Point filed civil charges against the Currys for nonpayment of a loan of $932.70. The money may have been used to build a new barn so the brothers could start a livery stable.

One old-timer, Bill "Milk River" Harmon, once a soldier at Fort Assinniboine, a Little Rockies prospector, and a bullwhacker for the Diamond B Ranch, was interviewed in 1935 by a Great Falls newspaper. He backed up the court records, saying that it was a common occurrence for one or maybe all three of the Currys to beat up some poor devil with a six-gun. He described them as "mean, bull-dozing cusses."

The North Montana Round-up Association, formed in 1896 to combat rustling activities, also looked askance at the Curry gang. Even Pike Landusky's bartender, Jake "the Jew" Harris, filed assault charges against the brothers. The Curry boys loved to "hurrah" that saloon, riding into the bar on their horses and shooting at the ceiling. Once, according to legend, one of the Currys and his horse went through the floor into the cellar. The story is also told that, after Pike Landusky's death in December 1894, the Currys decided to run Harris out of town, but he held them off with his shotgun and a washtub full of shotgun shells in a three-hour-plus fire fight. Other antics included breaking up a piano and smashing guitars over the musicians' heads during a saloon dance. Apparently the boys didn't like the music.

Some say the Currys had their own saloon in Landusky, but there is no evidence of such an establishment, though there were other saloons besides Pike's.

In later years, Judge Dudley Dubose had more insights into the Currys' behavior. He said they did well in the cattle business, building up a herd worth $15,000, but they were more interested in making it as badmen. They were "anxious to be called gunfighters," as he put it. The judge said he saw the Currys many times in court for their acts of assault and battery towards others, but added that no jury would convict them.

An anonymous Lewistown rancher—perhaps Jim Fergus—

said Kid Curry was "a little wild and somewhat restless" but could be a true friend and would give a man his last dollar. He said the outlaw always had his nose in "yellow-backed literature" about the exploits of outlaws like the James brothers. The rancher observed that it wasn't until the Kid moved on to the Little Rockies that he started imitating his outlaw heroes.

The Currys were not large men, but their lack of size was easily made up for by their ugly tempers, numbers, and proficiency with firearms. They spoke in a slow, deliberate drawl, but people soon learned they were anything but laid back.

Harvey, the Kid, was about five feet, seven and one-half inches tall, but stocky, weighing approximately 160 pounds. According to wanted posters that came later, brother Lonie was about five feet, six inches and on the slender side. Bob Lee was tallest, at five feet, nine inches and 175 pounds, with the same dark complexion. There are no statistics for Johnny and Hank Curry, since neither participated in any bank or train robberies. A supposed group photograph of John, Harvey and Lonie does exist from about 1890, however.

In a one-to-one match in July 1892, Johnny (who also liked to call himself "the Kid") came out second best. He had an altercation with "a well-seasoned German [?] ex-cowboy" named John Olson. Versions of the story vary. In one, Johnny Curry shot up a herd of sheep while Olson, the unarmed herder, stayed low. In the other, he made the man dance by shooting at his feet. Later the two met on the Rocky Point-Landusky Trail, only this time, Olson had a rifle. Both fired, and Johnny Curry's horse was shot out from under him. While Curry struggled to get to his feet, another round from Olson hit his right arm; yet another struck his right elbow. Johnny passed out from the pain, and Olson departed with only a bullet hole in his hat.

Somehow, Johnny made it back to the Currys' Rock Creek ranch and received first aid at either St. Paul's Mission or the Fort Belknap agency near Harlem. He was loaded aboard a GNR train at Harlem for his trip to the Saint Clare Hospital at Fort Benton.

Because the lower arm and joint were too badly shattered, the doctor had to amputate. The herder and one-time cowboy who shot Johnny disappeared without a trace; whether Kid Curry killed him or he simply left the country in a hurry isn't known.

Also there is a story that the Kid killed a miner during an argument because he said that the boys' mother was of mixed Black-White blood.[2]

More violence was impending as a friendship between the Currys and Landusky soured. Perhaps the trouble began over a new plow that Pike borrowed from the Curry brothers. When the Currys got it back, it had a broken handle and was useless. The Currys often visited the Landusky ranch three miles to the north up Rock Creek, perhaps because of the young ladies of the house: Laura, Julia, and Cindinilla, called "Elfia" or "Elfie."

Elfia may have been courted by all three Curry brothers, but Lonie won her over. He had quite the reputation with the ladies and is described as a charming "Beau Brummell" type who wore fancy checkered suits and dressed his horse with a silver-embossed saddle. He was also considered the best fiddler in the country.

Landusky brooded over his stepdaughter's involvement with the Currys, especially when he heard that she was meeting Lonie after dark at a secret rendezvous. It didn't help that Pike's barroom customers gave him a hard time about it. Landusky started calling Lonie a whoremonger and the Kid a brand artist. The more he drank, the more he hated the brothers.

Some of the miners began lining up with Pike, and a few cowboys sided with the Currys. But the tension was broken in the summer of 1894 when Chouteau County Undersheriff John Buckley, armed with a warrant, arrested Lonie, the Kid, and later Jim Thornhill for allegedly rebranding some cattle of W. H. "Jim" Winters. The brands of these neighbors were quite similar. After the arrest, the lawman temporarily deputized Landusky and put the brothers in his custody while he investigated the charges and sought Thornhill, who was still at large. Buckley never forgave himself for deputizing Landusky, it is said.

The two brothers were handcuffed and their feet manacled. Lying helpless on the floor, the boys received the full brunt of Landusky's pent-up fury as he beat, cursed, and kicked them, then spat chewing tobacco on their open wounds. Pike rested on a chair between beatings and drank whiskey. When he was too full of alcohol, he relieved himself on them. Bored with all of that, he took out a knife and threatened to make eunuchs of them. Kid Curry told Pike that if he used the knife he would be the first man the town ever lynched. The Kid demanded to be let go for a fair fight, but Landusky declined, believing they were going to prison and would finally be out of his hair. Curry promised they would meet again, and that he would return the favor, only worse.

The brothers survived the beating, and, to Pike's chagrin, the charges. The Currys and Thornhill were quickly bailed out by the Coburn family, and no trial occurred because of insufficient evidence. Dad Marsh said Landusky felt remorse after he calmed down, and he tried to regain the Currys' friendship, but to no avail.

Nothing transpired between the Currys and Landusky for several months. The town's name was made; it boasted a booming business district with four saloons, two stores, a restaurant, a livery barn, a newspaper, boarding houses, and blacksmith shops. Landusky owned the saloon and general store, which served as a post office. Jake Harris, a tough character himself, operated it. Harris had lost a leg in a shootout in Great Falls with a Cascade County law officer. He used only one crutch when tending bar so he could reach for his shotgun if necessary.

The Kid and his brothers came to town to vote on October 15, 1894. The local citizenry planned a big Christmas get-together, and the Currys volunteered their new barn. Lonie offered to play fiddle and assembled a band. A rancher kindly volunteered his family pipe organ which to that point had only been used for hymns. The townspeople decorated the community, and in addition ordered fresh oysters packed in barrels from Baltimore to complete the feast. Apparently no one complained that the stage driver brought canned from Minneapolis instead. The celebration brought about 100 people to the town and the Curry barn to eat, drink, and dance, with Johnny calling the turns.

No violence occurred, although unrecorded words are supposed to have been exchanged between the Kid and Landusky. Perhaps Pike was trying to be conciliatory; or perhaps Curry repeated his promise to beat Pike. Whatever transpired, Pike stayed close to his saloon after the festivities, in the company of Harris and a gunman friend and employee named Hogan.

On the late morning or early afternoon of December 27, 1894—a cold, snowy, and overcast day—Lonie Curry and Jim Thornhill entered the saloon. Johnny Curry guarded the door and Lee Self may have stayed with the wagon and team. Thornhill and Lonie bought some apples while waiting for the Kid's entrance. Finally he arrived and headed directly for Landusky, who was drinking at the bar. The boys kept the others covered while the two men went at it. Landusky tried to throw his glassful of whiskey in Kid Curry's face, hoping to follow up with the bottle in his other hand, but Curry spilled the glass and knocked the bottle out of Pike's hand. Pike whirled around and took a punch to his jaw with all the Kid's weight behind it. The fight continued on the floor. Curry was the eventual winner, although he almost had an eye gouged out.

Curry was about 60 pounds lighter than Landusky, but he was also 23 years younger and more muscular. Pike was hampered by a heavy coat and rheumatic hands, although this condition hadn't interfered with his earlier beating of Curry.

Curry didn't fight to the death as some had predicted; he let the well-battered and bloody Landusky up. Pike then reached into his pocket for a handkerchief—or so the boys thought. Instead he pulled out a newfangled semi-automatic foreign pistol and aimed it at Curry, whose revolver had fallen to the floor during the fight and been picked up by Thornhill. Landusky pulled the trigger. The gun failed to fire, however; either a round wasn't chambered or it jammed or the safety was on. Before Landusky could correct what was wrong, Thornhill threw Curry his Colt .45. Curry fired three rounds and killed Landusky.

The Curry gang immediately left town for the ranch, where they held a conference. The Kid decided to return to Wyoming. He wasn't going to risk a trial, so Thornhill bought him out by selling his cattle to the Coburns.

The flight to Wyoming apparently wasn't immediate. First the Kid hid out at a cabin located at the "big bend" of the Missouri River below Rocky Point while the financial arrangements were worked out. It is also said that he feared the law less than the possibility of Jake Harris seeking revenge—so he stayed clear of town.

During the same time, back in the mining town, a messenger named Fred Smith rode to Harlem and informed the sheriff's office of the shooting. The undersheriff and coroner left Fort Benton immediately, and warrants were issued for the Currys, Thornhill, and Lee Self after the coroner's jury brought in a verdict of murder.

Lonie Curry stood trial as an accessory to murder. However, his case was dismissed for lack of evidence. Johnny's charge of assault with a deadly weapon was reduced to a $50.00 fine for simple assault. A jury found Thornhill not guilty in connection with the murder, and Self wasn't charged at all. It's strange that Thornhill and Lonie weren't at least found guilty of Johnny's lesser charge, since they too had pointed their weapons at the barroom crowd.

From all reports, Thornhill is the one who told Curry to let Landusky up and then to kill him when he pulled the pistol. The last command decided Curry's fate and determined which road he now must ride. The Kid was never brought to trial, though. He went on to become a major outlaw-killer in the American West, running with both George "Flat Nose" Currie's Hole-in-the-Wall gang and later Leroy "Butch Cassidy" Parker's Wild Bunch.

Federal and local lawmen, railroad and express agents, and the Pinkerton Agency credited Kid Curry with at least 15 killings, as well as a number of assaults with revolver, rifle, shotgun, or fists. Agency Director William Pinkerton said that Curry had not a single redeeming feature, yet Curry himself was proud of his reputation as a badman and such monikers as "the Napoleon of Crime," "the noted Western Desperado of Crime," etc.

George Bolds, a Kansas gunman, called Curry "the executioner of the Wild Bunch," and "one of the fastest guns in the West." Most lawmen agreed about his shooting expertise, adding that they regarded him as one of the most dangerous men in the West; he had a sense of suppressed violence about him that men never forgot. While short in height, he was very strong, and women flocked to him.

Utah historian Pearl Baker said of the Kid:

> Harvey Logan was always a killer, and would wait for years to even the score with someone. With the exception of the banker at the Delta [Colorado] shot by [gang member] Billy McCarty, practically every killing laid at the door of the Wild Bunch was committed by Harvey Logan.

Author Eugene Cunningham told how Curry would place a poker chip on the back of his hand at shoulder level and get off three shots before it hit the floor.

Pinkerton Special Agent Lowell Spence, Curry's primary tracker and adversary, said that lawmen knew if they went after him "it was almost suicide." Curry wouldn't run or hide. He would instead plot to ambush his pursuers. Spence also said that the "cold, calculating killer" was an expert with handgun and rifle alike.

According to historian Larry Pointer, Butch Cassidy called Curry "the bravest man I ever knew." Pointer contended that only Cassidy could control Curry, and it was through respect, not fear. Consequently, several of Curry's potential victims owed their lives to the Wild Bunch's leader.

While friends such as the Coburns said the Currys were generally well liked by the people of the Little Rockies, others contended "they were an overbearing and cowardly lot and never brought anything but a bad name to Landusky."

With his bloody and violent career ahead of him, Kid Curry rejoined George Currie in Johnson County, Wyoming. Now big-time outlaws, the Currie gang operated out of the Hole-in-the-Wall valley and the K C Ranch, 30 miles to the east on the Powder River. From rustling livestock, they had gone on to plundering ranches, post offices, mercantiles, banks, and even trains. The outlaw gang moved south to Powder Springs in about 1897 and joined Butch Cassidy's Wild Bunch when the authorities and large ranchers made the country too hot for them. This band, made up of the remnants of several gangs, operated throughout the West from hideouts in southern Wyoming, northwest Colorado, southern Utah, New Mexico, and southwest Texas. It received the full attention of all law enforcement agencies: federal, state, county, city, and private detective and express companies.

According to several sources, including Judge Dubose, Kid Curry took a short vacation to France between the fall of 1897 and the early spring of 1898. The wanted man boarded a steamer, perhaps at Savannah, Georgia, and sailed to Le Havre, taking a train from that port to Paris. Among other night life, he took in one of the biggest, fanciest brothels of the city but reportedly cut his visit short because of the impending Spanish-American War.

Unfortunately, the Kid's exit from the Little Rockies country did not end the violence there. Johnny Curry began feuding with neighbor "Uncle Dan" Tressler over irrigation and water rights. Johnny also had gotten involved with Tressler's young wife, Lucy, said to have been a "striking-looking blonde woman." So, in disgust, fear, or both, the former Pennsylvanian left his wife, sold his six-year-old ranch in 1894 to Jim Winters, and moved with his teenage son and five young daughters to the Harlem area on the Milk River.

Locals just shook their heads at anyone dumb enough to get involved in a dispute with the Currys. Still, Winters loved "the long ranch house built upon a grand bench overlooking the badlands breaks of the Missouri River with a wonderful view of the Judith Mountains" across the river to the south. To the east stood the Curry-Thornhill ranch in plain view across Rock and Warm Springs creeks.

Johnny Curry and Lucy Tressler decided they were entitled to half the profits or the ranch itself. They demanded that the new owner, Winters, pay up or leave. However, Winters didn't feel he owed the couple anything. Besides, he had no use for the Currys or their stealing ways, and he made his views public, pointing out the changed brands on their horses, or the cattle they butchered with no hides in evidence because they had other ranchers' brands on them.

Winters was no novice cowboy. He had begun his career by working for some of the famous cattle outfits on his way north. He hailed from Jacksonville, Florida, where he was born in 1858. He was said to have been the son of a Confederate States of America soldier killed in action, and he was reared and educated by Dr. Charles Gill of New York City. Before coming to the Little Rockies, he had operated a saddlemaking and tack shop in Malta. The townspeople there thought well of him, as did the "better class of ranchers." Winters also may have once worked with the Currys at the Circle C Ranch.

Winters' stubbornness did not sit well with Johnny Curry, who was working hard on his desperado image and attempting to instill fear in all who crossed his path. Still, Winters was good with a gun himself and kept Curry off the ranch. Johnny and brother Lonie warned Winters to leave the area. At night Winters kept the window shades down so as not to be an easy target. Johnny would come within shooting distance in the darkness and make more threats. Finally, on the night of February 21, 1896, he gave Winters a final warning: leave in ten days or you'll be a dead man.

A visitor to the Winters ranch had a close call. When he borrowed a horse, he was shot at during a ride around the countryside. Luckily, the bullet only went through the crown of his hat. Winters was quoted afterward as saying, "If they want me, they know where I am."

True to his word, Johnny returned alone ten days later, on March 1, at about 10 a.m. Winters came to the door, leaving it open, with a shotgun just inside. Because Curry had the use of only one arm, he kept the bridle rains tied so he could quickly drop them across the saddle horn, leaving his gun hand free. He drew his revolver and fired, missing Winters' head by only inches. The bullet slammed into the overhead door jamb. The sudden movement and noise spooked Curry's horse, and he wasn't able to fire again quickly. Winters grabbed his shotgun and fired once, hitting his target. Wounded, Curry managed a second shot before Winters finished him off with a second barrel of buckshot. Curry's revolver discharged as he fell from his mount. The frightened horse took off for home.

Winters believed that when the horse was found, Lonie and friends would come after him. So he decided to seek the protection of the law at Fort Benton. He saddled up and headed for a High Line train station to the north, but his horse gave out before he got there. He stopped at the John Brown ranch on the Fort Belknap Reservation. He scribbled a note about what had taken place, and Brown delivered the message to Malta businessman and rancher R. W. Garland. Garland in turn telephoned the Chouteau County authorities, who escorted Winters to Fort Benton.

Later, a posse found no trace of any Currys or associates in the area and left. The coroner's jury found Winters had acted in self-defense, and the incident was considered closed. Johnny Curry, would-be outlaw, was buried on the home ranch without ever having appeared on a wanted poster.

People said Winters had surely signed his own death warrant by refusing to leave the area. The Kid was certain to avenge his brother's death. But who would buy the Winters ranch now, with such a history? The answer was no one. Thornhill and perhaps the Coburns would see to that. So Winters decided to stay and protect his investment at whatever cost.

From then on, always reminded by Johnny's grave across the creek, Winters kept hired hands on the place and never went anywhere without an escort. He had no immediate worry from Lonie Curry. He had also left the area, joining his brother in Wyoming. Supposedly, a warrant had been issued for Lonie's arrest for "hammering a Shorty Parker at the Perry store on the Belknap Reservation." Before he died, Johnny may have been involved in the same incident.

There was little sympathy for Johnny's death in Malta. Winters was well-liked there and had many friends in both Valley and Chouteau counties. Winters' friends considered him a quiet and peaceful man in contrast to the Currys and their violent ways.

Lonie Curry returned quietly to the Landusky area every once in a while, since Elfia Landusky had two children by him: Lonie, Jr., and Mamie. Authorities described Elfia as "a well-built woman, good-looking with long, black hair, fair skin, and brown eyes." Another beauty, the now very pregnant Lucy Tressler, took up with Jim Thornhill after Johnny's death; the child was said to be her former husband's.

Although the Kid stayed away, he did send word that he would never forget that Jim Winters had killed his younger brother. And Kid Curry knew about the comings and goings in the Little Rockies thanks to the Coburns, Jim Thornhill, and Northern District Chief Brand Inspector John Lee.

Part II

Jim Winters received company and a much-welcomed morale boost in the form of Abraham Ditmars Gill, his stepbrother. "A gentleman by breeding and by nature," as Walt Coburn described him, Abe Gill fit the stereotype of an Eastern dude traveling west to become a cowboy and cattleman, as the Curry brothers had. He was described as a tall, well-proportioned, and handsome gentleman with an olive complexion and jet black hair. He had an eastern accent, and was well-mannered and soft-spoken. He was a graduate of Brooklyn Polytechnic Institute and came from a prominent New York State family. His reading preferences leaned towards the philosophical, and he especially enjoyed Walt Whitman's poetry, as well as the essays of Ralph Waldo Emerson and Henry David Thoreau. The Gill family claimed as friends the acclaimed naturalists John Burroughs and John James Audubon.

Gill came to love the rugged Little Rockies country, although locals always considered him an outsider. Besides Gill's intellectualism and rigid sense of right and wrong, Walt Coburn said, he wore clothes straight out of a Frederic Remington painting: a wide-brimmed hat turned up in front and creased in the middle, and spurs with rowels that dragged on the floor. As one writer put it, "His being in the wild country was as natural as a banana tree in the Arctic zone."

Abe Gill was born in Brooklyn, New York, in March of 1873. His father, Dr. Charles Gill, was a native New Yorker from one of the oldest families in the state. Dr. Gill died in 1891 on the family farm on the Hudson River. Abe's mother, Maria Gill, was of Spanish descent, tracing her family roots back to world explorer Juan Ponce de Leon. Her father was governor of the Cuban province of Matanzas. The Gill family included at least five other sons who all lived in New York, except John, who ran the family plantation in Georgia.

After Abe graduated from college in 1893, he joined the U.S. Naval Reserve. In his college years he had been quite athletic and had been captain of his football team. He moved to the Little Rockies in the winter of 1895-1896 and formed a partnership with Jim Winters. The following winter, he returned to the East Coast and served as chief gunner's mate in the Atlantic Coast defense system. He also served shipboard, salvaging Spanish warships off the coast of Cuba once the Spanish-American War began in 1898. He returned to Montana in 1899.

Gill was appointed a U.S. land commissioner in 1897 and served in some capacity with the U.S. Department of Agriculture. He was active in the Chouteau County Democratic Party and had a wide circle of friends, mostly influential ones. No wonder his "ordinary" neighbors couldn't relate to him.

Of course Gill's involvement in the disputed ranch property immediately earned him the dislike of the Curry, Thornhill, and Coburn clans. And, too, he gained the animosity of a portion of Little Rockies settlers by trying to impose his stricter views of right and wrong on them, and reporting them to the law for the slightest infraction.

For all his brilliance, Gill seemed to lack insight into the westerner's pragmatic nature versus that of the more civilized and industrialized easterner. Out West, nature was still in command, and many of the men and women struggling to survive felt they had few restraints upon their acts. Hence the rugged individualist of fact and fiction was born.

The year 1899 brought another individual back to the mountain country—Lonie Curry, accompanied by his cousin Bob Lee. Lee had worked as a miner and card player in such places as Black Hawk and Cripple Creek, Colorado, before joining up with the Currie and Cassidy gangs. His role in the gangs is still disputed.

It was a significant year. Government and private law enforcement agencies were closing in on the outlaw bands. Some gang members were already in jail or dead. From the Pinkerton Agency's nerve center in Denver came information from law officers, express companies, railroad detectives, and paid informants all over the West. The agency learned the outlaws' identities, descriptions, backgrounds, habits, activities, and suspected hiding places. The information was carefully indexed and filed. The identities of the many informants were closely guarded and only code names were used.

The last robbery Lonie and possibly Bob Lee participated in was the June 2, 1899, holdup of the Union Pacific Overland Flyer train at the Wilcox railroad siding in Wyoming near the town and waterway of Rock Creek.[3] The holdup netted the six robbers about $30,000 in unsigned bank notes. In the ensuing chase north of Casper on the Salt Creek Road, Kid Curry killed Converse County

Sheriff Joe Hazen of Douglas and cowhand Tom McDonald, plus he shot four bloodhounds worth $1,000 each. The group separated after meeting up with Butch Cassidy at a hideout in north Fremont County. The main group went south to Alma, New Mexico, after a short recuperative stay at the Robbers' Roost outlaw ranch on a high, rugged, and isolated plateau in the canyon country of the San Rafael Desert. It was about 65 miles south of Green River, Utah, in eastern Wayne County.

Judge Dudley Dubose saw Lonie Curry in Helena before the Wilcox train robbery. Dubose learned later that Curry needed money to ride the train to the point of the robbery and had Dubose help him cash a check for $50.

Lonie was wanted for more than just the Wilcox robbery. Under the name Roberts, he and Kid Curry had apparently participated in the June 1897 robbery of the Belle Fourche, South Dakota, bank. The "Roberts brothers" and other gang members were captured by a posse before an abortive attempt to rob a Red Lodge, Montana, bank, but they escaped from the Deadwood City jail. The same year Lonie was believed to have been present at the killing of Johnson County, Wyoming, Deputy Sheriff Billy Deane. In a complete loss of sanity, Deane attempted to capture the whole gang by himself at their KC Ranch headquarters.

Lonie apparently arrived alone in the Little Rockies, leaving Lee and a partner prospecting near Helena. Curry visited Harlem, Gilt Edge, Lewistown, and Rocky Point before going to the old ranch now owned by Thornhill and his wife, the former Mrs. Tressler. Supposedly, Curry was in the market for mining equipment, but the visit may have been an attempt to set up an alibi for the Wilcox train robbery. Lee may have been doing the same by prospecting.

Lonie, Elfia, and the two children were reunited in September and rented a house in Harlem, Montana. The Curry brothers bought a half-interest in George Bowles's Club Saloon on the north side of the railroad tracks. Next, Lonie went to Helena for Bob Lee and his mining partner, a man named Luske. They stopped at

Great Falls to visit an old friend, former Valley County sheriff and Glasgow saloon owner Sid Willis, at his Mint Saloon. Lonie had too much to drink and passed some distinctive currency with crudely forged, mutilated signatures and dynamite-singed edges. Lonie passed more of these bank notes in Harlem. An alert employee at the Stockmen's National Bank of Fort Benton recognized them from the Pinkerton Agency's circular and notified the authorities. Meanwhile, foolhardy Lonie and Bob Lee bought the other half-interest in the saloon. Luske wisely moved on.

Bob and Lonie redecorated the saloon and enlarged the cellar as well. For the grand opening on December 28, a turkey shoot was planned for behind the saloon.

Lonie played banjo and fiddle for the Harlem New Year's dance, not knowing that Pinkerton Agency operative W. O. Sayles had visited Harlem. For the first time, lawmen knew the true identity and background of the Curry brothers. Their knowledge came just when Lonie and Bob had been accepted socially by Harlem's residents. Lonie had even changed his mode of dress to suits and added a mustache, and he had participated in the printing of the first *Harlem Enterprise* newspaper with the rest of the townspeople by helping ink the forms. He was popular partly because of his willingness to "always help a fellow out," as Harlem resident Phil Buckley put it. Being Kid Curry's brother didn't hurt him, either.

Apparently the saloon wasn't profitable, perhaps because of too many drinks on the house and unpaid tabs. Lonie and Bob tried to cash a $1,000 bank note with store owner and postmaster W. E. French. The robbers kept their cache of stolen funds in the safe at the Cecil Hotel.

Pinkerton Agency operative Sayles planned another trip to Harlem from Helena, and he contacted French to set up a poker game with the boys at their saloon. Meanwhile, Denver Pinkerton Superintendent J. P. McParland ordered operative Charlie Siringo to join Sayles for the capture. But the cousins were warned before the scheme could be enacted. They sold the saloon to rancher George Ringwald on January 6 for $300 down and a promissory note for the balance payable to Jim Thornhill. Ringwald operated a store near the Milk River bridge south of Harlem. Lonie and Bob took the receipts from a community raffle for traveling money—thus ending their good reputations with the Harlem folks.

The men rode 12 miles west to the community of Zurich, boarded a westbound GNR train for Shelby Junction, and transferred to a southbound train for Butte. From the mile-high mining city, they took the Union Pacific Railroad to their final destination: Cripple Creek, Colorado.

Former lawman Phil Buckley believed the pair rode to the Little Rockies and visited with Lonie's wife before catching the train at Zurich. In contrast to a prevalent view, Lonie gave her money during that brief visit to send their two children to the mission school.

The Curry home was re-rented, and Elfia and the young children returned to the Little Rockies. She took employment as a servant with the Ellis family in Landusky. John Ellis owned the Clark Hotel in Harlem. Lonie, Jr. or Eddy, was enrolled in St. Peter's Mission school near Cascade under the Ursuline Sisters at the cost of $10 tuition a month—paid to Mother Amadeus with a $100 bill from the Wilcox robbery. It was paid back finally, however. Daughter Mamie was informally adopted by Paul and Mary Sunday of Harlem. Elfia eventually moved to Great Falls and worked at both the Mint and Silver Dollar saloons. She is said to have eventually come into some money from either Lonie's mining claims or robbery proceeds or both.

In another recent account, Al Brekke of Harlem claimed that the Curry children were raised by a trusted Havre friend who was employed by the Great Northern Railway.

At Cripple Creek, Bob Lee returned to dealing cards, while Lonie, under the alias of Frank Miller, waited for a registered letter from Jim Thornhill with the rest of the money from the saloon sale. When he got it, he returned to his aunt Elizabeth Lee's home in Dodson, Missouri. The Cripple Creek postmaster there immediately notified the Pinkertons, but Lonie had boarded a train for Missouri by the time they discovered his whereabouts. It isn't clear whether he was tracked to Dodson because of intercepted mail from Elfia or from passing more of the stolen, forged bank notes. Regardless, the following February a local police and Pinkerton task force surrounded the Lee home, and Lonie was killed while trying to escape. Chouteau County Sheriff Cleary traveled to Kansas City to identify the body. Cleary reported that Lonie had shaved off his mustache.

The Pinkertons also found an address for Mrs. Lee's son Bob amongst some mail she was attempting to burn in the stove. He was captured and went to prison for ten years. He reportedly returned to Kansas City and operated a saloon there after his release.

A handwritten manuscript recently discovered and attributed to Kid Curry claims that Lee was framed for the Wilcox train robbery because he was a Curry cousin.

Disguised as a wanted Texas outlaw, Charlie Siringo spent some time in the Little Rockies country working for Thornhill. Thornhill later claimed to have been aware of his real identity. Siringo became friendly with Elfia Curry and reportedly talked with Jim Winters, learning that Winters expected Curry to kill him to avenge the death of his brother Johnny. Siringo left the Little Rockies after another Union Pacific train robbery by the Wild Bunch near Tipton, Wyoming. Other robberies followed, including the First National Bank of Winnemucca, Nevada, which netted an estimated $32,000.

The gang members spent some of their loot in the red-light districts of Fort Worth and San Antonio, Texas. Back at their Powder Springs, Wyoming, headquarters, Kid Curry may have convinced Butch Cassidy to pull one more robbery before departing for South America. Others say Cassidy wasn't involved at all. Harry Longabaugh ("the Sundance Kid") and Etta Place had already headed for South America via New York City, so they certainly did not participate.

Robbing any more Union Pacific trains was out; the company now carried a crack force of men, the Union Pacific Rangers, on a special car with their horses to track down thieves right after a robbery. Led by U.S. Deputy Marshal Joe Lafors and assisted by local lawmen and Union Pacific and Pinkerton agents, they made the country too hot for any additional attempts. The advance of civilization had also eliminated many of the gang's potential hiding places.

Curry had an idea how and where to get money without interference from the Pinkerton Agency. He thought he could take care of a long-overdue bit of personal business, too....

On the sultry afternoon of July 2, 1901, in a Malta, Montana, saloon about half a block from the Great Northern Railway station, the bartender and a customer, George Campbell of Big Sandy, looked on while an ordinary-looking cowboy kept watch out the front window. When the westbound Number Three Coast Flyer whistled its impending departure, the cowboy headed for the station. The bartender remarked that he looked sort of familiar. Campbell replied matter-of-factly that it was Kid Curry.[4] When they saw the Kid hop aboard the blind baggage car, they knew that a robbery was imminent. Campbell left town with his herd of Circle Diamond horses and continued into Canada. He knew that when a posse was called, the law would confiscate his horses for the saloon bums to ride and ruin.

On the train, Curry crawled over the coal tender and dropped down into the locomotive cab. He ordered the engineer to put on the brakes at a prearranged stop near the Exeter Creek siding near Wagner. A burning barricade had been placed on the tracks to insure compliance. Another outlaw was aboard a passenger car, and two other bandits waited with the horses. With Curry were O. Camille "Deaf" Hanks, Ben "the Tall Texan" Kilpatrick, and possibly Butch Cassidy. Laura Bullion, Kilpatrick's girlfriend, may have been in the neighborhood, too. Some have mentioned Jim Thornhill as a participant, while others said only that his ranch house was used as the final staging area. He is also believed to have scouted out when the money shipment would be carried, and on which train.

Others disagree with Thornhill's supposed intelligence role. Author F. Bruce Lamb cites Teddy Blue Abbott's opinion that Cassidy got the information for Curry at St. Paul. In another view, an anonymous Fergus County rancher said that Curry learned the information himself in Helena. Also, a rumor circulated of an insider at the railroad being involved.

While the passenger cars were disengaged from the express car and locomotive tender,[5] the outlaws kept up a steady stream of rifle fire along both sides of the coaches, wounding two train men and an eighteen-year-old passenger, Gertrude Smith. Curry enlisted fireman Mike O'Neil[6] to help blow the express car safe, which finally yielded after three charges of dynamite. A rider named John Cunningham showed up to find out what was going on and had his horse shot out from under him for his trouble. Cunningham hotfooted it back to Wagner and gave the alarm.

Once $40,000 or so in bank notes,[7] money orders, eight gold watches, and a bolt of silk for Curry's "old lady" were collected, the boys mounted and rode around the bend before crossing the river by raft. They changed mounts at the Circle C Ranch and headed for the Circle C line camp on Rock Creek near the Missouri River. It was said that they stashed the loot at a place called Walsh Coulee, and that it was later retrieved by Laura Bullion in a buggy rented in Hinsdale.

The gang met two ranch hands from the Ben Phillips ranch and told them to inform the posse that they were heading south. Two of the wanted men were riding on one horse, with one spent horse lagging behind. The ranch hands also observed that one of the outlaws had a bloody cheek. Since no heavy luggage was observed, the story about Bullion's pickup is even more believable.

If Jim Winters' fate wasn't sealed by then, Abe Gill guaranteed it by inviting the 60-man posse to stay at the Winters ranch. He supplied them with fresh horses, to boot. The ragtag posse was of little use, however, having eaten spoiled beans at the Coburn ranch earlier and drunken rotgut whiskey at the local saloons. They never went near any of Curry's old haunts or explored any new ones.

Curry put out the word and distributed written notices that anyone who helped the posse was dead unless they left the country. This meant Gill had joined Winters on the death list. The Coburns had already warned Winters to get out.

The posse spent a week's worth of taxpayer money stumbling about the immediate countryside raising dust. Posses from other towns and counties had no better luck at finding their prey.

Supposedly Curry went to Great Falls and asked an old Glasgow friend, former sheriff Sid Willis, to get someone to forge officials' signatures on the bank notes. But Willis declined and told Curry to leave and never return; he had already had enough trouble from the stolen bills Lonie had used. It is believed that the rest of the gang left two days after the robbery with their share of the still-unsigned notes; and that they changed horses at a ranch on Porcupine Creek near Forsyth, passed through Miles City, and went south along the Tongue River into Wyoming.

The posses left the Winters-Gill ranch by month's end. They were replaced by six college students from Gill's alma mater, Brooklyn Polytechnic. Believing as Aristotle did that "in all things of nature there is something of the marvelous," the students intended to spend an idyllic summer working on a real Western ranch. They didn't expect the drama that ensued.

The early morning of July 25 began peacefully enough, with student Alfred Nicholson going for a ride before breakfast. Jim Winters left the cabin to use the outhouse. As he stepped from the porch, two rifle bullets pierced his stomach—a calculated injury that ensured a slow, painful death. Thus Curry returned the two shots for Johnny and on almost the same piece of ground.

Neither the students nor Gill were able to reach the bleeding Winters for a while because of continuous gunfire. Finally three of them brought Winters inside. In the meantime, two others went to Landusky for help, returning with mine owner J. P. Guy Manning. A rider also was dispatched to Harlem to get the doctor, but Winters lived only a few agonizing hours. Law officers arrived from Fort Benton about 40 hours later.

Gill didn't leave the cabin until the posse arrived, or he would probably have been killed, too. Shell casings and the stubs of hand-rolled cigarettes were found in the nearby brush and willows along the creek. Some brush had been broken off, and the ground bore horses' hoof prints and manure. The outlaws had led their horses some distance before mounting, according to the signs.

At least two or three men had waited for Winters at that secluded location. Law enforcement officials speculated that after Curry shot Winters, he left the area, leaving someone to keep up the shooting to give him a head start and to ensure that Winters didn't receive swift medical attention. Thornhill reportedly had an ironclad alibi, since he was visiting a neighbor at the time, but still he and the Circle C men were suspected as Curry's accomplices. It was no secret that they bore ill will towards both Winters and Gill.

Even with a reward of $1,400 offered by Chouteau County officials for information leading to Curry's capture, as well as a $6,500 reward offered by the Pinkerton Agency, the state, and the railroad express company for information about the train robbers, there were no takers. It didn't take much brain power to realize that dead people couldn't spend much.

A second posse stayed at the Winters-Gill ranch, but a more professional one this time, from Chouteau County. The trail of the attackers was soon lost, and no further leads developed. All the chief suspects had impeccable alibis. The college students were sent home, their romantic cowboy notions ruined, but they had something to talk about for a lifetime. Winters was buried on the ranch, across the creek from Johnny Curry's resting place and only a few miles south of Pike Landusky's grave.

Gill was now in quite a predicament. He had a ranch to run, and he had to survive at the same time. If some sources can be believed, Gill took what looked like a controversial course. He made it abundantly clear that he would take no active part in the capture of Curry, deciding against being an informant for local law enforcement officers or the Pinkerton Agency. Because the hideout on Thornhill Butte to the west was almost always occupied by outlaws, Gill knew that word would get to Curry, wherever he roamed.

At the same time, according to other sources, Gill became Mr. Law-and-Order, keeping authorities informed of all lawless acts of residents. His ranch was the headquarters for lawmen who had business in and around the Little Rocky Mountains. Gill was shot at on occasion, but this didn't deter him. He just rode at nighttime and never publicly told anyone of when or where he was going.

Gill must have been greatly cheered by the December 1901 news that Curry had been captured in Knoxville, Tennessee, after a pool-hall brawl in which he wounded two policemen and a customer. Pinkerton sources said that Curry visited Kansas City (Dodson) after the GNR train robbery and Winters' murder. He then returned to Texas, picked up his companion Annie Rogers, and began a tour of Arkansas, Louisiana, and Tennessee. Ben Kilpatrick and Laura Bullion had tried to do the same via the Midwest, but were tripped up by the unsigned currency and crude forgeries they attempted to pass. Meanwhile, Cassidy had joined Harry Longabaugh and Etta Place in South America.

Kilpatrick went to prison, but Curry escaped 18 months later from the Knoxville County Jail, just after being sentenced to prison.[8] He may have been aided in some way by Thornhill. There was talk of a $10,000 bribe. In his escape, Curry took the sheriff's conveniently located horse, and no alarm was sounded. It was suspicious enough that the U.S. Attorney's and U.S. Marshal's offices filed charges of negligence against the sheriff and won. Curry was not recaptured.

In one popular version of Curry's route after his escape, he roamed all around the local countryside and mountains. But in another, he rode the rails as a hobo north to Minneapolis, Minnesota, to visit his sister Allie and her second husband Manuel Rodriguez. In yet a third version, Curry visited Allie and Manuel in Kansas City, and an older sister in Minneapolis. This was after spending a few days in a safe house near Knoxville, possibly that of a relative. Curry began a westward journey in boxcars after resting up and arrived back at Wagner, Montana, the site of the train robbery. He went back to all his old haunts around Landusky and was seen by many. In the next few months he reportedly visited with friends all over northern Montana. Once such friend was James T. Moran of Yantic; another was Tom Conant of Vernon, British Columbia.⁹

That Curry didn't bother with Gill is not surprising. He was the most wanted outlaw in the United States, and he had no intention of calling attention to himself.

According to some sources, Curry next hopped a freight train to Seattle and secured employment on a ship to South America. He jumped ship upon arrival at the Chilean port of Valparaiso. Some said this was only a temporary diversion and alleged that he returned to America in March 1904, when he was supposedly seen in Rock Springs, Wyoming.

Curry supposedly sent postcards to many friends back home during his intercontinental journey. His activities in South America reportedly included staging holdups, working in a Chilean copper mine and a Brazilian logging camp, and working a mining claim. He also was credited with having been jailed twice for being drunk and disorderly, and he reportedly visited the Argentine ranch of Cassidy, Longabaugh, and Place. This would have been just before their South American outlaw career began.

No concrete proof substantiates these South American adventure stories or another story in which Curry stayed at the Lamb brothers' ranch on Sand Gulch in Fremont County, Colorado.¹⁰

Whether or not Curry ever left the country, he was officially sighted in Denver, Colorado, on February 16, 1904. A man identified as Curry checked into the Oxford Hotel. The desk clerk recognized him from his boyhood days in Missouri, but said nothing when he registered. The man carried his own bag, but gave the bellhop a dollar anyway. He asked the boy for a pitcher of water, which he got about 15 minutes later. The bellhop entered the man's room without knocking and saw an open valise containing new-looking currency and a large revolver lying beside it. The man swore at him and ordered him out of the room. By the time police came, the man had ducked out a side door.

Curry had been in Denver other times before the trip to the South that had landed him in the Knoxville County, Tennessee, jail. Local newspapers speculated that the money the bellhop had glimpsed was the remainder of the unsigned bank notes from the Wagner, Montana, train robbery. Of the $40,000 or more taken, only $18,000 had been accounted for.

There are two earlier stories of Curry's supposed activities after the escape, and both take place near the Hole-in-the-Wall country in Johnson County. Former junior gang members Walt Punteny and Tom O'Day are used interchangeably in these stories. Both men had been released from prison in April of 1898 for their participation in the Belle Fourche, South Dakota, bank robbery. Punteny was said to have gone straight and left the area, while O'Day returned to his horse-thievin' ways. But there were few outlaws left in the country, and law enforcement was stronger. Even the former outlaw valley was occupied by legitimate ranchers.

In the folktales, Curry teams up with one of them and steals some horses—and perhaps saddles. They are pursued by a posse and Curry is wounded. In one version The Kid dies; the other he recovers. In both cases he is attended by a physician: either a Doctor Hale or a Doctor Schuelke, both of Thermpolis.

This "incident" actually incorporates parts of two separate events, years apart. In 1899 the Wild Bunch robbed a Union Pacific train near Wilcox, Wyoming. After a harrowing escape in which Curry killed a sheriff and posse member, the gang hid out at a secluded ranch on Muddy Creek, about 25 miles south of Thermopolis through the Owl Creek Mountains. There is a grave on that ranch where a badly wounded member of the gang died and was buried a short time after their arrival. Author Larry Pointer believed that the outlaw who died there was Harvey Ray, since he is the only one never heard of again.[11]

Enter German-born doctor Julius Schuelke of Lander, Wyoming, formerly of St. Louis. Schuelke was responsible for naming the new town of Thermopolis and promoting its thermal hot springs for health treatments. He moved there in 1897 after helping to negotiate the sale or lease of the springs from the Shoshone Indians on the Wind River Reservation. Schuelke bought property nearby and was channeling the springs to his property to treat patients. The doctor was said to have a problem with alcohol and narcotics. In 1890, he shot Lander's pharmacist to death, but he was ably defended by Wild Bunch attorney Douglas Preston and received only a slap on the wrist.

Schuelke told of a night when two masked men blindfolded him and took him on a long buggy ride to treat a wounded comrade. Upon entering a house, he was taken to a room around which blankets had been hung so he couldn't later identify the place. The wounded outlaw had a serious groin wound. The doctor did what he could for the man and returned a few nights later under the same circumstances. Schuelke told the outlaws that the patient was dying from the seriously infected wound. His only description of the man's features was that he was "of very dark complexion." The description fits Harvey Ray. The date of this incident was changed in later years to fit with Kid Curry's Knoxville escape.

The second story took place in 1903, a few months after Curry's escape. Schuelke had died, and doctors Richards and Hale were in residence at Thermopolis. Hale covered for Richards while the latter treated a wounded Curry at a ranch east of Thermopolis. Curry survived and escaped the law.

There doesn't appear to be any documentation for this story, other than the version that appeared in the book *Stories of Early Days in Wyoming*, written by Tacetta B. Walker in 1936. The only facts that remotely conform to any part of this folktale occurred on November 23, 1903. On that date Natrona County Sheriff Frank Webb of Casper captured Tom O'Day at a cabin in the Big Horn Mountains. O'Day was headed for Montana with 23 horses stolen from Natrona and Converse counties. The sheriff and his two deputies returned with the prisoner two days later. O'Day got six years in the state penitentiary for the theft. The incident took place nowhere near the outlaw valley or the lost cabin as portrayed in the Curry story.

The next incident said to involve Curry was the robbery July 7, 1904, of a Denver and Rio Grande Western Railway Co. train near Parachute, Colorado, high in the Rockies. The tracks paralleled the Colorado River (then called the Grand River). The robbery began in the usual Wild Bunch fashion: one robber hopped aboard as the train left the station, climbing over the baggage car to the tender and locomotive. About two miles below Parachute on Streit Flats, he ordered the crew to stop the train and separate the passenger cars from the express car and engine, then pull ahead until they reached a small campfire by the roadbed. At that point, they were to signal with the train whistle.

Once the train stopped, another two holdup men moved to the express car and blasted it open with dynamite when loyal company mail clerk, Fred Hawley, refused to open it. Hawley stuffed the registered mail down his overalls and threw the first-class mail sack into a dark corner to avoid confiscation. It worked. The robbers found the safe empty except for a small package. What it held was never publicly revealed. They had robbed the wrong train! Their intended victim, a Colorado Midland train carrying $150,000, was running late. It had been passed by the Denver and Rio Grande train, which used the same stretch of track.

The dynamite explosions brought the conductor and brakeman running. The nervous bandits shot out the brakeman's lantern and shot the conductor in the thigh. The conductor returned to a passenger car, and the brakeman ran back to the Parachute station to sound the alarm. Soon after, Garfield County Sheriff Adams dispatched a force of deputies by special train from the county seat at Glenwood Springs, Colorado, approximately 60 miles to the east.

At the same time the three bandits headed southeast, crossed the river in a stolen boat, and headed up thickly forested Battlement Mesa. They stopped at the Gardiner ranch for fresh horses and then headed east. At first, the posse had no trouble tracking the three since their horses had recently been shod. The lawmen lost the trail on Cache Creek, but figured the outlaws would continue south through the mountains to the Gunnison River. But the outlaws headed east, and the posse eventually found their trail and followed.

The locals couldn't understand why the outlaws didn't go south, following the isolated Dog Creek over the Grand Mesa Mountains to the Gunnison River Valley instead of going east through all the communities and stirring them up by stealing their horses. None of them cared about the train robbery.

The cat-and-mouse game progressed to the Silt area, some 50 miles to the east. The robbers stopped at the Banta ranch on Mamm Creek the third morning of the chase, June 9. There they had breakfast, procured fresh mounts, and left a smashed telephone behind. They changed horses again at the Todd ranch; the thin mountain air took its toll on the hard-driven mounts. Later that day, they stopped at the Larsen ranch in Divide Valley. Except for Mrs. Larsen and her young sons, all hands were out with the posse.

Mrs. Larsen saw the bandit trio at the corral getting fresh horses and ran out of the house yelling at them to leave her animals alone. She retreated to the house after being threatened. This didn't deter her for long, though; she sent her sons out with rifles.

At that point the posse arrived. The outlaws rode to a nearby deep gulch, abandoned their horses at the entrance, and began to climb the steep hillside. The deputies stayed mounted and lost two horses to gunfire because of it. The action took place about fifty yards from the Larsen place.

Deputy Elmer Chapman received a slight cheek wound and started to retreat. The closest bandit aimed at the fleeing Chapman, but was shot by Deputy Rolla Gardiner. The deputies heard the wounded bandit's companions encourage him to climb higher, saying "Come on, Sam!" But he told them he was too badly wounded, and they should go on without him. In a dramatic action worthy of the best Shakespearean tragedy, "Sam" stood up in front of his pursuers and shot himself fatally in the head.[12]

Upon reaching and examining the body, the officers found that Gardiner's shot had hit "Sam" in the left shoulder. The outlaw had two revolvers, and a Winchester rifle lay next to his body. In the dead man's pockets were a pair of field glasses, a large supply of ammunition, a compass, railroad time tables, and a crudely drawn map of the immediate area.

The other two bandits escaped to higher, rougher, brush-covered ground along East Divide Creek and disappeared in spite of a massive manhunt with bloodhounds. The posse members thought the fugitives didn't know the area except by the map and were heading back to the river.

Conflicting reports filtered into the sheriff's office at Glenwood Springs. One report said the outlaws were surrounded on Garfield Creek near New Castle. Another said they had been seen at Divide Creek again, near Silt; others said they were seen at a cabin back at Parachute or that they had shot a rancher—or maybe it was a cow—on Divide.

The search was called off after a week when it was learned that the fleeing duo had procured horses and ridden through Glenwood Springs, heading north to Wyoming. The two reportedly stopped at Shoshoni, Wyoming, for supplies on their way to the Big Horn Mountains. A local rancher, Jim Cox, even followed them at a distance until they reached the mountains, then returned home, his curiosity satisfied.

But the most attention was focused on the identity of the dead bandit. The initial identification came from Otto Barton, the Globe Express agent in Glenwood Springs. Barton said the deceased had brought a suitcase to the express office for shipment to Pueblo, Colorado, about 160 miles to the southwest. At that time, he had given his name as J. H. Ross. It was believed, then, that the dead man was Ross—until it was reported that Ross was alive and residing in a Pueblo hotel.

Next, "Sam" was identified as George W. Kendricks, a wanted man with many aliases who had come from the East and specialized in burglaries. However, the name Ross cropped up again when it was learned that the previous week three individuals calling themselves J. H. Ross, Charles Stubbs, and John Emmerling had worked as section hands for the railroad between Parachute and DeBeque. Here they supposedly planned the robbery and made themselves familiar with the country in order to plot an escape route. Their employment was short, earning them only $5.85 apiece. They called at the railroad office at New Castle on Saturday morning, June 4, to pick up their checks and learned they wouldn't be available until Tuesday. Two of them worked in a local restaurant for meals until payday. They were last seen riding a westbound freight train.

On Tuesday, June 14, a week after the robbery attempt, "Sam" was taken from the undertaker's parlor and buried in a cheap pine coffin in a pauper's grave. Beforehand, photographs were taken of the corpse from four different positions; these were to be circulated throughout the country.

The local folks didn't think that was necessary, since several had identified the dead man as "Tap" Duncan, a San Saba County, Texas, cowboy who had worked on several local ranches that summer around Glenwood Springs and New Castle. Duncan was related by blood or marriage to the notorious outlaw "Black" Jack Ketchum.

The Pinkerton Agency had a different opinion about the dead man's identity. Denver Superintendent James McPharland identified the corpse in the photo as that of Harvey "Kid Curry" Logan.

William Pinkerton assigned Lowell Spence, now the assistant superintendent of the Chicago office, to investigate the possibility that the deceased was actually Kid Curry. After all, Spence had been Curry's chief pursuer and knew him best. Spence interviewed many people who had known the cowboy called Duncan and came to the conclusion that the dead man was indeed Curry. Curiously, he assumed Duncan was a Curry alias and never checked out whether or a cowboy named Duncan ever existed. Spence requested that the body be exhumed for further investigation.

The body was unburied on July 16. Present at the exhumation, in addition to Spence, were R. Brunazzi, special agent for the Denver and Rio Grande Western Railroad and Globe Express Company; W. S. Canada, special agent for the Union Pacific Railroad; deputy sheriffs Mohn and Crissman; doctors Clark and McAllister; and other officials.

Spence definitely identified the deceased as Curry; all the others disagreed. Moreover, some Pinkerton men disagreed. Spence took the photos of the body to Knoxville, where everyone in the sheriff's office agreed with him that it was Curry. Local authorities and the railroad detectives claimed that the Pinkerton man only identified the deceased as Curry so he could collect the large rewards offered. Others said the railroads were hedging so they wouldn't have to pay their share of the rewards.

Agent Brunazzi decided to prove the identity of the deceased with the support of Canadian and Garfield County authorities. They couldn't understand why Spence was so sure it was Curry, although they conceded the dead man was roughly Curry's size. But they found no deep scars on the right arm or wrist from the gunshot wound Curry received during his capture near Lavina, Montana, in 1897. Also, the deceased had a peculiar scar on the end of his nose and buckshot wounds on his abdomen, which Curry did not have. Nor did Curry have a scar extending from the crown of his head to the base of his skull or a deep scar on his right shoulder—probably from a knife wound—extending half the length of his arm, as the dead bandit did. These were old wounds—nothing Curry could have acquired recently. Finally, among other discrepancies, the amount of body hair on the two men was completely different.

And contrary to some reports, the body was in a good enough

state of preservation to determine what identification marks, etc., the deceased had or hadn't in comparison to Harvey "Kid Curry" Logan's medical records.

Local physicians and authorities concluded that the description of the dead bandit did not match that of Curry. But the railroad detectives did not stop there. Brunazzi began his investigation by tracing an address on an envelope found in the dead man's coat. It led him to Olga Kilpatrick of Knickerbocker, Texas (now part of San Angelo). He also learned that in March, Tap Duncan, George Kilpatrick, and Jack Sheffield had left Crocker County, Texas, where the Kilpatricks resided, well-armed and provisioned for a long journey, destination unknown. Sheffield may have been a relative of the Kilpatricks by marriage.

George Kilpatrick's brother Ben, "the Tall Texan," was serving a fifteen-year prison term for his participation in the Great Northern Railway robbery near Wagner, Montana. Their brother Boone was also under indictment for passing some of the unsigned bank notes from the robbery. Sheffield was "a notorious Texas outlaw and rustler," according to historian James Horan.

Neither Kilpatrick nor Sheffield had been seen nor heard since the robbery attempt, Brunazzi learned. He was positive that they were the other two participants in the train robbery, and he matched the descriptions relatives and friends gave to those given by witnesses at the crime scene. Brunazzi was equally certain that Duncan was the bandit buried at Glenwood Springs. Duncan's friends and relations identified the man in the photo as him, and the sheriff in Brady, Texas, also gave a positive identification. The sheriff said Duncan's nose wound had been inflicted several years before by his deputy, Joe Arkery, when Duncan was resisting arrest. The buckshot wounds on his stomach occurred during another arrest attempt, when Duncan was shot off his horse by the county authorities. Duncan almost died from these wounds, Brunazzi learned.

The detective's report went on to say that the Duncan and Kilpatrick homes had been the winter rendezvous for both the

Ketchum and Cassidy gangs for several years.

Brunazzi's findings gained credence when a John Ring, formerly of Waco, Texas, then residing in Des Moines, Iowa, identified a photograph hanging in the Waters Gallery as that of Duncan, formerly of Iowa. Ring said Duncan was "a disagreeable sort of fellow and had but few friends, being possessed of unfortunate domineering qualities which brought to him a feeling of antipathy from people who might otherwise have been called friends." Ring also said the nickname "Tap" came from his practice of claiming poker winnings—"tapping the pot"—whether or not he had the winning cards. Duncan followed the county fair circuit for such games. Ring also said Duncan had permanently left Iowa about three years earlier and returned to Texas.

But what was Duncan's first name? Was it Sam? Or Tom, as others claimed? Might the bandits have been urging "Tap" to come along? The answer was not clear. So while some of the Pinkerton officials and Knox County authorities thought they had Curry in the ground, the railroad sleuths continued to look for him and for Duncan's former partners in crime.

Kilpatrick eventually returned home and was killed when he became entangled while roping a steer. He had suffered health problems since 1901 due to five bullet wounds received in a Sonora gunfight with the law. Sheffield was never found.

Curry's U.S. bandit career was resurrected briefly on November 1, 1904, when a would-be robber matching his general description, accompanied by a taller man, attempted to rob the First National Bank of Cody, Wyoming. The afternoon holdup resulted in the death of cashier L. O. Middaugh after he wrestled with the gunman. Middaugh had attempted to leave the bank by a rear door to summon help. The outlaws engaged in a brief gun battle with some townspeople before departing. A posse of about 20 men led by Big Horn County Deputy Sheriff Jeff Chapman pursued them through the hills to the southwest. There was a continuous exchange of gunfire until the posse lost the bandits at dark near Meeteetse, about 30 miles to the south, when they turned into a canyon. The outlaws were believed to have had a relay team of horses waiting for them, provided by accomplices. The posse reorganized and continued the hunt later that night, then returned to Cody after following the outlaws' trail as far as Thermopolis, another 40 miles to the south. The Cassidy gang had once frequented the town and surrounding area.

Buffalo Bill Cody cashed in on the publicity generated by the crime by telling citizens of Omaha, Nebraska, that he would take a hunting party and pursue the outlaws; he actually continued on to the wilds of the Yellowstone River country with his friends.

Interest in the Cody, Wyoming, bank robbery spread nationwide when county authorities said the outlaws had operated like the Wild Bunch, using accomplices and relief horses. They reported that Kid Curry had led the robbery attempt, and speculated that the robbers were now hiding in the Hole-in-the-Wall country. This was refuted by ranchers of Johnson and Natrona counties, who by that time occupied the area.

The *Sheridan Post* editor agreed with the ranchers, editorializing that "the Hole-in-the-Wall no longer exists, save in the novelist's fancy and the space-writer's imagination." Still, some storytellers and historical writers today use this supposed sighting of Curry as evidence that he didn't die in Colorado. But further investigation does not bear this story out.

One of the Cody bank robbers was a man matching Curry's general description, but he was larger and taller. The same outlaws were also thought to have been the culprits in the robberies of several area saloons. A man fitting the robber's description, going by the name of George Merritt, had appeared in Thermopolis buying supplies before the Cody bank robbery attempt.

The Curry connection unraveled on November 16, 1904, when the "Curry bandit" was captured by two Hot Springs County deputy sheriffs at the mouth of Owl Creek Canyon north of Thermopolis. The robber offered no resistance and came apart emotionally—hardly the Kid Curry type. Then, on November 18, another man answering the description of the killer of bank cashier

Middaugh ordered supplies at a store on the western Idaho border. His two companions were to pick up the goods, but they never did, even though they had been seen riding through town.

Big Horn County lawmen captured this second suspect in late December near Basin, Wyoming, north of Thermopolis. He gave his name as Irvin, and witnesses placed him at scene of the Cody robbery. The Curry connection was severed for good, although the bank job still figures in Curry folktales in Wyoming.

The fact that this supposed Curry character wasn't very tough brings up another reason for doubting the Curry death near Glenwood Springs. The real Curry might be expected to go out with his guns blazing rather than surrendering or committing suicide. He would have made a grand, Hollywood-type exit.

Back in the Little Rockies, Abe Gill preferred to believe the official news from Knoxville that the dead bandit buried at Glenwood Springs had been identified as Kid Curry. Still, stories of Curry's continued appearances wouldn't go away. On or about February 11, 1905, the Tarapaca and Argentine Bank, Ltd. in Santa Cruz Territory, was robbed—by Butch Cassidy, the Sundance Kid, and a third individual. This was some six hundred miles southeast of the Cassidy-Longabaugh-Place ranch on the Patagonian Pampas. The alleged third bandit somewhat matched Curry's description, and it was said he even had deep scars on the back of his right wrist. Initial Argentine police reports, however, were disputed by the Pinkerton Agency, which identified the third male as an outlaw named McVey, "a young gunslinger" from the States.

In their second 1905 South American robbery of the Bank de la Nacion at Villa Mercedes, San Luis Province, the Cassidy-Longabaugh-Place team was said by Pinkerton to have been accompanied by a young Texas outlaw named Dey, a "construction worker down on his luck." This again stirred Curry stories.[13]

Curry was implicated in no more of the robberies committed by Butch Cassidy and the Sundance Kid, but he surfaces again in South America nonetheless—in connection with other former

Montana bandits.

Curry, using the name Andrew Duffy, was supposedly in-volved in South America with Montana outlaws Robert Evans (a.k.a. Hood) and William Wilson (a.k.a. Gray). This group, prior to 1906, had supposedly been part of a larger gang whose other members returned to the U.S. Duffy was in fact the man who had ridden with the Dutch Henry Ieuch gang in Montana, Canada, and North Dakota. And Duffy did in fact go to South America in about 1905 with at least one partner, George Whitney (alias Tom Ryan), and possibly others (such as Johnny Woodruff). A Decem-ber 27, 1910, report to the Pinkerton Agency from the police chief of the Territorio del Chubut reported that there were several Montana outlaws in Argentina.

Arthur Jordan, a friend to many eastern Montana outlaws, claimed that Whitney, Kid Curry, and two others were killed in a gun battle at a cabin in the Argentine interior. This somewhat corresponds with a December 1911 report that Wilson and Evans were killed by a contingent of frontier police and provincial soldiers near Rio Pico in the Andes of western Argentina. They were suspected of having robbed a store at Arroyo Rescado, Chubut Province, in December 1909, killing the manager in the process. A third man, either Curry or Duffy, was reportedly killed by his partners near the Chilean Gulf of Corcavado, across from Cholila. Duffy was well known by the Argentine militia as a companion of Wilson and Evans. In 1910, Pinkerton learned that Wilson had also been associated with Duffy in northern Montana. Duffy's nickname was "Diente de Oro" because he had a gold tooth. He and the others also frequented the ranch of Cassidy, Longabaugh, and Place. It is possible that Duffy was in the company of George Whitney and perhaps Johnny Woodruff.

The Pinkerton Agency clung to its tenuous belief that Kid Curry was dead, at least through 1906, and there was no evidence to the contrary. Prior to the 1904 Colorado train robbery, Pinkerton agents had prowled the Little Rockies, but they had since ceased any active investigations there. Still, they did get nervous when

Curry's name surfaced in South America.

PART III

In late 1905 or early 1906, John Survant and James Peck of Malta and William Coburn of Brookside traveled with Abe Gill to the vast Pampas country of Argentina for four months. Survant was the manager of the Bloom Land and Cattle Company, the Circle Diamond brand, and he represented the Swift Company, the owners of which were interested in developing a large ranch operation in Argentina. The Coburn boys were interested in relocating, since homesteaders were taking up so much land in Montana.

As Cassidy and Sundance had discovered earlier, vast amounts of land were available in Argentina under a law similar to the U.S. Homestead Act. The sandy soil of the high plains country near Patagonia was much like that of southern Utah and other cattle-raising states. Thousands of acres could be leased long-term for only a few cents an acre, if a party knew how to deal with the politicians. This is where Gill came in; he was handy as both interpreter and diplomat, to smooth the way.

Gill stayed in Buenos Aires while the others toured the vast interior. Whether Gill was intimidated by the Curry sightings or whether he stayed as a matter of diplomacy is unclear. The others took a train inland to the end of the line, and Will Coburn went on alone with a pack train outfit. Supposedly he stopped at the outlaw ranch and visited with Kid Curry; this was reported by both Walt Coburn and Joseph Kinsey Howard in their respective books *Pioneer Cattleman in Montana* and *Montana: High, Wide, and Handsome*. This is the only known "official" sighting of Curry in South America—although there were no witnesses.

Walt Coburn believed that Gill notified the authorities in the provincial capital of Curry's presence, but they showed no interest. Next, Gill notified the Pinkerton Agency, either while he was in South America or when he returned to Montana. One thing was certain: he was in no hurry to go home. He wrote letters to friends postmarked in the Windward Islands telling of his leisurely steamship cruise through the West Indies.

Reports of Kid Curry living in South America surfaced in the Montana papers in October 1906. They said that Curry had been seen there by a "Montana man" within the last 6 months. Obviously they were referring to Coburn's visit, but they didn't explain the several months' delay in reporting it. It is apparently because of this incident that the Pinkertons showed renewed interest in Curry's case. Addressing a police chief convention at Jamestown, Virginia, in 1907, William Pinkerton said Curry had turned up in Argentina. His brother and partner, Robert Pinkerton, expressed the same belief in an internal memo in January 1907. A wanted poster for Curry, printed in both Spanish and English, was circulated in South America as early as 1903.

According to Walt Coburn, Abe Gill was "a troubled, worried man." Finally, Gill decided to sell his Montana ranch and return to New York, since he felt it was only a matter of time before he was killed. His ranch would become the property of the Coburns, and Gill would go into partnership with some of his brothers. Gill wrote home to his family in October that he was leaving near the end of the month. He placed his luggage on the Landusky stage bound for the Harlem train station and planned to follow on horseback the following day.

He never arrived.

Was the Curry sighting for real or was it just a scheme to get Gill to leave Montana? No other verified identification of Curry occurred. Jesse Cole Kenworth, author of *Storms of Life: The Outlaw Trail and Kid Curry*, said Curry never did go to South America. Kenworth's words are important because he interviewed the grandchildren of Lonie and Elfia Curry and had access to an unpublished manuscript written by Elfia, as well, perhaps, as biographical family documents.

Assuming then that Curry never left the U.S., why would the Coburns want Gill out of the Little Rockies country, especially at this particular time?

The answer is perhaps partially to be found in chapter four of Walt Coburn's book *Pioneer Cattleman of Montana*. Entitled "The Great Land Swindle," it tells of the homesteaders coming in droves, lured by the "pie in the sky" bait of free land by James J. Hill and his Great Northern Railway; and of their taking up land and water previously used by cattle ranchers. The Coburns fought this invasion as did other ranchers in the West. One of their methods was to have their cow hands file homestead claims on the former Circle C range, then, after prove-up, to have them deed it to the Coburns. Burning homesteaders' shacks and tarring and feathering them were other, more direct, means used by resisting ranchers. These activities would have been fought by U.S. Land Commissioner Abe Gill. Also, with Gill permanently gone, his land was a welcome addition to the Coburn ranch.

If Gill had been a local boy without connections, perhaps the furor over his disappearance would have died down more quickly. But he was known all over Montana. This was especially true in Helena, due to his political work and his job as land commissioner. Plus, he was a well-educated man with good social connections. He had attended the Democratic Party state convention in Helena and had made regular stops in Fort Benton, Havre, Malta, Harlem, and other places to visit friends, take care of his own ranching business, and provide land to settlers under the Homestead Act. He also issued deeds after the proving-up process, the very thing the Coburns were fighting. He was a good friend of U.S. Congressman Charles N. Pray of Fort Benton, formerly the Chouteau County attorney, and of Undersheriff Merritt Flannigan, among others. A woman Gill had courted, May Flannigan, was probably a relative of Merritt.

It wasn't until early December that Chouteau County officials mounted a search for Gill after local friends and his family in New York became alarmed at his disappearance. Yet by January 6, 1907, no trace of him had been found. His friends concluded that Gill had been killed by someone connected with the Currys.

There was even the question of whether Curry himself had returned to do the job. Again, we can return to Kenworth's book for the most likely answer: "Harvey did not kill Abe Gill, as Harv was not even in the country [Montana] at the time of Gill's demise." Yet Kenworth did believe that Curry had killed Winters, saying, "At that time, shortly after the Kid pulled off the Great Wagner, Montana, Train Robbery, Harvey gutshot Winters with two well-placed shots." Note that Kenworth said Curry was "not even in the country" in 1906, and did not say he was dead at the time (meaning he couldn't have been the Colorado corpse of 1904).[14]

Gill's detractors and enemies said no one had murdered him; he had met with a fatal accident on the wintry prairie. The list of suspects questioned by the authorities included the Coburns, their foreman Jake Myers (a reputed former top gunman from Oklahoma), and of course Jim Thornhill, whose ranch hands were said to have usually been men on the dodge from somewhere on the Texas-Montana outlaw trail.

Walt Coburn claimed to have witnessed a conversation between Gill and Montana brand inspector and former Havre lawman George Hall at the Coburn ranch in August 1906. Hall told Gill that he believed Curry was back in the states and was hiding in the Hole-in-the-Wall country of Wyoming. Hall also said he expected Curry would eventually show up in the Little Rockies. Gill admitted to Hall that this was one of the reasons he was selling out; he thought it was only a matter of time before he was killed.

One has to believe that Hall was involved in the conspiracy to scare Gill into leaving, since he had to have known that the Hole-in-the-Wall valley had long been abandoned as an outlaw refuge.

Authorities attempted to track Gill's movements during what were apparently his last days on earth. The previous September 12 he had been at the Republican nominating convention at the Chinook Opera House to support a friend's candidacy. The campaign began on July 16, 1906. Gill delayed his departure from

Montana for seven months because of this campaign—a delay that may well have cost him his life.

On Sunday, September 30, Gill wrote from Harlem (Montana) to Joseph Sullivan, a Fort Benton saddle and harness maker, requesting some leather work. He wrote that he was leaving for his old ranch location and would return to Harlem the following Thursday, October 4, when he would board a train for the East. Gill also planned a trip to a ranch on the Missouri River, but authorities were not sure if he attempted such a trip.

There was some speculation that Gill and his horse had drowned in the ice-clogged Missouri River. Crossing the river would have been particularly perilous since Gill traveled mainly at night because of death threats and potshots taken at him. Supposedly, the last anyone saw of him was when he collected the down payment on the sale of his ranch to the Coburns and rode off towards the Missouri River.

The following spring, two of Gill's brothers, Thomas and James, came to Montana for a month to personally check on their brother's last movements and sort through the many bogus stories that had come out of the woodwork—particularly when they offered a $500 reward for information.

One story told of a young Metis (French-Indian) boy who stumbled on the carcass of a recently killed horse bearing Gill's brand. The horse reportedly had bloodstains on its back that were inconsistent with its own fatal wounds. The boy guessed that the horse had died weeks earlier from a bullet to its brain. Another Metis named Sorrette traveled to Harlem and talked to the visiting Gill brothers. He related this same story, saying that only the bones remained now. In his inspection of the site, Sorrette found the remains of a large campfire where he thought a man's body had been burned. He could find only a lower arm and jawbone at the scene, which was east of the Coburn Buttes, just south of the Coburns' Beaver Creek ranch.

Justice P. Baird of Landusky made the trip to the supposed murder scene at a small limestone cave measuring five feet high, five to six feet wide, and about ten feet deep. But all Baird found was a bed of ashes and some animal bones. He theorized that the place was used by wanted men on the outlaw trail.

The next story, datelined Landusky, is even more bizarre. It received statewide press coverage with no follow-up or explanation. The storyteller announced that Gill's remains had been found under the floor of a cabin on an adjoining ranch—the Curry-Thornhill place. The body was identified by personal effects found on it, the story said. A horse's body was found in a second cabin close by. Both had died from gunshots.

The Gill brothers even contacted a woman in Norway who claimed to have been an eyewitness to Gill's murder when she lived in the Little Rockies. The unidentified woman said she saw two men quarreling and one killed the other. She implied that several important individuals would be implicated in the crime and eventually brought to justice.

The searches continued. Gill was a constant topic of conversation, with many suppositions advanced as to his whereabouts. No clues were discovered, however, and all the stories brought forward were found to be baseless.

Newspapers around Montana, particularly the *Helena Herald*, decried the area's evil ways. Little Rockies prospector and mine owner Tom Carter replied to the criticism in the *Little Rockies Miner*, saying that Gill was eccentric, a mystery to locals, even before his death. Furthermore, he often went off for days without letting anyone know his destination. In fact, Gill had told a few trusted friends of his various travels, but he was selective because of his fear of ambush.

Carter also said that Kid Curry was a good guy, just an average citizen except for his misguided acts of robbing. (He forgot to excuse Curry's killings.) Offering nothing new, Carter suggested that Gill either, one: fell into the river, two: was murdered, or three: froze to death.

The Gill family not only looked for Abe, they also sued the Coburn Cattle Company for the balance due in the sale of Gill's ranch. Gill had received only $2,000 of the $10,000 selling price on the day he disappeared. Robert Coburn, Sr., was served the summons at his Great Falls home. The Coburns had also purchased Gill's and partner Andrew Newman's interests in two mining claims, the Hawkeye and Eagle Eye, for $30,000 in October 1905. Only a small down payment was given, the balance to have been paid in one year. The remainder was due about the time of Gill's death. Was this a sufficient motive for murder? The question may never be answered.

Along with the litigation, the bogus stories concerning Gill's whereabouts continued. Friends of Gill received word that he was alive and well somewhere. A rancher east of Billings named P. J. Walters, listed as the foreman of the Six B Nine brand on Porcupine Creek, claimed that Gill not only stayed at his ranch but left there for South America. He said he last saw Gill heading out in a wagon with a trunk aboard. Walters further claimed that Gill wrote him postcards.

Chouteau County Surveyor Arthur Irelan spent two weeks in the mountains looking for Gill's body but was unsuccessful. Next to the locals, he probably knew the area best. He had just completed surveying a new county road on the east side of the mountains from Wilder's Landing, formerly Rocky Point, on the Missouri River.

Charles Crawford, a former Chouteau County undersheriff, then a policeman at Havre, led another search party. Chouteau County Undersheriff Merritt Flannigan also searched in vain.

Walt Coburn said a prevailing rumor in the Little Rockies was that the Pinkertons combed the area, perhaps in the employ of the Gill family.

On August 27, 1910, the *Havre Plaindealer* facetiously suggested that "apparently the earth opened and swallowed him." As Walt Coburn pointed out, there were many canyons and coulees where a dead man could be left to the coyotes, wolves, and mountain lions. Besides, the spring thaw would obliterate any remaining trace. Coburn concluded that Gill was murdered and his body disposed of. That was that.

What he didn't mention was that the locals supposedly knew more, but kept their mouths shut out of fear.

No other author offered any specifics on Gill's disappearance until Helen Duvall-Arthur and her father Walt, with the remembrances of her grandfather Charlie, published *Memories of a Filly Chaser* in 1992. According to this book, Charlie had been given an envelope by Charlie Baird, the justice of the peace, containing what the Duvall family thought was an explanation of what had really happened to Abe Gill. Baird had written on the envelope, "Not to be opened until my death." But Baird outlived Duvall, and the letter apparently disappeared.

Charlie Duvall, besides having been a rancher on the edge of the Missouri Breaks, a store owner, and a former freight and team driver, was also the Landusky correspondent for the *Great Falls Tribune*. He had two theories about what happened to Gill. In the first, he gives the following chronology of Gill's last day on earth: The cheerful Gill went off to the Coburn ranch near Beaver Creek on the morning of Tuesday, October 2, 1906, to collect his down payment on the ranch. He returned to Zortman where he stayed the night at the local hotel.[15] The following day, he sent his luggage ahead on the stage to Harlem's train station. From Zortman he rode his old white horse southwest, paralleling Rock Creek, to the Gregory Doney ranch on the opposite shore of the Missouri River bottoms, where he collected his laundry.

Duvall wrote that Gill left the Doney ranch that evening in the company of a cowboy, Pat Herron, who lived two miles west of the river on Coburn Bottoms. Herron claimed he left Gill when they took the road out of the river bottoms.

Duvall believed that somewhere on his solitary northward journey back to Zortman, Gill came upon several Indians of an unknown tribe butchering a Coburn steer. They fired a warning shot at Gill, but he kept approaching, so they killed his horse. Gill got up and approached them with his hands up, but they shot him anyway—the party apparently fearing the Coburns' wrath more than a murder charge. Duvall said they hurriedly skinned and butchered Gill's horse and loaded the hides along with Gill and his saddle gear aboard their wagon. They knew of a seemingly bottomless hole in the limestone rock at the eastern edge of the mountains and threw the wagon's entire contents into it. They went back to the scene of the crime, loaded the two animal carcasses, and went home.

Duvall said that the old Indian who told him the story said brush had grown up around the crevice, making it difficult to find. Author Helen Duvall-Arthur believes she can still find it today. One can only hope she will.

But there are obvious problems with this story. Why would Gill ride some 20 miles to have his laundry done when it could have been done locally?—particularly when he would have been exposing himself unnecessarily to harm and giving his enemies one last chance to assassinate the "daring young rancher," as the *Fort Benton River Press* put it. Also, the Doney ranch was near the Circle C line camp, used as a hideout by the Currys and possibly others. And according to Doney family members James Kelsey and Lillian Short, Gregory Doney never knew Gill; he never ferried across the river to the ranch that day or any other; and the Doneys never took in anybody's laundry or had any of Gill's clothes.

Still, Charlie Duvall believed the story until 1914, when Pat Herron, who was working for Duvall, told him he had to leave the country. "It's them sons-of-bitches that killed Gill," he said. "I know too much." Pat left that night and was never seen again. Duvall also learned from Herron's neighbors on the Missouri River that Herron suspected his wife and Gill of having an affair and that "Pat had threatened to kill Gill a number of times." Duvall began to wonder if Herron had killed Gill—but then who was Herron afraid of? Duvall concluded that Herron must have known the Indians who killed Gill and was afraid of them.

There is, of course, another possibility—that Herron acted as a Judas steer for the real killers, who were not Indians, but old enemies of Gill; and that the Herron place had been Gill's real destination. One of the main suspects in this theory was Jake Myers, who became foreman on the B. D. Phillips ranch when the Coburns sold out to him in 1916. The scourge of small farmers and ranchers, Myers was said to have ended his days at the old Great Northern Hotel in Malta, attended by a local physician. Supposedly he relieved his conscience by telling the good doctor everything before he died. Folks always wondered if he confessed to Gill's murder or implicated others, but the man of medicine never revealed the dying man's words.

One suspicion about what happened to Gill's body centered around the Ruby Gulch mining operation. In 1904, the Coburn brothers, Bob and Bill, with ranchers Charles Whitcomb and B. D. Phillips (first state senator from the future Phillips County) acquired the rights to the Ruby Gulch and Little Alder Gulch properties. The new mining company became one of the most profitable operations in the state.[16] The partners set up a hundred-ton cyanide mill to process the gold ore; the cyanide process could extract the metal from low-grade ores. The plant burned down in 1912 and was replaced. Supposedly a skeleton was found in the old processing vat during the rebuilding process. Some believed this was what was left of Abe Gill, which pointed the finger of suspicion at the Coburns once again. Adding to the Curry connection, the Coburns' mining partner, Charles Whitcomb, was married to one of Lucy Tressler's daughters.

Valley County Deputy Sheriff Hugh Calderwood told of a skeleton that had been found that might have been Gill's, but he didn't say where and when it was discovered. And lastly, there is the story about Gill's last night as told by the Walsh family.

The Walsh home on Beaver Creek, west of the Coburn ranch near the Zortman-Malta trail, was a halfway house for travelers. Gill supposedly came by for a meal on his way to pick up his check at the Circle C Ranch. Later, about midnight, the Walshes heard the hoof beats of a single horse crossing their wooden irrigation bridge. The rider was followed shortly by other horsemen. The family always wondered if that single rider was

Gill on his way back to Zortman, followed by his killers.

In 1968, Walt Coburn wrote of Gill: "Sixty years have now passed, and to the best of my knowledge the mystery of Abe Gill's disappearance has never been solved."

Whatever happened to Harvey "Kid Curry" Logan is no less a mystery, at least to most researchers. Curry is credited with going to South America; returning to die after the Colorado train robbery; going back to South America to live or die again; and returning again to the United States! Some say his final return to the U.S. (or last hold up) was celebrated with the $3,000 cash robbery of the Gila Valley Bank of Morenci, Arizona, in September 1910. This was not far from where the Will and Bob Coburn had relocated on the San Carlos Indian Reservation near Globe, Arizona. The bank robber was pursued by two deputies, but they lost his trail about seven miles south of the San Francisco River. Retired Pinkerton man Charlie Siringo was brought in by the Burns Detective Agency. He concluded from his investigation that the lone bandit was Kid Curry.

Diligent Curry researcher Jesse Cole Kenworth wrote that Curry robbed the bank in Clifton, Arizona, in about 1898, taking over $10,000 with the help of Ben Kilpatrick. Clifton was only a few miles southeast of Morenci. At the time, the Wild Bunch had returned to its hideout near Alma, New Mexico. So the country was familiar to Curry.

Ross Santee, author of *Lost Pony Tracks*, quotes a conversation he had with Thornhill at his Cross S Ranch at Cutter, Arizona. The Thornhill family had moved to Arizona after the Coburn ranch was sold in 1916 to the Phillips family. Thornhill supposedly said to Santee, "Kid's still alive, of course. We don't dare write, but I've had word from him." In *Pioneer Cattleman in Montana*, Walt Coburn said Thornhill told him later that Curry had gone to South America. Others in the Little Rockies and north-central Montana claim that Curry lived in Arizona for several years.

Lastly, Ruel Horner, who came to the Little Rockies country in 1903, and was one of the last stagecoach drivers between

181

Zortman and Malta, was quoted in a 1959 *Great Falls Tribune* article as saying that he ran into Elfia Curry a "few years back" and that she said "the Kid died of injuries he had received in a car accident in the state of Washington not too many years ago." Apparently Elfia and a sister visited the Harlem-Landusky area in about 1956, when Elfia was about 78 years old.

In the same article, Horner told of having seen Kid Curry with a local rancher at Zortman after his June 1903 escape from the Knoxville County, Kentucky, jail. "There wasn't a man or woman in Zortman who recognized him," he said. "Publicly, that is. The Kid was well liked," he concluded. Horner's property was near the Curry-Thornhill ranch.

The Curry/Logan grandchildren apparently still live in Montana, and at least two or more researchers have had access to the Curry family papers. Elfia's daughter died in Great Falls in 1961, leaving five sons and five daughters.

Perhaps more information will be discovered about the possible Arizona and Washington state segments of Curry's life.

The Curry question intrigues historical researchers, but Gill's whereabouts seem to be of little interest, perhaps because he was a law-abiding man who represented the civilized East. Being a policeman of sorts as a U.S. land commissioner and helping the homesteaders get established pitted him against the local ranchers. Perhaps Walt Coburn summed it up best when he wrote, "Because of his mysterious disappearance, Abe Gill played a minor role in the saga of violence and bloodshed in the feud between Jim Winters and the Curry boys." Yet, as an administrator, he played a major part—and might have played a larger one if he had stayed in Montana and survived—by contributing to the orderly democratic process of distributing public lands in a fair and honest manner.

Kid Curry's role, of course, was hardly minor from the folklore standpoint.[17] Yet because he killed many lawmen who were well-liked and respected, and because he treated his holdup victims poorly, he hardly fits the mold of a socially conscious Robin Hood. Nor does it work to defend him by saying he only killed those who were trying to kill him, since some of his victims were neither armed nor aware of his presence. Unlike the American Robin Hood-types such as the James and Younger brothers, the Daltons, and the Doolin-Dalton gang, Curry didn't have wide support in the areas (besides the Little Rockies) where he operated. Through his involvement with Butch Cassidy, who had a popular following, he did garner some respectability, however.

Curry seemed to operate more as a terrorist. The handwritten posters he put up in the Little Rockies after the Wagner train robbery, warning people what would happen to those who informed on him, hardly showed him to be a Jesse James-type; James wouldn't have needed such intimidation tactics and wouldn't have been afraid of a murder trial, either. No, Curry operated almost exclusively among his own kind with no popular following.

From the settled regions came the social outcasts, sociopaths, and psychopaths who thrived in the Western vacuum of few settlers and fewer lawmen. Some, like Curry, thought only of their own preservation and had the tempers and reckless natures to match their fast trigger fingers. Usually they took one fatal step from which there was no turning back, as in Curry's killing of Pike Landusky.

Today, the controversy over where and when Curry died seems to overshadow his outlaw career. Perhaps there is a reformed Curry yet to learn about.

As Wild Bunch researcher James Horan concluded of these outlaws, "They were desperate men, evil men, but for all that they were fascinating men." ★

NOTES

Chapter 1

1. The City of Helena started as a group of placer miner's cabins in July of 1864 when four men returning from an unsuccessful prospecting trip at Alder Gulch in Virginia City agreed to give the area "their last chance." They struck it rich, and Last Chance Gulch eventually yielded $30,000,000 in paydirt.

Chapter 2

1. Ritch claimed that Pike Landusky was as proficient with a weapon as Thompson, but he never mentioned Curry, even though he knew him. This probably had to do with Ritch's likes and dislikes of those individuals.

2. Ben Thompson (1842-1884) was born in England and raised in Austin, Texas. His claim to fame was his standing as a professional gambler, soldier of fortune, Civil War veteran, and town marshal. He was considered the best, most precise, most dangerous, and most ruthless killer the American West ever saw, according to William "Bat" Masterson. Only John Wesley Hardin was considered his near-equal with a gun, and only Kid Curry matched him for cold-bloodedness.

3. This story may have been confused with one about the origins of the Curry/Logan brothers.

4. This date would obviously have to have been at least 1889,

given Thompson's age.

5. This story only adds to the confusion because the author cannot find reference to any deputy U.S. marshals killed during that period. In fact, finding definitive information on Thompson in either Oklahoma or Texas has proved fruitless.

6. See Helena Huntington Smith, *War on Powder River*, chapter 34.

7. Allison's real name was Martin Allison Tisdale, and he was the black sheep of a respectable Texas family. He was part of both the Hat Cattle outfit and the "Red Sash" outlaw gang. His older brother, John, was a legitimate, wealthy rancher who was murdered in Johnson County, Wyoming, in 1891. Tisdale/ Allison was killed in a gunfight on a Glasgow street by George Dunnell in 1894.

8. The name "High Line" referred to the railroad that ran through this part of the country. It was not only the farthest north of three railroad lines in Montana, it also had a gradually ascending roadbed from Havre west to Marias Pass. Eventually, the name was applied to all the Great Northern rails in northern Montana east to Minot, North Dakota, paralleling present-day U.S. Highway 2 along the Milk and Missouri rivers. This section, beginning east of Havre, was originally called "the Long Level."

9. Investigation by this author and English outlaw historian Ralph Bradley failed to verify or disprove any gunfights or killings in which Thompson participated prior to coming to Montana.

10. The original boundaries of Valley County stretched from the Canadian line to the Missouri River and from Malta to the North Dakota line. The county eventually was broken into five separate counties.

11. No records of this case exist, and only brief newspaper accounts are available.

Chapter 3

1. After the Battle of the Little Bighorn in 1876, some 5,000 Sioux (Dakota) and Cheyenne people fled to the Wood Mountain area, giving the site particular historical significance.

2. This would appear to have been Tom Courchen's combination restaurant-saloon, livery barn, and corrals. It was located about a block and a half north of the railroad siding and its 45-acre stockyards. Courchen (a.k.a. Courching or Cushing) was an ex-soldier from Fort Buford. He also had a ranch near town.

3. The town of Buford got its start when the military buildings at Fort Buford, a mile to the northwest, were auctioned off in 1895, and some were moved to form the new community. Buford originally had a population of ten and included a post office, two hotels, several stores, and a Great Northern Railway passenger station. In the beginning, it was a major stopping place for outlaws and other travelers and a receiving place for stolen livestock.

4. There are conflicting stories as to whether the cars were actually disconnected or whether the passengers were told to move back a car so they would not be harmed by the impending explosion.

5. The Mounties disagreed. They said Jones had no redeeming features at all. The Pinkertons said the same of Kid Curry.

6. In another version, King found no one at the Mounted Police post.

7. East Scobey was to become the town of Scobey and seat of Daniels County, created in 1920. The city was once advertised as the world's largest wheat shipping point.

8. This may actually have been Buffalo Gap, just northwest of Big Beaver.

9. Birch was captured two years later and sentenced to a term in a Canadian prison.

10. According to Terry Kincannon of Peerless, Montana, Pete Ieuch may have lived out his years at Cascade, Montana, going by the name of Tucker. A local saloon owner boarded Tucker when he got too old to work. Apparently there were some similarities between Ieuch's and Tucker's lives.

Chapter 5

1. According to another report, the payroll was escorted by six men and was dispatched from Fort Shaw, located on the Sun River about 120 miles to the southwest. But since this was the first payroll and since hostilities were intense, it's more likely a larger detail of soldiers was used. Also, the outlaws would have been less likely to attempt this robbery so far from their Sun River base.

2. The Blackfoot Confederacy was made up of the Blackfeet proper, Blood, and Piegan tribes. For treaty purposes, the Gros Ventres (Atsina) were originally classified as part of the confederacy; in their own language they call themselves the Rapids, Waterfalls or White Clay People, referring to their former lands along the south Saskatchewan River in western Canada.

3. Sam Bass, Joel Collins, Tom Price, and Persimmons Bill Chambers led other major gangs operating in the area. In 1878, these various gangs robbed twelve of the Cheyenne-to-Deadwood stagecoaches.

4. This was true as of June 1981.

Chapter 6

1. Colin Taylor of Casper, Wyoming points out that Casper did not exist as a town until 1888. In 1884, Fort Casper would have existed to guard the wagon trains using the Platte River log bridge against Indians. Taylor also concludes that one year was too short a time for the Currys' Kansas-Missouri-Texas-Wyoming- Montana trip. It has been suggested that their trip

began in early 1883. In addition, Colin believes that Hole-in-the-Wall was not being used as an outlaw haven when the Currys first arrived in Montana. Outlaw author Charles Kelly felt that it was used, however, not extensively.

2. In yet another tale, Curry was credited with robbing the bank at Roy, Mont., and having to hide out at the nearby town of Gilt Edge when his horse gave out.

3. Rock Creek was soon abandoned by the railroad, and a new station complex and town were established at Rock River.

4. Hanks may also have frequented a local saloon(s) before the train robbery.

5. As previously mentioned, there are conflicting stories as to whether or not the cars were separated, or the passengers were told to move back one car because of the impending explosions.

6. O'Neil had once been a partner of Long George Francis and allegedly had been involved in Francis' rustling operation around Havre, Beaver Creek Valley, and Chouteau County.

7. Other sources put the total at between $65,000 and $70,000.

8. On November 30, Curry received ten sentences of 130 years at the Columbus, Ohio federal prison for forging and passing the Helena banknotes. Curry's legal expenses total over $3,000. His state appeal was denied on December 13, and it was appealed to the U.S. Circuit Court of Appeals. Shortly after his conviction was upheld, he escaped before he could be transported to prison—just as the Pinkertons had predicted.

9. See this author's book *Tall in the Saddle*, page 29, and Alan Brekke's *Kid Curry: Train Robber*, page 91.

10. Frank Lamb and his son F. Bruce Lamb both wrote books contending that Kid Curry stayed at their Fremont County, Colorado, ranch both before and after his Knoxville jail escape, and that he only briefly stayed at Landusky after his Tennessee jail break, and hid out at their ranch before being "killed"

during the attempted holdup near Parachute, Colorado. However, these two books contradict each other and conflict with official reports and documented facts.

It is hard for this author to accept that Curry stayed on the Lambs' ranch during the fall and winter of 1903 and the spring of 1904 without being discovered. For one thing, the ranch was near the county seat at Canon City, Colorado, and not far from the urban centers of Pueblo, Colorado Springs, and Denver (where the Pinkertons were headquartered). It is inconceivable to me that, with the whole country looking for Curry, the large rewards offered, and given his tendencies to brag, drink, and fight, someone would not have noticed his presence in the area.

Also, Curry's death at Parachute is very questionable, casting more doubt on the Lambs' accounts, since their stories revolve around this supposed event.

Still, Jesse Cole Kenworth, in his book *Storms of Life*, accepts the Lambs' story, although he doesn't explain why. Since he had the cooperation of the Logan family during this research, his words cannot be ignored. Perhaps the complete publication of Kenworth's vast research materials would help clear up this mystery.

A man who could very well help resolve this question is Larry Pointer, who has been researching Curry for several years and who also has some Logan family papers in his possession. But Pointer has not replied to my inquiries. The mystery continues.

The Montana Historical Society has recently received information from the Coburn family about a diary Kid Curry supposedly kept while in jail at Knoxville. If it surfaces, it may also shed some light on matters.

11. See Larry Pointer, *In Search of Butch Cassidy*, page 185.

12. The *Glenwood Springs Post* reported the name as "Sam," but the *Rocky Mountain News* said "Tom."

13. Researchers Daniel Buck and Anne Meadows contend that this was the first Cassidy-Longabaugh-Place robbery and that others had committed the previous robbery at the Tarapaca-Argentine Bank.

14. This author believes that Kenworth tripped himself up because, out of acquired loyalty, he was trying to keep the family secret—that Curry survived his outlaw days.

15. It was said that the page from the hotel register with Gill's signature disappeared after Gill did.

16. This was not true for O. Pete Zortman. He eventually squandered the riches gained from the August Mine on other mining ventures in Butte, Montana, and Bellview, Idaho. Thirty-five years later, he reportedly died a pauper at Big Timber, Montana.

17. A Malta (MT) restaurant even has a "Kid Curry Lounge."

Acknowledgments

My deepest thanks to those descendants of the pioneers of the North American West whose shared oral and written recollections have substantially contributed to this text.

Home base for my research is the Havre-Hill County Library under librarian Bonnie Williamson, a caring and talented administrator. This institution is the closest thing I have to an office (besides home), and luckily they don't charge me rent. Reference librarian Francine Brady could almost qualify as my unpaid administrative assistant. She is the key to making my research efforts jell with the most efficiency. Without Francine, my research endeavors would have suffered.

While the bibliography covers all (I hope) the people and organizations that have helped me, it doesn't tell the whole story of those who went the extra distance. First, thanks to Linda Caricaburu, then regional editor (now city editor of the *Great Falls Tribune*, who first published my early version of the Con Murphy story and rescued my Wickes story with a "daring daylight burglary."

Thanks to Jean Brainerd, senior historian of the Wyoming Historical Society (under its assorted names), who is the most enthusiastic and competent researcher I have ever come across—and who has a wonderful English accent, too. And thanks to Jim

Dullenty, founding board member of the Western Outlaw-Lawman History Association, for pointing me in Jean's direction, along with directing me to other important resource groups. Dullenty shares Jean's catchy enthusiasm. Thanks also to Dr. William Beahen of the Royal Canadian Mounted Police Archives in Toronto, Ontario, who provided me with important research materials from the other side of the line.

My research of the Little Rockies country would have been far from complete without the assistance of Great Falls-based author Helen Duvall-Arthur. Her expertise added so much to the Kid Curry-Abe Gill chapter. Also Gene Barnard, Manson Bailey, Jr., Joel Overholser, and Pam Linn added greatly to my two Valley County chapters—and not to forget Ralph Bradley of England, who was doing parallel research on Long Henry Thompson. Thanks also to Bob Mann of Plentywood, who had been researching Dutch Henry et al. for years.

My thanks to the personnel of the Crosby, North Dakota, and Roseau, Minnesota, historical groups, who filled in what their respective state historical societies couldn't produce. Dave Walter and the Montana Historical Society files added much to my knowledge of the Valley County outlaws.

The Valley, Sheridan, and Chouteau county offices were of significant assistance, as was the Scobey-Daniels County historical group. Although I never met the employees of the Glasgow and Sheridan offices, I really enjoyed the hospitality of those at the Fort Benton-Chouteau County courthouse. Unfortunately, I have lost all of their names.

My greatest fear is that over my off-and-on nine years of research, I have left out individuals and organizations that belong in the bibliography. My most sincere apologies if these fears prove valid.

My thanks to Donna Tweeten for her editing and proofreading skills. And to my son Michael and daughter Jeanne, who continue to be my best promoters in the state of Montana.

And, finally, thanks to God Almighty, who gave me this book, even though it wasn't really in my plans and was pushed in between my scheduled books. My efforts to fight it proved fruitless. Thy will be done!

While I have had many, many people to thank for their assistance, the ultimate responsibility for the facts and interpretations of history in this book rests with me. And that is always a heavy burden.

Gary A. Wilson
Bull Hook Siding, Havre
September 11, 1994

BIBLIOGRAPHY

BOOKS

Aasheim, Magnus, ed. *Sheridan's Daybreak, Sheridan County, Montana.* Plentywood, Mont.: Sheridan County Historical Society and Sheridan County Homemakers, 1970.

Abbott, E. C., and Helena Huntington Smith. *We Pointed Them North: Recollections of a Cowpuncher.* Reprint. Norman: University of Oklahoma Press, 1971.

Adams, Ramon. *Burs Under the Saddle: A Second Look at Books and Histories of the West.* Norman: University of Oklahoma Press, 1964.

——. *More Burs Under the Saddle: Books and Histories of the West.* Norman: University of Oklahoma Press, 1979.

——. *Six-Guns and Saddle Leather: A Bibliography of Books and Pamphlets on Western Outlaws and Gunmen.* Rev. ed. Norman: University of Oklahoma Press, 1969.

Alvin, John. *Eastern Montana, a Portrait of Its Land and People.* Helena: Montana Magazine, 1982.

Anderson, Norman, and Fern Wallen, eds. *Crosby Diamond Jubilee, 1904-1979.* Crosby, North Dakota: Historical Committee, 1979.

Archer, John. *Saskatchewan, a History.* Saskatoon, Sask.: Western Producers Prairie Books, 1980.

Baker, Pearl. *The Wild Bunch at Robbers' Roost*. Reprint. Lincoln: University of Nebraska Press Bison Books, 1989.

Bartholomew, Ed. *Black Jack Ketchem, Last of the Holdup Kings*. Houston: Frontier Press, 1955.

——. *Biographical Album of Western Gunfighters*. Houston: Frontier Press, 1958.

Bennett, Estelle. *Old Deadwood Days*. New York: J. W. Sears & Co., 1928.

Bertino, Belvino. *The Scissorbills*. New York: Vantage Press, 1976.

Bertins, Belle. *Culbertson Diamond Jubilee Book*. Culbertson, Mont.: Searchlight Publishing, 1962.

Betenson, Lulu, as told to Dora Flack. *Butch Cassidy, My Brother*. Reprint. New York: Penguin Books, 1976.

Billington, Ray. *Westward to the Pacific: An Overview of America's Westward Expansion*. St. Louis: Jefferson National Expansion Historical Association, 1979.

Breihan, Carl. *The Day Jesse James Was Killed*. New York: Bonanza Books, 1962.

——, with Charles Rosamond. *The Bandit Belle*. Seattle: Superior Press, 1970.

Breitmeir, Stella, ed. *Thunderstorms and Tumbleweeds: East Blaine County, Montana, 1887-1987*. Harlem, Mont.: Centennial Book Committee, 1986.

Brekke, Alan. *Kid Curry, Train Robber*. Chinook, Mont.: Privately printed, 1989.

Brown, Mark. *Plainsmen of the Yellowstone: A History of the Yellowstone Basin*. New York: G. P. Putnam's Sons, 1961.

Brown, Mark, and W. R. Felton. *Before Barbed Wire: The Frontier Years*. New York: Henry Holt & Co., 1955.

Burlingame, Merrill, and K. Ross Toole. *A History of Montana*. 3 vols. New York: Lewis Publishing Co., 1957.

Cheney, Roberta. *Names on the Face of Montana*. Rev. ed. Missoula, Mont.: Mountain Press, 1984.

Cheney, Truman, and Roberta Cheney. *So Long, Cowboys of the Open Range*. Helena, Mont.: Privately printed, 1990.

Coburn, Walt. *Pioneer Cattleman in Montana: The Story of the Circle C Ranch*. Norman: University of Oklahoma Press, 1972.

Costello, Gladys, and Dorothy Whitcomb Klimper. *Top o' the Mountain: Charley Whitcomb, Mining Man in Zortman*. Great Falls, Mont.: Privately printed, 1976.

Cunningham, Eugene. *Triggernometry*. Reprint. Caldwell, Idaho: Caxton Printers, 1971.

David, Robert. *Malcom Campbell, Sheriff*. Casper, Wyo.: S. E. Boyer & Co., 1932.

Davis, Jean. *Shallow Diggin's*. Caldwell, Idaho: Caxton Printers, 1962.

Dawson County Bicentennial Committee. *Montana Stockgrowers 1900 Directory of Marks and Brands*. Reprint. Glendive, Mont.: Dawson County Bicentennial Committee, 1974.

Dempsey, Hugh A. *Big Bear: The End of Freedom*. Lincoln, Neb.: Bison Books, 1984.

Didier, Hazel, ed. *The Yesteryears*. Malta, Mont.: Phillips County Historical Society, 1978.

Drago, Harry. *Great American Cattle Trails*. New York: Bramhill House, 1965.

Duvall, Walter, with Helen Duvall-Arthur. *Memories of a Filly Chaser*. Great Falls, Mont.: Privately printed, 1992.

Eide, Marlene, ed. *The Wonder of Williams County, North Dakota*. 2 vols. Williston, North Dakota: Williams County Historical Society, 1975.

Engbretson, Dave. *Forgotten Names, Empty Saddles: Outlaws of the Black Hills and Wyoming*. Aberdeen, South Dakota: North Plains Press, 1982.

Ernst, Donna. *Sundance, My Uncle*. College Station, Texas: Creative Publishing Co., 1992.

Federal Writers' Project, Works Progress Administration. The American Guide Series:

Colorado. Reprint. New York: Hastings House, 1946.

Idaho. Reprint. New York: Oxford University Press, 1960.

Montana. Reprint. New York: Hastings House, 1946.

North Dakota. Reprint. New York: Oxford University Press, 1950.

Oklahoma. Norman: University of Oklahoma Press, 1941.

South Dakota. Reprint. New York: Hastings House, 1952.

Texas. Reprint. New York: Hastings House, 1940.

Wyoming. Reprint. Lincoln, Neb.: Bison Books, 1981.

Fletcher, Robert. *Free Grass to Fences*. New York: University Publishers, 1960.

Franzen, Doris, ed. *Footprints of the Valley*. 3 vols. Glasgow, Mont.: History Committee, 1991.

French, William. *Some Recollections of a Western Ranchman*. New York: Argosy-Antiquarian, 1965.

Friesen, Gerald. *The Canadian Prairie, a History*. Toronto: University of Toronto Press, 1984.

Garcia, Andrew. *Tough Trip through Paradise, 1878-1879, [the autobiography of] Andrew Garcia*. Edited by Bennett H. Stein. Reprint. Sausalito, Calif.: Comstock Editions, 1986.

Giebel, Doug, ed. *In Print: Havre, Montana*. Vol. 1. Big Sandy, Mont.: Privately printed, 1987.

Hegne, Barbara. *Border Outlaws of Montana, North Dakota and Canada*. Eagle Point, Ore.: Privately printed, 1993.

Horan, James. *The Gunfighters: The Authentic Wild West*. New York: Crown Publishers, 1976.

———. *Desperate Men: The Rise, Reign, and Fall of the West's Most Notorious Outlaws*. Rev. ed. New York: Ballantine Books, 1974.

———. *The Pinkertons: The Detective Dynasty That Made History*. New York: Crown Publishers, 1967.

———. *The Wild Bunch*. New York: Signet Books, 1958.

Horan, James, and Paul Sann. *Pictorial History of the Wild West*. New York: Crown Publishers, 1954.

Howard, Joseph Kinsey. *Montana: High, Wide, and Handsome*. New Haven, Conn.: Yale University Press, 1974.

Jordan, Arthur. *Jordan*. Missoula, Mont.: Mountain Press, 1984.

Kelley, Charles. *The Outlaw Trail: A History of Butch Cassidy and His Wild Bunch*. Rev. ed. New York: Bonanza Books, 1959.

Kennedy, Michael, ed. *Cowboys and Cattlemen, a Roundup from "Montana, The Magazine of Western History"*. New York: Hastings House, 1964.

Kenworth, Jesse. *Storms of Life: The Outlaw Trail and Kid Curry*. Bozeman, Mont.: Quarter Circle Enterprises, 1990.

Kirby, Edward. *The Rise and Fall of the Sundance Kid*. Iola, Wis.: Western Publishers, 1983.

Kuykendall, W. L. *Frontier Days*. Cheyenne, Wyo.: Privately printed, 1917.

[Lamb, Frank.] *The Wild Bunch*. Edited by Alan Swallow. Denver: Sage Books, 1924.

Lamb, F. Bruce. *Kid Curry: The Life and Times of Harvey Logan and the Wild Bunch*. Boulder, Co.: Johnson Books, 1991.

Lefors, Joe. *Wyoming Peace Officer*. Laramie, Wyo.: Powder River Publishers, 1953.

Lenz, Louis. *The N.P.R. Data Tables*. Walla Walla, Wash.: Privately printed, 1978.

Long, Phillip. *Forty Years a Cowboy*. Billings, Mont.: Cypress Press, 1976.

Loomis, John A. *Texas Ranchman: The Memories of John A. Loomis*. Edited by Herman Viola and Sarah Loomis Wilson. Chadron, Neb.: Fur Press, 1982.

McAuliffe, Eugene. *Early Coal Mining in the West*. Omaha, Neb.: Newcomen Society, 1948.

Malone, Michael, and Richard Roeder. *Montana, a History of Two Centuries*. Seattle: University of Washington Press, 1976.

Meloy, Mark. *Islands on the Prairie*. Helena: Montana Magazine, 1986.

Mercer, A. S. *The Banditti of the Plains*. Reprint. Norman: University of Oklahoma Press, 1987.

Merriam, H. G. *Way Out West*. Norman: University of Oklahoma Press, 1969.

Miller, Nyle, and Joseph Snell. *Great Gunfighters of the Kansas Towns, 1867-1886*. Lincoln: University of Nebraska Press, 1963.

Mokler, Alfred. *The History of Natrona County* [Wyo.]. Chicago: R. R. Donnelly & Sons, 1923.

Montana Writers Project Inventory: Livestock History for Daniels, Sheridan, and Valley Counties, Circa 1939. In Montana Historical Society Archives, Helena.

Murray, Erlene Durrant. *Lest We Forget: A Short History of Early Grand Valley, Colorado, Originally Called Parachute, Colorado*. Grand Junction, Colo.: Quahada, 1973.

Noyes, Alfred. *In the Land of Chinook, or, The History of Blaine County.* Helena, Mont.: State Publishing Co., 1917.

O'Neal, Bill. *Encyclopedia of Western Gunfighters.* Norman: University of Oklahoma Press, 1979.

Overholser, Joel. *Fort Benton, World's Innermost Port.* Fort Benton, Mont.: Privately printed, 1989.

Paladin, Vivian, ed. *From Buffalo Bones to Sonic Boom: Seventy-fifth Anniversary Souvenir.* Glasgow, Mont.: Jubilee Committee, 1962.

Parker, Watson. *Deadwood: The Golden Years.* Lincoln: University of Nebraska Press Bison Books, 1981.

Patterson, Richard. *Historical Atlas of the Outlaw West.* Boulder, Colo.: Johnson Books, 1985.

Phillips County Jubilee Committee. *Railroads to Rockets, 1887-1962: The Diamond Jubilee of Phillips County, Montana.* Malta, Mont.: Phillips County Jubilee Committee, 1962.

Pointer, Larry. *In Search of Butch Cassidy.* Norman: University of Oklahoma Press, 1977.

Progressive Men of Montana. Chicago: A. W. Brown & Co., 1901.

Rankin, M. Wilson. *Reminiscences of Frontier Days.* Denver: Privately printed, 1935.

Ranstrom, Barbara, and Dan Friede, eds. *Chinook: The First 100 Years.* Chinook, Mont.: Centennial '89ers, 1989.

Redford, Robert. *The Outlaw Trail: A Journey Through Time.* New York: Grosset & Dunlap, 1981.

Robbins, Vista, ed. *A Local Community History of Valley County.* Glasgow, Mont.: Montana Federation of Women's Clubs, 1925.

Rue, L. E., ed. *Plentywood's Golden Years, 1912-1962.* Plentywood, Mont.: Golden Anniversary Committee, 1962.

Russell, Charles M. *Good Medicine: The Illustrated Letters of Charles M. Russell.* Garden City, New Jersey: Doubleday, 1930.

——. *Trails Plowed Under.* New York: Doubleday, 1927.

Sandoz, Mari. *The Cattlemen.* Reprint. Lincoln: University of Nebraska Press, 1978.

Santee, Ross. *Lost Pony Tracks.* New York: Bantam Books, 1956.

Segars, Lorretta, ed. *One Hundred Years in Culbertson, 1887-1987.* Culbertson, Mont.: Steering Committee, 1986.

Selcer, Richard. *Hell's Half Acre.* Fort Worth: Texas Christian University Press, 1991.

Sharp, Paul. *Whoop-Up Country: The Canadian-American West, 1865-1885.* Norman: University of Oklahoma Press, 1973.

Shirley, Glenn. *Henry Starr, Last of the Real Badmen.* New York: David McKay, 1965.

——. *Law West of Fort Smith.* Reprint. Lincoln, Neb.: Bison Books, 1968.

——. *West of Hell's Fringe: Crime, Criminals, and Federal Police Officers in Oklahoma Territory, 1889-1907.* Norman: University of Oklahoma Press, 1978.

Sirango, Charles. *A Cowboy Detective: A True Story of Twenty-two Years with a World Famous Detective Agency.* Reprint. Lincoln: University of Nebraska Press, 1981.

Smith, Helena Huntington. *The War on Powder River: The History of an Insurrection.* Reprint. Lincoln: University of Nebraska Press Bison Books, 1967.

Stone, Elizabeth. *Uinta, Its Place in History.* Laramie, Wyo.: Privately published, 1924.

Syverad, Edgar. *Historic Sheridan County.* Plentywood, Mont.: Privately printed, 1939.

Thiessen, Nancy. *Empty Boots, Dusty Corrals*. Salt Lake City: Sterling Press, 1986.

Thomas, Lewis, ed. *The Prairie West to 1905: A Canadian Sourcebook*. Toronto: Oxford University Press, 1975.

Turner, Peter. *North-West Mounted Police*. 2 vols. Ottawa: King's Printer and Controller of Stationery, 1950.

Walker, Don. *Cleo's Cowboys*. Lincoln: University of Nebraska Press, 1981.

Walker, Tacetta. *Stories of Early Days in Wyoming, Big Horn Basin*. Casper, Wyo.: Prairie Publishing Co., 1936.

Waller, Brown. *Last of the Great Western Train Robbers*. New York: A. S. Barnes, 1968.

Warner, Matt, as told to Murray King. *Last of the Bandit Riders*. New York: Bonanza Books, 1938.

Watts, Peter. *A Dictionary of the Old West*. New York: Promontory Press, 1987.

Webb, Walter Prescott. *The Great Plains*. Reprint. New York: Grosset & Dunlap, 1972.

———. *The Texas Rangers*. Boston: Houghton-Mifflin, 1935.

Wellman, Paul. *A Dynasty of Outlaws*. Lincoln: University of Nebraska Press Bison Books, 1986.

Willard, John. *Adventure Trails in Montana*. Helena, Mont.: State Publishing Co., 1964.

Wilson, Gary A. *Tall in the Saddle: The Long George Francis Story, 1874-1920*. Havre, Mont.: High-Line Books, 1989.

Wolle, Muriel Sibell. *Montana Pay Dirt*. Denver: Sage Books, 1982.

Young, Paul. *Back Trail of an Old Cowboy*. Lincoln: University of Nebraska Press, 1983.

ARTICLES

"Acquisition of Dutch Henry's Gun Inspires Investigation," *Montana Post* [Montana Historical Society newsletter], April 1964.

"Beaver Creek Originally Part of Military Post," *Great Falls Tribune*, June 6, 1943.

Breihan, Carl. "Big Nose George Parrott," *The Branding Iron* [newsletter of the Los Angeles Corral of the Westerners], September 1955.

Brekke, Al. "The Currys Were a Wild Bunch, Harlem to Hole-in-the-Wall," 2 parts in *Chinook Opinion*, June 29 and July 6, 1988.

Buck, Dan, and Anne Meadows. "The Wild Bunch in South America," 4 parts in *The Journal* [of the Western Outlaw-Lawman History Association], 1991-1992.

———. "Where Lies Butch Cassidy?" *Old West*, Fall 1991.

Coburn, Walt. "The Night 'Dutch Henry' Played Santa Claus," *True West*, September-October 1969.

Cochran, Keith. "A Bisley With a History," *Gun Report*, September 1966.

Costello, Gladys. "A Frontier Marshall Turns in His Star," *Great Falls Tribune*, November 4, 1954.

———. "Former Stagecoach Driver [Ruel Horner] Recalls Little Rockies Boom," *Great Falls Tribune*, November 22, 1959.

———. "Malta Cattle Country," *Montana Magazine*, Spring 1977.

DeMattos, Jack. "Gunfighters of the Real West," *Real West*, October 1983.

"Dr. Schuelke, a Brilliant but Eccentric Man," *Wind River Mountaineer* 7, 1991.

Donovan, Roberta. "Ghost Towns Haunted by Feel of Montana's Past," *Great Falls Tribune*, June 18, 1978.

Dullenty, Jim. "He Saw Kid Curry Rob Great Northern Train," *Quarterly of the National Association and Center for Outlaw and Lawman History*, 1985.

Dullenty, Jim, and Ben Garthofner, with Robbie Lucke. "New Gold Rush in the Little Rockies," *True West*, March 1984.

Duvall, C. W. "Milk River Bill Harmon, Seventy-five," *Great Falls Tribune*, November 17, 1935.

"Early-day Athlete [Charles Whitcomb] Became Mine Owner," *Great Falls Tribune*, Montana Parade section, August 27, 1961.

Ferris, Robert, ed. "Prospector, Cowhand, and Sodbuster," in *The National Survey of Historic Sites and Buildings*, Vol. 11. Washington, D.C.: National Park Service, 1967.

Fletcher, Bob. "Smoke Signals," *Montana the Magazine of Western History*, April 1952.

Gilette, F. B. "Many Notorious Badmen Were at Saco," *Nashua Independent*, March 23, 1931.

Gunderson, Carl. "The High Line," in Chapter XX , *A History of Montana,* Burlingame and Toole. New York: Lewis Historical Publishing, 1957.

Johnson, Dorothy M. "Durable Desperado Kid Curry," *Montana the Magazine of Western History*, April 1956.

Kindred, Bruce. "Harvey Logan's Secret Letters," *True West*, October 1994.

Lamb, John A. "Harvey Logan's Lost Journal," *True West*, October, 1994.

Larson, Kim. "Ursulines Return to Roots for 100th Anniversary: Early Days Come Alive," *Billings Gazette*, November 13, 1983.

McBryde, Carolina Bullion. "Love Behind Bars: The Prison Correspondence of Ben Kilpatrick and Laura Bullion," *True West*, April 1992.

Mann, Robert. "Outlaws of the Big Muddy: The North End of the Outlaw Trail," *The Journal* [of the Western Outlaw-Lawman History Association], Spring-Summer 1992.

Miller, Gladys. "The Death of Jim Winters." *W.P.A. Livestock History*, April 25, 1940.

Miller, Robert. "Kid Curry, Montana Outlaw," *Montana Magazine*, Spring 1976.

Morin, Marvin. "Two Graves in Montana, Mute Evidence of Frontier Violence," *True West*, March 1984.

O'Malley, D. J. [The N Bar N Kid]. "Ed Starr, Gunman-Killer, Worked as [Brand] Inspector Unknown," *Montana News Association*, May 10, 1937.

———. "Long Henry Thompson," *Montana News Association*, July 18, 1938.

Powers, Jacob Mathew. "Montana Episodes: Tracking Con Murphy," *Montana the Magazine of Western History*, Autumn 1980.

Ritch, John. "Two Two-Gun Gunners of the Ranges Were Real: He-Men of the Golden West," *Miles City Star*, Golden Jubilee issue, May 24, 1934.

Saindon, Bob. "Stealing of Coat Finally Led to Man's Hanging by Mob," *Glasgow Courier*, Diamond Jubilee issue, October 9, 1962.

———. "The Shooting of Long Henry," *Glasgow Courier*, Diamond Jubilee issue, October 9, 1962.

Steckmesser, Kent. "Lawmen and Outlaws," in *A Literary History of the American West*. N.p.: 1987.

Walker, Wayne. "Born and Ieuch: The Two Dutch Henrys," *Real West*, October 1983.

"Where Was Loney Curry at Train Robbery Holdup?" *Great Falls Tribune*, Montana Parade section, November 17, 1957.

White, Richard. "Outlaw Gangs of the Middle Border: America's Social Bandits," *Western Historical Quarterly*, October 1981.

Wilson, Gary A. "Con Murphy, Montana's Last Vigilante Hanging," *Great Falls Tribune*, September 23, 1984.

——. "Havre Could Have Been Lohman Instead," *Great Falls Tribune*, January 12, 1986.

NEWSPAPERS

Colorado:

    Denver Post, Denver Republican, Glenwood Springs News

Minnesota:

    Minneapolis Tribune, Roseau County Press, Roseau County Times, Roseau Region, Roseau Times-Region

Montana:

    Basin Times, Boulder Age, Butte Evening News, Chinook Opinion, Culbertson Searchlight, Fairfield Times, Fallon County Times, Fort Benton River Press, Glasgow Courier, Glasgow Herald, Glasgow Record, Great Falls Tribune, Harlem News, Harlem Enterprise, Havre Plaindealer, Havre Promoter, Helena Weekly Herald, Helena Independent, Helena Daily Record, Hinsdale Tribune, Jefferson County Sentinel, Judith Basin County Press, Judith Gap Journal, Lewistown Democrat News, Little Rockies Miner, Malta Enterprise, Malta News, Miles City Daily Star, Milk River Eagle, Montana Daily Record, Nashua Independent, Nashua News, North Montana Review, North Montana News, Park

County News, Plentywood Herald, Phillips County News, Producer's News, Saco Enterprise, Saco Independent, Sheridan County News, Townsend Messenger, Valley County Gazette, Valley County News, Virginia City Madisodian, Yellowstone Journal

North Dakota:

Ambrose Newsman, Grand Forks Daily Herald, Minot Journal, Walsh County Record, Williston Herald

Saskatchewan:

Regina Leader, Regina Leader-Post

Wyoming:

Cheyenne Daily Leader, Rawlins Daily Times, Sheridan Post, Wyoming State Journal

INSTITUTIONAL SOURCES

Albany [N.Y.] Institute of History and Art

Blaine County offices of Clerk & Recorder and Clerk of Court, Chinook, Mont.

Borough of Brooklyn [N.Y.] Department of Health, Vital Records

Chouteau County offices of Clerk & Recorder and Clerk of Court, Sheriff's Department, Fort Benton, Mont.

Colorado Historical Society, Denver, Colo.

Crosby-Divide County Historical Society-Museum, Crosby, North Dakota

Daniels County Museum Archives, Frontier Town; Clerk & Recorder's Office, and Clerk of Court, Scobey, Mont.

Eden [Texas] Public Library

Funeral Home Records:

> Adams Funeral Home, Malta, Mont.
>
> Benton Funeral Home, Fort Benton, Mont.
>
> Edwards Funeral Home, Chinook, Mont.
>
> Holland & Bonine Funeral Home, Havre, Mont.
>
> Riverside Funeral Home, Fort Benton, Mont.

Garfield County Library; main library, Glenwood Springs; and branch library, Parachute, Colo.

Garfield County Clerk & Recorder's Office, Jordan, Mont.

Havre-Hill County Library, Havre, Mont.

Jefferson County Clerk of Court's Office, Boulder, Mont.

Mesa County Library, Grand Junction, Colo.

Montana Historical Society Library & Archives, Helena

MSU-Northern Vande Bogart Library, Harrison Lane Collection of Western Americana, Havre

Nebraska State Historical Society, Lincoln

New York Department of Health, Albany

Oklahoma Historical Society, Oklahoma City

Ontario State Records Unit, State Military and Transportation Records, and Government Archives Division, Ottawa

Phillips County offices of Clerk & Recorder and Clerk of Court, and Historical Society-Museum, Malta, Mont.

Pinkerton Security and Investigative Services, Van Nuys, Calif.

Polk County Recorder's Office, Crookston, North Dakota

Polytechnic Institute of New York, Office of the Registrar, Brooklyn

Roseau County Administrator's Office, Roseau, Minn.

Roseau County Historical Museum and Interpretive Center, Roseau, Minn.

Royal Canadian Mounted Police Archives, Ottawa, Ontario

Royal Canadian Mounted Police Museum & Archives, Regina, Sask.

Sheridan County Clerk & Recorder's Office, Plentywood, Mont.

State Historical Society of North Dakota, Bismarck

Texas State Library, Austin

Valley County Clerk of District Court, Glasgow, Mont.

Western Outlaw-Lawman History Association, Hamilton, Mont.

Wyoming Division of Parks and Cultural Resources, Cheyenne

CORRESPONDENCE AND INTERVIEWS

Aasheim, Magnus. Antelope, Mont.

Albers, Donna. Fort Benton, Mont.

Aldridge, Lorene. Blanco, Texas

Bailey, Jr., Manson. Glasgow, Mont.

Barnard, Gene. Malta, Mont.

Bauer, Mildred. Little Rockies, Mont.

Bertino, Belvina. Culbertson, Mont.

Beyer, Viola. Malta, Mont.

Billing, May. Jordan, Mont.

Blue, Wallace. Glasgow, Mont.

Boynham, Walter. Saco, Mont.

Bradley, Ralph. Bourne, Lincolnshire, England

Brekke, Alan. Harlem, Mont.

Broadbrooks, Dan. Malta, Mont.

Broadbrooks, Joe. Malta, Mont.

Broome, Sherwood. Darnling Park, Fla.

Buck, Dean. Washington, D.C.

Caricaburu, Linda. Great Falls, Mont.

Cheney, Roberta. Cameron, Mont.

Cole, Oscar. Columbus, Ohio

Conlon, Dorothy. Saco, Mont.

Crush, Eric. Bainville, Mont.

Dempsey, Hugh. Calgary, Alta.

Desonia, Fred. Nashua, Mont.

Dolson, Wilber. Glasgow, Mont.

Donovan, Roberta. Lewistown, Mont.

Doolan, Andy. Liverpool, England

Duvall-Arthur, Helen. Great Falls, Mont.

Eaton, Richard. Hinsdale, Mont.

Etchhart, Gene. Hinsdale, Mont.

Etchhart, John. Hinsdale, Mont.

Gerspacher, Ed. Hinsdale, Mont.

Gone, Ray. Fort Belknap, Mont.

Holman, Charles. Havre, Mont.

Kelsey, James. Zortman, Mont.

Kincannon, Terry. Peerless, Mont.

Konareck, Joe "Speed." Roy, Mont.

Linn, Pam. Saco, Mont.

Lucke, Alvin "Al". Havre, Mont.

McBryde, Caroline Bullion. Big River, Calif.

McKeever, Anna. Fort Benton, Mont.

Meadows, Anne. Washington, D.C.

Magera, Jim. Havre, Mont.

Mann, Bob. Plentywood, Mont.

Minugh, Al. Dodson, Mont.

Mitchell, Winston. Little Rockies, Mont.

Overholser, Joel. Fort Benton, Mont.

Parsons, Chuck "The Answer Man." Smiley, Texas

Reese, Thomas "Dock." Havre, Mont.

Richardson, Edgar. Scobey, Mont.

Richardson, Mary. Scobey, Mont.

Robinson, Mrs. George. Saco, Mont.

Rue, Thorbjorn. Crosby, North Dakota

Saindon, Bob. Wolf Point, Mont.

Sands, Gordon. Havre, Mont.

Seaforth, Harvey. Libby, Mont.

Seel, Gene. Malta, Mont.

Shirley, Glenn. Stillwater, Okla.

Short, John. Malta, Mont.

Short, Lilly. Malta, Mont.

Smith, Charles. Harlem, Mont.

Spangelo, Jim. Havre, Mont.

Stoner, Helen. Outlook, Mont.

Swanson, Debbie. Havre, Mont.

Taylor, Clifford. Helena, Mont.

Taylor, Colin. Casper, WY.

Teske, Edna. Havre, Mont.

Veseth, Mrs. Myron. Havre, Mont.

Welsh, Carmelita. Little Rockies, Mont.

Williams, Paul. Fort Benton, Mont.